A Connecticut Yankee
in Lincoln's Cabinet

A Connecticut Yankee in Lincoln's Cabinet

Navy Secretary Gideon Welles Chronicles the Civil War

Edited by J. Ronald Spencer

The Acorn Club
Hartford, Connecticut

Published by The Acorn Club c/o Richard Malley, Connecticut Historical Society, 1 Elizabeth Street, Hartford, CT 06105

Distributed by Wesleyan University Press, Middletown, CT 06459
www.wesleyan.edu/wespress

Book design by David Wolfram

5 4 3 2 1

Library of Congress Cataloging-in-Publication Data

Welles, Gideon, 1802-1878.
A Connecticut yankee in Lincoln's cabinet : Navy Secretary Gideon Welles chronicles the Civil War / Gideon Welles ; edited by J. Ronald Spencer.
   pages cm
Includes bibliographical references and index.
ISBN 978-0-615-96103-3 (pbk. : alk. paper) -- ISBN 978-0-8195-7498-5 (ebook)
1. Welles, Gideon, 1802-1878—Diaries. 2. United States—Politics and government—1861-1865. 3. United States—History—Civil War, 1861-1865—Naval operations. 4. United States—History—Civil War, 1861-1865—Sources. 5. Lincoln, Abraham, 1809-1865—Friends and associates. 6. Cabinet officers—United States—Diaries. I. Spencer, J. Ronald. II. Title.
E467.1.W46A3 2014
973.7092--dc23
                   2014004776

Frontispiece: Gideon Welles, Secretary of the Navy, 1861–1869.
Engraving of a photograph taken ca. 1865.
Source: The Connecticut Historical Society, Hartford, CT

In Memory of

Milton P. DeVane, 1929 – 2012
Donald B. Engley, 1917 – 2012
Ellsworth S. Grant, 1917 – 2013
Edward W. Knappman, 1944 – 2011
Edward W. Sloan III, 1931 – 2012

Contents

Acknowledgments

A Connecticut Yankee in Lincoln's Cabinet is the thirty-seventh publication of the Acorn Club, which was founded in 1899 to publish books of enduring value in Connecticut history. The book is dedicated to the five former members of the Club who have died since the appearance of the Club's last publication: Milton P. DeVane, Donald B. Engley, Ellsworth S. Grant, Edward W. Knappman, and Edward W. Sloan III.

A number of individuals – both Club members and non-members – were instrumental in moving this book from conception to publication. As the editor, I am pleased to acknowledge their contributions.

First, I am grateful to the five Club members who volunteered to serve on the publications committee for the book. Richard Buel, Jr., who edited or co-edited the last three Acorn Club volumes, made astute comments about an early draft. Briann Greenfield did a similarly thorough and constructive critique of the manuscript and offered thoughtful advice throughout the project. Richard Malley, the Club's secretary, provided assistance with multiple matters, great and small. Patrick Pinnell not only reviewed the manuscript but took the excellent photograph of the statue of Welles at the State Capitol and worked with the book's designer to incorporate it into the book's cover. William Peterson recommended several important additions to the text and stood watch to prevent the editor, a landlubber, from making mistakes about maritime matters.

Several other Club members also helped make the book a reality. During a conference call of the Club's executive committee in March 2013, Helen Higgins, the Club's treasurer, asked a question that prompted me, on the spur of the moment, to propose a book based on Gideon Welles's wartime diary. George Willauer, who stepped down as the Club's president in May 2012 following six years of service, generously agreed to reassume the presidency on an interim basis so I, who had succeeded him, could concentrate on preparing this book. James English, a member of the Club for more than 30 years, was a source of encouragement from the project's start, and his close reading of the manuscript caught many infelicities I had missed. Ann Smith cast her lawyerly eye over the publication and distribution agreement between the Club and the Wesleyan University Press. And Robert Smith, Jr. arranged for Jacqueline Pennino Scheib, a publications and copyright specialist at his law firm, to advise me on copyright issues and also to review the agreement with the Press.

Michael Lestz, chair of the history department at Trinity College, granted me permission to use departmental equipment to make scans of the 1911 edition of Welles's diary; and Gigi St. Peter, the department's administrative assistant, made sure I knew how to operate it. Jack Chatfield, my longtime friend and colleague in the department, reviewed the introduction. The book also benefitted from the attentions of Suzanna Tamminen, the director and editor-in-chief of the Wesleyan University Press, and David Wolfram, the book's designer.

Finally, a special note of appreciation to two people who provided indispensable help from start to finish. Louis P. Masur, who became a valued friend during his nine years as a member of the Trinity College faculty and is now Distinguished Professor of American Studies and History at Rutgers University, confirmed my initial sense that the book was worth doing, critiqued the manuscript with care and discernment, and provided good counsel each of the many times I sought it. My wife, Linda S. Spencer, who was a National Register Specialist-Historian at the Connecticut State Historical Commission and its successor agency for nearly three decades, not only tolerated endless table talk about Welles's diary but also read the manuscript at multiple points in its evolution and each time made recommendations that significantly improved it.

Thanks to all.

J. Ronald Spencer, Editor
November 1, 2013

INTRODUCTION

Gideon Welles, a native of Glastonbury, Connecticut, was one of the state's most influential journalists and politicians during the three decades preceding the Civil War. Today, however, he is usually remembered as Lincoln's secretary of the navy – "Father Neptune" (or just "Neptune") as the president called him. He was only the fourth Connecticut resident appointed to a cabinet post, which he continued to hold throughout Andrew Johnson's presidency.[1]

Historians usually credit Welles with being an energetic and effective administrator who did much to modernize a service in the grip of an aging uniformed leadership that was rigidly set in its ways. When in July 1861 Congress authorized him (and also the secretary of war) to take into consideration merit as well as seniority in making assignments, Welles proceeded to appoint younger, less tradition-bound officers to key positions. He also oversaw the Navy's growth from fewer than 100 ships to 671 and the organization and implementation of the increasingly effective blockade of 3500 miles of Confederate coastline. Furthermore, after some initial hesitation, he pushed for the development of ironclad warships, including the famous USS *Monitor* that fought the ironclad CSS *Virginia* (formerly the USS *Merrimack)* to a draw on March 9, 1862, thereby saving the wooden Union warships stationed in Hampton Roads, Virginia, from virtually certain destruction.[2] He was, in short, one of the architects of Union victory.

---

[1] The first three were Oliver Wolcott, Jr., secretary of the treasury under Washington and John Adams; John M. Niles, postmaster general during the Van Buren administration; and Isaac Toucey, who was both attorney general in the Polk administration and Buchanan's secretary of the navy.

[2] Of the 671 warships, 559 were powered wholly or in part by steam, and more than 70 were ironclads. James M. McPherson, *War on the Waters: The Union and Confederate Navies, 1861 – 1865* (Chapel Hill: University of North Carolina Press, 2012), pp. 35-36, 98-105, and 224. On the initiation of the blockade, see McPherson, Chapter 2, and Craig L. Symonds, *Lincoln and His Admirals* (New York: Oxford University Press, 2008), Chapter 2.

For many historians, however, what is most interesting about Welles is the extensive diary he kept during the war.[3] It provides first-hand information, and often perceptive insights, about Lincoln, Welles's cabinet colleagues, and their conflicts and rivalries. It also covers a wealth of other topics – topics as varied as a cabinet discussion of what the track gauge of the planned transcontinental railroad should be (Welles favored 4 feet, 8½ inches, which became standard for American railroads); home-state pressure on Welles to establish a navy yard in New London; the July 1863 New York City draft riots, which Welles blamed mainly on New York's Democratic governor, Horatio Seymour, whom he dubbed "Sir Forcible Feeble;" Welles's fear, as a lifelong hard-money man, that the government's issuance of paper currency not convertible to gold would lead to financial disaster; and the cabinet's opposition to a proposed constitutional amendment declaring the United States a Christian nation.

Despite his achievements as navy secretary, Welles was often the target of public criticism. When rebel cruisers wreaked havoc on American maritime commerce, merchants and ship owners blamed him for their losses. Newspapers regularly faulted him because so many blockade-runners managed to evade navy patrols and bring cargo into and out of Confederate ports. Armchair admirals were quick to second-guess his decisions. And cartoonists had a field day at his expense. Welles rarely replied to his critics, but he sometimes vented his anger in the diary. For instance, on December 26, 1863, he wrote

> In naval matters . . . those who are most ignorant complain loudest. The wisest policy receives the severest condemnation. My best measures have been the most harshly criticized. . . . Unreasonable and captious men will blame me, take what course I may.

The diary also provided an outlet for Welles's resentment that the War Department failed to give the navy due credit for its contribution to such successful combined army-navy operations as the capture of Vicksburg on the Mississippi River in 1863. He was confident, however, as he wrote on August 23, 1864, that "history will put all right," although he predicted it would be a generation or more "before the prejudices and perversions of partisans will be dissipated, and the true facts be developed."

---

[3] This was not Welles's first turn as a diarist. In earlier life he also had kept a diary periodically. The manuscript of his 1836 diary is on deposit at the Connecticut State Library, and diaries he kept in various years between the 1820s and the mid 1850s are held by the Connecticut Historical Society.

Welles began the diary sometime between July 14 and August 11, 1862 (the first entry is not dated), started keeping it on a regular basis shortly thereafter, and continued to make regular entries in it through the Johnson administration.[4] In the entry for October 20, 1863, he noted that work on it "usually consumes a late evening hour, after company has gone and other labors of the day are laid aside." He rarely went more than a few days without making an entry.

The diary has an immediacy rarely found in memoirs, since it records the rush of events as they happened, when it was uncertain what they signified, how the Lincoln administration should respond, or how they would look in retrospect. As Welles acknowledged in a passage inserted into the September 19, 1862, entry at a later date, "I am not writing a history of the War. . . . But I record my own impressions and the random specula- tions, views, and opinions of others also." Moreover, since he usually wrote about events the day they occurred or soon thereafter, the diary's pages are largely unaffected by the hindsight that often distorts the recollections of memoirists writing well after the events they discuss.[5] The sense of imme- diacy is further heightened by Welles's forceful, often impassioned prose.

This book contains some 250 excerpts from the wartime portion of the diary. They are organized into 10 topical chapters, and many of the excerpts are annotated by the editor.[6] In an Afterword, Welles's post-war activities

---

[4] Published editions of the diary contain an opening chapter entitled "The Beginning of the War" in which Welles discusses such major events of 1861 and early 1862 as the Fort Sumter crisis, the Confederates' seizure of the Gosport (Norfolk, Virginia) Navy Yard, the replacement of Secretary of War Simon Cameron by Edwin M. Stanton, and the panic in Washington that the *Merrimack* would steam up the Potomac and bombard the capital. Welles says nothing, however, about navy Captain Charles Wilkes's forcible removal of two Confederate envoys, James Mason and John Slidell, from the *Trent*, a British mail packet, in November 1861, which precipitated a crisis in Anglo-American relations that could have led to war. It did not because the Lincoln administration decided in late December to free the envoys and allow them to go on their way (Mason to England and Slidell to France). The omission is curious given the episode's intrinsic importance and the navy's central involvement in it. In any event, this chapter was not a part of the diary *per se*, having been written no earlier than 1864 and probably not until the 1870s. Since it was not written contemporaneously with the events it recounts, it is used sparingly in this book. When it is cited, it is as "Chapter 1," followed by the page number.

[5] After the war – probably in the 1870s – Welles made numerous revisions to the diary. Some of them *did* reflect the influence of hindsight. For example, he softened some of his criticisms of the martyred Lincoln and modified some passages to cast a less favorable light on men with whom he had bitter political differences during Reconstruction. Further revisions were made by his son Edgar, who edited the edition published in 1911. How these revisions are treated in this book is explained in the Editorial Note following the Introduction.

[6] Most passages are excerpted from diary entries in which Welles discusses multiple subjects. Some entries that deal exclusively with a single topic are reproduced in their entirety.

in the Johnson administration and then in retirement are summarized.

Some diary entries appearing here, such as those about the Emancipation Proclamation, the attempt by Senate Republicans to force Lincoln to reorganize his cabinet in December 1862, and the scene at the Petersen house as Lincoln lay dying, have often been cited by historians (though rarely reproduced in full). Many of the lesser-known passages are included for what they reveal about important historical figures and events; others offer interesting sidelights on the war or illuminate Welles's personal qualities.

Welles recorded numerous comments about Lincoln, whom he liked and respected, but of whom he could also be critical, as is evident in multiple excerpts. Lincoln likewise held Welles in high regard, valued his advice, and apparently enjoyed his company, except on those occasions when he rushed to the White House in high dudgeon over some issue. The Welles-Lincoln relationship was strengthened because Welles's wife, Mary, was among Mary Todd Lincoln's few close female friends in Washington. One bond between them was that they both lost a child in 1862. Mary Welles helped nurse the dangerously ill Tad Lincoln when his mother was prostrate with grief over the death of his older brother Willie in February. Nine months later Mary's youngest child, Hubert, died at age four – the sixth of the Welles children to die in childhood or adolescence. She also rose from a sick bed to attend Mrs. Lincoln following Lincoln's assassination.[7]

The diary is studded with Welles's usually shrewd, often caustic, sometimes unfair characterizations of his cabinet colleagues, senior army and navy officers, and other prominent public figures. Many such passages are found in the ensuing pages.

The book also contains excerpts about numerous other subjects. Among them are a scheme to colonize freed slaves in Central America; the debate over whether Lincoln should authorize the use of privateers against blockade-runners and Confederate commerce raiders; Welles's disagreements with Secretary of State William Henry Seward – and sometimes with Lincoln – about enforcement of the blockade; the adverse impact of conscription on navy recruitment of able-bodied seamen; various Connecticut-related matters in which Welles perforce became involved; his resistance to attempts to politicize hiring and firing at the navy yards; and his periodic musings about the war's causes, course, and probable consequences.

---

[7] Jean H. Baker, *Mary Todd Lincoln: A Biography* (New York: W.W. Norton, 1987), pp. 212 and 247; Catherine Clinton, *Mrs. Lincoln: A Life* (New York: Harper Collins, 2009), p. 248; and Welles's diary entry for April 14, 1865.

✻ ✻ ✻ ✻ ✻ ✻ ✻

Welles was born in 1802 into a relatively prosperous family, the fourth of five sons of Samuel and Anne Hale Welles.[8] The family traced its lineage to Thomas Welles, an early settler of Hartford and the fourth man to serve as governor of Connecticut colony. Samuel was successively a farmer, merchant, exporter of agricultural products to the British West Indies, and money lender. He was also active politically. At a time when the Federalist Party dominated Connecticut politics, he enthusiastically supported Thomas Jefferson. Glastonbury voters elected him first selectman and later sent him to the state legislature. He also represented the town at the convention in 1818 that framed Connecticut's first constitution.[9]

Gideon Welles was educated at the local district school, the Episcopal Academy in Cheshire, Connecticut, and the American Literary, Scientific, and Military Academy in Norwich, Vermont. As a young man he lacked direction. He twice began the study of law, but each time abandoned it essentially out of boredom. He helped his father with his investment and mortgage business; and a paternal loan enabled him to try his hand at wholesale merchandising. In 1823 and 1824 he published, under a pen name, five vignettes in the *New York Mirror and Ladies Literary Gazette*. But after this initial success, a series of rejection letters from the *Mirror* and other publications ended his hopes for a literary career.

In 1825, during his second try at mastering the law, Welles finally discovered the dual vocation to which he would devote most of his adult life: journalism and politics. These occupations were closely linked in the 19th Century, when most newspapers were party organs and editors were well-represented among party leaders at the local, state, and national levels.

Welles began writing for the *Hartford Times* in 1825 and assumed editorial direction of the paper the following year. He quickly distinguished himself as an outspoken champion of Andrew Jackson's presidential candidacy. Over the next several years, he concentrated on making the nascent Democratic Party an effective vote-getting organization and

---

[8] Most of the factual material in this overview of Welles's pre-war life and career is drawn from John Niven, *Gideon Welles: Lincoln's Secretary of the Navy* (New York: Oxford University Press, 1973; paperback edition, Baton Rouge: Louisiana State University Press, 1994), Chapters 1 – 17. The Afterword also draws on Niven's book, Chapters 26 – 30, as well as on the postwar portion of Welles's diary.

[9] This topic is treated in Richard J. Buel, Jr., and George J. Willauer, eds., *Original Discontents: Commentaries on the Creation of Connecticut's Constitution of 1818*, published by the Acorn Club in 2007.

the *Times* its leading editorial voice in the state. Although Jackson lost Connecticut in both 1828 and 1832, the party steadily gained strength, partly because of Welles's efforts. In 1836, Martin Van Buren, Jackson's hand-picked successor, carried the state. And in 1835, 1836, and 1837, the Democrats elected the governor and won majorities in the state legislature.[10] This enabled them to enact several reforms Welles advocated, including a mechanic's lien law, the end of imprisonment for debt, and the nation's first general incorporation law. As an exponent of the egalitarian strain of Jacksonian Democracy, Welles supported the latter measure out of a conviction that if the state intended to continue issuing corporate charters, it should make them generally available, not grant them only to the wealthy, politically well-connected few.

Welles continued to play a major leadership role in the state party well into the 1840s. Although he turned the editorship of the *Times* over to Alfred E. Burr in 1837, he still wrote many of its editorials. He also crafted many of the party's annual campaign platforms, influenced the distribution of federal patronage in the state, maintained extensive correspondence with prominent Democrats in other states, and traveled to Washington periodically to talk strategy with other party leaders. From 1836 to early 1841 he was Hartford's postmaster, a plum patronage appointment. In 1846, President Polk named him to head the Navy Department's Bureau of Provisions and Clothing, a post he held until June 1849, when President Zachary Taylor replaced him with a fellow Whig.

In the later 1840s, Welles's influence declined as other ambitious – and in his view unprincipled – men moved to take over the state party. The issue of slavery's expansion into the western territories deeply divided Connecticut Democrats, as it did Democrats throughout the free states. Welles personally favored the Wilmot Proviso, which, if enacted, would have barred the institution from the vast area the United States acquired from Mexico at the close of the Mexican-American War in 1848. As a patronage appointee in the Polk administration, however, Welles had to be very circumspect about the Proviso, which was anathema to the president.

Welles's enemies in the state party – foremost among them Isaac Toucey – were eager not to offend their southern Democratic brethren.[11] Thus they rejected the Wilmot Proviso in favor of the doctrine of "popular sovereignty," which left it to the settlers of each territory to decide whether to permit slavery. Welles was sure popular sovereignty would lead to the

---

[10] Connecticut held legislative and gubernatorial elections annually, in early April.

[11] See Chapter 7 for an account of how Toucey, as Buchanan's secretary of the navy, advocated appeasing South Carolina during the crisis over Fort Sumter.

institution's spread.

In 1848, some Connecticut Democrats bolted to the new Free-Soil Party, which was committed to confining slavery within its existing geographic boundaries. Although sympathetic to the Free-Soilers, Welles did not join them, lest he jeopardize his job in the Navy Department.[12] The bolt further weakened his position within the state Democratic Party, since many of the bolters had been his allies in the struggle for control of it.

Returning home from his three years in Washington, Welles signaled his dissatisfaction with the conservatives now dominating the party in Connecticut by identifying himself as an "independent Democrat" whose politics, he liked to think, were determined by principles and conscience, not party bosses or political expediency. He hoped President Franklin Pierce, the dark horse candidate the Democratic national convention nominated in 1852 after 49 contentious ballots, would move the party in a free-soil direction. But Pierce soon proved to be a "doughface" – a northern man with southern principles who faithfully did the bidding of the party's slave-state wing.[13]

Welles's already tenuous party loyalty was further weakened by the passage of the Kansas-Nebraska Act in 1854. The act repealed the ban on slavery above 36° 30' of north latitude in the Louisiana Purchase, a ban adopted as part of the Missouri Compromise 34 years earlier. Sponsored by Democratic Senator Stephen A. Douglas and backed by President Pierce at the insistence of southern Democrats, the act was widely seen in the North as betraying a time-hallowed covenant between the free and the slave states. Like countless northerners, Welles attributed its passage to an increasingly aggressive "slave power."

The act proved to be disastrous for the Democratic Party: in the ensuing Congressional elections the party lost 67 of the 92 northern House seats it had held in the Congress that enacted the measure. Many of these losses came at the hands of insurgent "anti-Nebraska" candidates backed by an *ad hoc* coalition of outraged Whigs, dissident Democrats, and Free-Soilers, a coalition that prefigured the Republican Party.[14] The nativist American Party (discussed below) also contributed to the Democratic debacle in Connecticut and some other states.

---

[12] If Welles had gone over to the Free-Soilers, Polk surely would have sacked him. For financial and other reasons, Welles was eager to retain his position.

[13] On the doughfaces, see Leonard L. Richards, *The Slave Power: The Free North and Southern Domination, 1780 – 1860* (Baton Rouge: Louisiana State University Press, 2000).

[14] For a perceptive account of the Kansas-Nebraska Act and its consequences, see David Potter, *The Impending Crisis: 1848 – 1861*, completed and edited by Don E. Fehrenbacher (New York: Harper & Row, 1976), Chapters 7 – 10.

By mid 1855, Welles had concluded that the Democratic Party was beyond redemption – a conclusion he arrived at in part because under relentless pressure from conservative Democrats Alfred E. Burr, editor of the *Hartford Times*, had closed the paper's pages to him. For a time he was uncertain whether and where he would find a new political home. In early February 1856, however, with a presidential election on the horizon, he was among about a dozen ex-Whigs, Free-Soilers, and independent Democrats who met in Hartford to found the state's Republican Party. Again he immersed himself in building a new party from the ground up. His first step was to establish the *Hartford Evening Press*, which would do for the fledgling Republican Party what the *Hartford Times* had done for the fledgling Democratic Party three decades earlier. He declined the editorship, but wrote many of the paper's editorials during its start-up phase.

Welles represented Connecticut on the Republican national committee and attended the party's first presidential nominating convention at Philadelphia in June 1856. Named to the 22-member platform committee, he, together with his Jackson-era friend Francis Preston Blair, Sr., drafted much of the party's first national platform.

John C. Fremont, the Republican presidential nominee, carried Connecticut in the November election. For the Republican Party to become a lasting force in the state's politics, however, it would have to meet two challenges. First, the former Whigs, who constituted the party's largest component, and its much smaller contingent of ex-Democrats, would have to put aside their old partisan animosities in the interest of party unity. This they managed to do despite lingering tensions.

A greater challenge was posed by another new political organization, the American (or Know-Nothing) Party. Running on an anti-immigrant and anti-Catholic platform, it did remarkably well in the 1854 legislative elections and continued to prosper for several years, taking the governorship and three of Connecticut's four seats in the U.S. House of Representatives in 1855 and winning the gubernatorial contest again in 1856. Many Connecticut Know-Nothings were not only nativists but also opposed to slavery's extension; and many anti-slavery Republicans also harbored nativist sentiments. Thus some leaders of the two parties favored bringing them together in a formal alliance, or even merging them into a single entity. Detesting ethnic and religious bigotry, Welles opposed any merger. He was enough of a practical politician, however, to support cooperation between Republicans and Know-Nothings, provided that his party avoided taking a nativist stance.

The two parties did cooperate during the 1856 presidential race, when many of the state's anti-slavery Know-Nothings, like their counterparts elsewhere in the North, were so outraged by the American Party's tacit endorsement of the Kansas-Nebraska Act that they backed the breakaway *North* American Party, which endorsed Fremont. The result in Connecticut was a hybrid Electoral College ticket composed of three Republicans and three North Americans. The following year the two parties held a joint convention at which Alexander Holley, whose support came largely from the Know-Nothing delegates, won the gubernatorial nomination by a wafer-thin margin over the candidate preferred by most Republican delegates, William A Buckingham, who was free of any Know-Nothing taint.

Ultimately, the Republican Party won over a large share of Connecticut's Know-Nothing voters and absorbed many of the American Party's leaders. To Welles's satisfaction, it did so largely on its own terms as nativist passions subsided while hostility to slavery's extension and the "slave power" continued to intensify. The turning point came in 1858, when the party spurned Governor Holley's bid for a second term, nominated Buckingham instead, and went on to win the gubernatorial race without making significant concessions to the Know-Nothings.[15]

By 1860, the Know-Nothing movement was defunct; the Democratic Party's perceived subservience to the "slave power" had seriously weakened it in Connecticut (as it had in much of the North); and relative harmony prevailed between the ex-Whig and ex-Democratic components of the Republican Party, as was exemplified by Welles's selection to head the state's delegation to the Republican national convention at Chicago in May.

Welles was optimistic about the party's chances of taking the White House in 1860. But he strongly opposed the frontrunner for the nomination, William H. Seward, a U.S. senator since 1849 and previously a two-term governor of New York. He not only distrusted Seward as a longtime leader of the Whig Party but also believed he was an unprincipled opportunist who wanted to centralize power in Washington at the expense of the states and was tainted by the corruption characteristic of Empire State politics. In the months preceding the Chicago convention, Welles wrote several forceful anti-Seward articles for influential newspapers in New York City and Washington, helped convince the Connecticut delegation not to cast any of its 12 votes for him, and worked to deny him support in other New England states, which Seward was

---

[15] On the relationship between Republicans and Know-Nothings in the North, including Connecticut, see William E. Gienapp, *The Origins of the Republican Party, 1852-1856* (New York: Oxford University Press, 1987) and Tyler Anbinder, *Nativism and Slavery: The Northern Know Nothings and the Politics of the 1850s* (New York: Oxford University Press, 1992).

counting on to back him heavily.[16]

Welles favored Salmon P. Chase, formerly a U.S. senator and governor of Ohio, for the nomination. But he had also been impressed by Lincoln when the two men talked during the Illinoisan's visit to Hartford in early March as part of a speaking tour in New England following his heralded Cooper Union address in New York City.[17]

At the Chicago convention, Seward led on the first ballot, but to Welles's satisfaction he drew far fewer votes from New England delegates than expected. Thereafter, his candidacy stalled, and on the third ballot Lincoln was nominated, mainly because a majority of the delegates concluded that he had a much better chance than Seward of carrying the key battleground states of Pennsylvania, New Jersey, Indiana, and Illinois, all of which the party had lost in 1856.[18]

Although Welles voted for Chase on all three ballots, he deemed Lincoln a worthy candidate and would give him unqualified support in the general election. He was part of the delegation of Republican leaders that traveled to Springfield after the convention to formally notify Lincoln of his nomination. The nominee greeted him warmly and made reference to their conversation in Hartford the previous March.

Lincoln learned early in the morning of November 7th that he had won the election and within hours began the politically delicate task of forming a cabinet. Determined to maintain sectional and political balance, he intended to give one seat to a prominent New Englander, preferably a former Democrat. Welles was on the short list from the start. But cabinet-making took time and involved the juggling of numerous competing claims. Thus Welles didn't receive definitive word that Lincoln had chosen him until February 28th, just four days before the inauguration. Even then it was uncertain whether he would become postmaster general or secretary of the navy. That question was answered on March 5th when the president submitted his name to the Senate for confirmation as the latter.

✳ ✳ ✳ ✳ ✳ ✳ ✳

---

[16] As will be seen in several of the ensuing chapters, Welles's suspicion and mistrust of Seward persisted during their years as colleagues in Lincoln's cabinet.

[17] Lincoln spoke in five Connecticut cities between March 5th and 10th. In addition to Hartford, they were Norwich (where he met with Governor Buckingham, who was in a very tight race for reelection), Meriden, New Haven, and Bridgeport. See Harold Holzer, *Lincoln at Cooper Union: The Speech That Made Abraham Lincoln President* (New York: Simon & Schuster, 2004), pp. 192-201.

[18] A detailed account of the balloting is given in Murat Halstead, *Caucuses of 1860: A History of the National Political Conventions of the Current Presidential Campaign* (Columbus, Ohio: Follett, Foster, and Co., 1860), pp. 146-149.

Welles brought to the cabinet a number of political convictions and personal characteristics he had exhibited in the pre-war decades. Like his father, he revered Thomas Jefferson and believed the key to Jefferson's greatness was his faith in the capacity of ordinary people for self-government. Lincoln and Welles both understood that the fate of democracy was at stake in the Civil War. As Lincoln declared in his July 4, 1861, message to a special session of Congress:

> [Secession] presents to the whole family of man, the question, whether a constitutional republic, or a democracy – a government of the people, by the same people – can, or cannot, maintain its territorial integrity, against its domestic foes . . . . It forces us to ask: "Is there, in all republics, this inherent and fatal weakness?" "Must a government, of necessity, be too *strong* for the liberties of its own people, or too *weak* to maintain its own existence?"[19]

Over the next four years, both men exerted themselves unrelentingly to ensure that those daunting questions were answered in the negative and the country would emerge from its severest trial with democracy intact.

In keeping with his Jeffersonian predilections, Welles had always advocated strict construction of the Constitution and staunchly defended states' rights, believing it was the states, not the federal government, that could best safeguard the rights and liberty of the individual. Yet unlike many proponents of strict construction and states' rights, northern as well as southern, his thinking took a decidedly anti-slavery turn. He viewed the Constitution's fugitive slave clause as exclusively an agreement among the states to return runaways to their owners, not a grant of power to the federal government. Thus he thought the Fugitive Slave Act adopted as part of the Compromise of 1850 was unconstitutional. He also rejected slaveholders' claims that they had the right to take their human property into the territories, since he found nothing in the Constitution that authorized the federal government to establish or protect slavery anywhere that it had exclusive jurisdiction, which he believed it did in the territories.

As to slavery in the southern states, Welles deemed it a local institution that was created by state law and shielded from federal interference by the Constitution. Under the impact of secession and war, however, he, like Lincoln and many other northerners, concluded that the president, as commander in chief of the armed forces, could emancipate the slaves

---

[19] Roy P. Basler, ed., *The Collected Works of Abraham Lincoln* (New Brunswick, New Jersey: Rutgers University Press, 1953), Vol. IV, p. 425.

in the rebellious states on grounds of military necessity, which overrode the constitutional protection slavery enjoyed as long as the people of those states had remained loyal to the Union.

Welles was sincere in espousing states' rights and always feared that creation of an over-mighty central government would jeopardize individual liberty. Thus he was privately critical of the Lincoln administration's wartime infringements of civil liberties.[20] And as will be seen in the Afterword, his states' rights convictions caused him fervently to oppose the entire Reconstruction program the Republican-controlled Congress adopted after the war. Yet he was also a nationalist. Like Andrew Jackson, he rejected John C. Calhoun's theory that each state's rights included the right to nullify federal laws. And he of course denied that states had a right to secede.

Finally, Welles personified many traits of character and personality associated with the stereotypical Yankee. He was a man of stern moral rectitude who set great store by honor, integrity and propriety. Strong-willed, high-minded, and judgmental, he sometimes fell prey to self-righteousness and was frequently irascible and short on tact. He occasionally lost his temper, but rarely lost his composure during a crisis. Conscientious to a fault, he had an abiding sense of patriotic *duty* (a word that appears frequently in his diary) and was severely critical of men he thought were putting personal or partisan interests ahead of their country's welfare. He believed politics should be about principle, not the mere pursuit of power and patronage. He drove himself hard, since his conscience would tolerate nothing less. (On March 31, 1863, he noted in the diary that during a two-week illness he had missed only one day at work.) He had a pessimistic streak and was something of a stoic, which helped him cope with political disappointments and military setbacks – and also with the ordeal of having six of his nine children predecease him. Despite his sometimes unruly wig, in photographs the mature Welles looks very much the dignified, sober-sided, austere Yankee gentleman that he was.

* * * * * * *

During the Civil War, a number of Connecticut men won distinction for their contribution to the Union cause. For example, William A. Buckingham, the "War Governor" who worked tirelessly to promote

[20] For instance, in his May 23, 1864, diary entry he condemned the government's temporary seizure of two Democratic newspapers in New York City that had been duped into publishing a phony presidential proclamation.

enlistments in the army; New Haven-born Admiral Andrew Hull Foote, whose gunboat flotilla played a key role in the campaign against Forts Henry and Donelson in February 1862; and General Alfred H. Terry, who commanded the troops that in combination with the navy took Fort Fisher in January 1865, thus sealing off Wilmington, North Carolina, the last major Confederate port that had remained open to blockade-runners. But it is Welles who stands foremost among them, for both his leadership of the Navy Department and the informative, insightful, often provocative diary he left to posterity.

EDITORIAL NOTE

The excerpts in this book come from the first published edition of Gideon Welles's diary. It was edited by his son Edgar, with an introduction by historian John T. Morse, Jr., and published in three volumes by the Houghton Mifflin Company in 1911. The main purpose of this note is to describe certain problems with that edition and to explain how the editor has dealt with them.

At various times after leaving office in 1869, Welles revised the manuscript diary, partially rewriting many entries, deleting others, and adding new material. It was this much-revised version that was published in 1911. But neither Edgar Welles nor Morse disclosed that Welles had written or rewritten parts of the diary years after the events he was recording occurred and that he had excised some passages. Furthermore, Edgar Welles not only made minor changes in the text (e.g., in punctuation and spelling), but also deleted a number of passages that were in the manuscript – some of them, presumably, because he did not want to offend still-living persons discussed in the diary or their descendants. Given his father's scathing criticisms of some individuals, he may even have been concerned about libel suits. In a brief preface, he acknowledged having made a "few" deletions, an understatement of their actual number.

Soon after the 1911 edition appeared, one reviewer suggested that it contained at least two passages that Welles had written at a later time. Additional doubts about its faithfulness to the original were expressed during ensuing decades. But the extent to which the 1911 edition diverged from the manuscript diary did not become clear until 1960, when historian Howard K. Beale, who had painstakingly compared the 1911 edition with the manuscript located at the Library of Congress, brought out a new edition, published by W. W. Norton & Company.[1]

---

[1] In a lengthy introduction to the 1960 edition, Beale, who had initially raised doubts about the 1911 edition in a paper he wrote for a Harvard graduate course in 1924, called

The new edition consisted of a verbatim reproduction of the earlier edition, together with Beale's extensive annotations.[2] Beale specified every change that had been made in the original text (except for corrections of Welles's misspellings), reproduced the language that had disappeared in the process of revision, and resurrected the passages that had been deleted.[3] He also identified a number of passages that were not in the manuscript diary. Although they apparently were written by Welles, it is unclear under what circumstances he wrote them, whether they were later additions, or why they existed apart from the manuscript diary.

The present editor checked all of the excerpts chosen for inclusion in this book against the Beale edition and found that many, but by no means all of them, had been revised to one degree or another. This raised the question of whether in all such instances he should revert to what Welles had originally written. After much deliberation, he adopted a more flexible approach instead.

As Beale himself acknowledged, many of the revisions were minor, such as the insertion of a missing word or a change in punctuation or paragraphing.[4] Furthermore, in many instances when Welles substituted one word for another or rewrote a phrase or clause, his purpose appears to have been not to alter his original meaning but to express it more clearly. In some other instances, he probably was exercising a writer's prerogative to burnish his language for purely stylistic reasons. (It is possible, as Beale noted, that Welles made some of these stylistic changes in the course of writing the original entry, not at a later time.) The editor has retained these kinds of revision, some of which make the text more readily comprehensible and none of which misrepresents what Welles had initially written.

It is quite another matter, however, when in a diary valued for its immediacy a revision *substantively* changed what Welles had written on the day the entry was dated. Thus the editor has substituted Welles's original language whenever, in his judgment, a revision altered a passage's

---

the diary an invaluable historical source, summarized earlier criticisms of the 1911 edition, described his editorial procedures, and identified seven different types of revision Welles had made, ranging from minor technical corrections to the insertion of language seemingly intended to make the diarist look more perspicacious.

[2] Beale did not, however, reprint Edgar Welles's preface or Morse's introduction, which were largely irrelevant to his goal of determining what Welles had originally written.

[3] The only passage deleted by Edgar Welles that is included in this book is the December 15, 1863, entry about the controversial appointment of a new U.S. marshal for Connecticut (see Chapter 7).

[4] Welles probably inserted most of the missing words, but it is likely his son made many of the changes in punctuation – especially the substitution of semicolons for the em dashes of which his father had made prolific use.

tone, emphasis, implications, or explicit meaning, or reflected the influence of hindsight, or seemed otherwise misleading about what the diarist actually had thought or observed at the time he first put the passage to paper. This proved to be necessary in only a relatively small number of instances because, as Beale noted in his introduction to the 1960 edition, Welles made far fewer substantive changes to the wartime portion of the diary than to the post-war portion.[5]

✴ ✴ ✴ ✴ ✴ ✴ ✴

Several additional explanatory comments are in order. First, in addition to writing a brief introduction to each chapter (printed in italics), the editor has inserted supplementary information (also in italics) immediately before or after selected excerpts. Supplementary material will also be found in many of the footnotes. Second, the bracketed language that appears in some excerpts was inserted by the editor. (Words appearing in parentheses were placed there by either the diarist or his son.) Third, Welles was inconsistent in how he indicated the date of diary entries. In this book, the date of each excerpt appears in boldface italics at the start of the passage. Finally, some of Welles's orthography will strike the modern reader as at best odd; for example, his hyphenation of "to-day" and "to-morrow," his use of the lower case "n" in "Negro," his spelling of "anyone," "someone," and "sometimes" as two words instead of one, and his preference for "intrenchment," "intrusted, and "indorsement" instead of "entrenchment," "entrusted," and "endorsement." These were all commonplace usages in Welles's day, and the editor has seen no need to clutter the pages with the notation [*sic*] when they appear.

---

[5] In several cases where a revision has been replaced with the original manuscript language, the revision is of sufficient interest that the editor has reproduced it in a footnote.

Chapter 1

THE EMANCIPATION PROCLAMATION AND BEYOND

Welles's entries on Lincoln's decision to issue the Emancipation Proclamation constitute one of the diary's most important contributions to historical knowledge. In Section I of this chapter those entries are reproduced in their entirety. Section II consists of excerpts about a number of related topics, including the possible colonization of African Americans outside the United States, the enlistment in the army and navy of contrabands (slaves who fled to Union lines) and free-born blacks, the limits of the Emancipation Proclamation, the massacre of African American soldiers at Fort Pillow in Tennessee, and Congressional approval of the 13th Amendment abolishing slavery.[1]

I

As Welles points out in the following excerpt, Secretary of State Seward and he were the first cabinet members Lincoln sounded out about the possible issuance of a proclamation freeing the slaves in the rebellious states. This was probably no accident. Although virtually all Republicans were opposed to slavery in principle, opinions about how to eliminate the institution ranged across a broad spectrum from gradual, state-initiated, compensated emancipation followed by the forced deportation of the former slaves, to immediate, federally mandated, uncompensated emancipation coupled with citizenship and equal rights for the freed people. It is likely that Lincoln viewed Welles and Seward as the cabinet's centrists – men who were generally less conservative than Interior Secretary Caleb Smith and

---

[1] Although most historians still employ the customary term "slaves," in recent years some scholars have advocated the use instead of "enslaved persons," a phrase they favor because it recognizes that those held in bondage were human beings, not simply property, which is how the laws of the slave states primarily defined them.

the two border-state members, Attorney General Edward Bates and Postmaster General Montgomery Blair, but more conservative than Secretary of War Edwin M. Stanton and Treasury Secretary Salmon P. Chase. As a centrist himself, Lincoln may well have wanted to try out the idea on his fellow centrists before soliciting the views of other cabinet members.

Undated[2]: On Sunday, the 13th of July, 1862, President Lincoln invited me to accompany him in his carriage to the funeral of an infant child of Mr. Stanton. Secretary Seward and his daughter in law Mrs. Frederick Seward were also in the carriage. Mr. Stanton occupied at that time for a summer residence the house of a naval officer, I think Hazard, some two or three miles west, or northwest, of Georgetown. It was on this occasion and on this ride that he first mentioned to Mr. Seward and myself the subject of emancipating the slaves by proclamation in case the Rebels did not cease to persist in their war on the Government and the Union, of which he saw no evidence. He dwelt earnestly on the gravity, importance, and delicacy of the movement, said he had given it much thought and had about come to the conclusion that it was a military necessity absolutely essential for the salvation of the Union, that we must free the slaves or be ourselves subdued, etc., etc.

This was, he said, the first occasion when he had mentioned the subject to anyone, and wished us to frankly state how the proposition struck us. Mr. Seward said the subject involved consequences so vast and momentous that he should wish to give it mature reflection before giving a decisive answer, but his present opinion inclined to the measure as justifiable, and perhaps he might say expedient and necessary. These were also my views. Two or three times on that ride the subject was adverted to, and before separating the President desired us to give the question special and deliberate attention, for he was earnest in the conviction that something must be done. It was a new departure for the President, for until this time, in all our previous interviews, whenever the question of emancipation or the mitigation of slavery had been in any way alluded to, he had been prompt and emphatic in denouncing any interference by the General Government with the subject.[3] This was, I think, the sentiment of every member of the Cabinet, all of whom, including the President, considered it a local, domestic question appertaining to the States respectively,

---

[2] This was the first entry in the manuscript of the diary. It apparently was written sometime between July 14 and August 11, 1862.

[3] In March 1862, however, Lincoln had secured a pledge from Congress to provide monetary assistance to any slave state that voluntarily initiated gradual emancipation.

who had never parted with their authority over it. But the reverses before Richmond,[4] and the formidable power and dimensions of the insurrection, which extended through all the Slave States, and had combined most of them in a confederacy to destroy the Union, impelled the Administration to adopt extraordinary measures to preserve the national existence. The slaves, if not armed and disciplined, were in the service of those who were, not only as field laborers and producers, but thousands of them were in attendance upon the armies in the field, employed as waiters and teamsters, and the fortifications and intrenchments were constructed by them.

On July 22nd Lincoln informed the entire cabinet of his intention to issue a proclamation of emancipation. Oddly, Welles made no diary entry on that date. But in his October 1st entry he discussed the July 22nd meeting (and a related one on July 21st). By the time that entry was written, Lincoln had issued the preliminary Emancipation Proclamation (on September 22nd), giving the rebellious states 100 days (i.e., to January 1, 1863) to return to the Union, or else he would declare their slaves emancipated. The October 1st entry is reproduced below, followed by Welles's September 22nd entry about the cabinet's final discussion of the preliminary Proclamation preparatory to its issuance later that day. This departure from the chronological order of the diary is necessary in order to see the sequence of events as Welles observed them.

October 1, 1862: When it [Lincoln's proposal for a proclamation of emancipation] was first brought forward [to the entire cabinet] some six or eight weeks ago,[5] all assented to it. It was pretty fully discussed at two successive Cabinet-meetings, and the President consulted freely, I presume, with the members individually. He did with me. Mr. Bates [a Missourian] desired that deportation, by force if necessary, should go with emancipation. Born and educated among the negroes, having always lived with slaves, he dreaded any step which should be taken to bring about social equality between the two races. The effect, he said, would be to degrade the whites without elevating the blacks. Demoralization, vice, and misery would follow. Mr. Blair [from Maryland], at the second discussion, said that, while he was an emancipationist from principle, he had doubts of the expediency of such a movement as was contemplated. Stanton, after expressing himself earnestly in favor of the step proposed, said it was so important a measure that he hoped every member would give his opinion,

---

[4] This is a reference to the failure of McClellan's Peninsula Campaign to take the Confederate capital (see Chapter 5).
[5] It was closer to 10 weeks.

whatever it might be, on the subject; two had not spoken – alluding to Chase and myself.

I briefly alluded to the strong exercise of power involved in the question, and the denial of Executive authority to do this act, but the Rebels themselves had invoked war on the subject of slavery, had appealed to arms, and they must abide the consequences. It was an exercise of war powers, and I was willing to resort to extreme measures. The blow would fall heavy and severe on those loyal men in the Slave States who clung to the Union, but they must abide the results of a conflict which they had deplored, and unless they could persuade their fellow citizens to embrace the alternative presented [i.e., to end the rebellion forthwith], they must suffer with them. The slaves were now an element of strength to the Rebels – were laborers, producers, and army attendants; were considered as property by the Rebels, and, if *property*, were subject to confiscation; if not property, we should invite them as well as the [loyal southern] whites to unite with us in putting down the Rebellion. I had made known my views to the President and could say here I gave my approval of the Proclamation. Mr. Chase said it was going a step farther than he had proposed, but he was glad of it and went into a very full argument on the subject. I do not attempt to repeat it or any portion of it, nor that of others, farther than to define the position of each when this important question was before them. Something more than a Proclamation will be necessary, for this step will band the South together, and unite the Border States firmly with the Cotton States in resistance to the Government.

An important outcome of the July 22nd meeting Welles does not mention was Lincoln's acceptance of Seward's recommendation that issuance of the preliminary Proclamation be deferred until the Union's military situation improved, lest it be seen as an act of desperation. The Union victory at Antietam on September 17th cleared the way for Lincoln to issue it five days later.

September 22, 1862: A special Cabinet meeting. The subject was the Proclamation for emancipating the slaves after a certain date, in States that shall then be in rebellion. For several weeks the subject has been suspended, but the President says [it was] never lost sight of. When it was submitted, and now in taking up the Proclamation, the President stated that the question was finally decided, the act and the consequences were his, but that he felt it due to us to make us acquainted with the fact and to invite criticism on the paper which he had prepared. There were, he had found, some differences in the Cabinet, but he had, after consulting each and all, individually and collectively, formed his own conclusions and made his own decision.

Alexander Hay Ritchie's engraving of Francis Bicknell Carpenter's 1864 painting *First Reading of the Emancipation Proclamation Before the Cabinet* (1866). Left to right: seated, Stanton, Lincoln, Welles, Seward, Bates; standing, Chase, Smith, Blair. Source: The Library of Congress

In the course of the discussion on this paper, which was long, earnest, and, on the general principle involved, harmonious, he remarked that he had made a vow, a covenant, that if God gave us the victory in the approaching battle [at Antietam], he would consider it an indication of Divine will, and that it was his duty to move forward in the cause of emancipation. It might be thought strange, he said, that he had in this way submitted the disposal of matters when the way was not clear to his mind what he should do. God had decided this question in favor of the slaves. He was satisfied it was right, was confirmed and strengthened in his action by the vow and the results. His mind was fixed, his decision made, but he wished his paper announcing his course [to be] as correct in terms as it could be made without any change in his determination. He read the document. One or two unimportant emendations suggested by Seward were approved. It was then handed to the Secretary of State to publish to-morrow. After this, Blair remarked that he did not concur in the expediency of the measure at this time, though he approved of the principle, and should therefore wish to file his objections. He stated at some length his views, which were that we ought not to put in greater jeopardy the patriotic element in the Border States, that the results of this Proclamation would be to carry over those States *en masse* to the Secessionists as soon as it was read, and that there was also a class of partisans in the Free States endeavoring to revive old parties, who would have a club put into their hands of which they would avail themselves to beat the Administration.

The President said he had considered the danger apprehended from the first objection, which was undoubtedly serious, but the objection was certainly as great not to act; as regarded the last, it had not much weight with him. The question of power, authority, in the Government to set free the slaves was not much discussed at this meeting, but had been canvassed by the President in private conversation with the members individually. Some thought legislation advisable before the step was taken, but Congress was clothed with no authority on this subject, nor is the Executive, except under the war power – military necessity, martial law, when there can be no legislation. This was the view which I took when the President first presented the subject to Seward and myself last summer as we were returning from the funeral of Stanton's child, a ride of two or three miles beyond Georgetown. Seward was at that time not at all communicative, and, I think, not willing to advise the movement. It is momentous both in its immediate and remote results, and an exercise of extraordinary power which cannot be justified on mere humanitarian principles, and would never have been attempted but to preserve the national existence. These were my convictions and this [was] the drift of the discussion. The effect which the Proclamation will have on the public mind is a matter of some uncertainty. In some respects it would, I think, have been better to have issued it when formerly first considered. There is an impression that Seward has opposed, and is opposed to, the measure. I have not been without that impression myself, chiefly from his hesitation to commit himself, and perhaps because action was suspended on his suggestion. But in the final discussion he has as cordially supported the measure as Chase.

For myself the subject has, from its magnitude and its consequences oppressed me, aside from the ethical features of the question. It is a step in the progress of this war which will extend into the distant future. The termination of this terrible conflict seems more remote with every movement, and unless the Rebels hasten to avail themselves of the alternative presented, of which I see little probability, the war can scarcely be other than one of subjugation. There is in the Free States a very general impression that this measure will insure a speedy peace. I cannot say that I so view it. No one in those States dare advocate peace as a means of prolonging slavery, if it is his honest opinion, and the pecuniary, industrial, and social sacrifice impending will intensify the struggle before us. While, however, these dark clouds are above and around us, I cannot see how the subject could be avoided. Perhaps it is not desirable it should be.

Apropos Welles's statement that Seward supported issuance of the preliminary Proclamation as "cordially" as Chase did, it will be seen in Chapter 2 that just two weeks before he issued the final Proclamation, Lincoln confronted a crisis precipitated by the attempt of a caucus of Republican senators to force him to oust the secretary of state. This was in part because many of the senators had the erroneous impression that Seward was exerting a "conservative" influence on the president with respect to emancipation. Chase, who was Seward's foremost rival for influence and power within the administration, had done much behind the scenes to give Republican senators this impression. There was even concern that if Seward had his way, Lincoln would not issue the final Proclamation on January 1st.

September 24, 1862: As I write, 9 P.M., a band of music strikes up on the opposite side of the square,[6] a complimentary serenade to the President for the [preliminary] Emancipation Proclamation. The document has been in the main well received, but there is some violent opposition,

---

[6] Welles's home in Washington was located on the northern side of Lafayette Square, a short walk from the White House.

and the friends of the measure have made this demonstration to show their approval.

December 29, 1862: At the meeting to-day, the President read the draft of his Emancipation Proclamation, invited criticism, and finally directed that copies should be furnished to each [cabinet member]. It is a good and well-prepared paper, but I suggested that part of the sentence marked in pencil be omitted. Chase advised that fractional parts of States ought not be exempted. In this I think he is right, and so stated. Practically, there would be difficulty in freeing parts of States and not freeing others – a clashing between central and local authorities. [7]

December 31, 1862: We had an early and special Cabinet-meeting, convened at 10 A.M. The subject was the Proclamation of to-morrow to emancipate the slaves in the Rebel States. Seward proposed two amendments, one including mine, and one enjoining upon, instead of appealing to, those emancipated, to forbear from tumult.[8] Blair had, like Seward and myself, proposed the omission of a part of a sentence and made other suggestions which I thought improvements. Chase made some good criticisms and proposed a felicitous closing sentence.[9] The President took the suggestions, written in order, and said he would complete the document.

January 1, 1863: The Emancipation Proclamation is published in this evening's Star. This is a broad step, and will be a landmark in history. The immediate effect will not be all its friends anticipate or its opponents apprehend. Passing events are steadily accomplishing what is here

---

[7] Citing his war powers as commander in chief of the armed services, Lincoln justified the Proclamation constitutionally as an act of military necessity. He believed it would undercut that rationale if he applied the Proclamation to areas of the Confederacy where the Union army was in firm control and thus there was no compelling military necessity. This is why, contrary to Chase's advice, which Welles endorsed, Lincoln expressly exempted from the Proclamation certain parishes in southern Louisiana, together with the city of New Orleans, and certain counties in Virginia, together with the cities of Norfolk and Portsmouth. Since he did not include Tennessee on the list of rebellious states to which the Proclamation applied, it was also in effect exempted, but more for political than for constitutional reasons.

[8] Critics, both at home and abroad, had construed some ambiguous language in the preliminary Proclamation as serving to encourage a massive slave rebellion. The revision to the text of the final Proclamation to which Welles refers was designed to make clear that the administration wanted no such thing.

[9] This sentence, which provided a rhetorical lift to a document that was otherwise and by intent dryly legalistic, read: "And upon this act, sincerely believed to be an act of justice, warranted by the Constitution, upon military necessity, I invoke the considerate judgment of mankind, and the gracious favor of Almighty God."

proclaimed. The character of the country is in many respects undergoing a transformation. This must be obvious to all, and I am content to await the results of events, deep as they may plough their furrows in our once happy land. This great upheaval which is shaking our civil fabric was perhaps necessary to overthrow and subdue the mass of wrong and error which no trivial measure could eradicate. The seed which is being sown will germinate and bear fruit, and tares and weeds will also spring up under the new dispensation. [10]

II

The following two excerpts describe the efforts by a shady promoter, Ambrose Thompson, to colonize African Americans on the Chiriquí Strip, located on the Isthmus of Panama, which was then part of New Granada (now Colombia). The colonists would support themselves by mining the supposedly rich coal deposits located there. Welles resisted the scheme, despite the interest Lincoln took in it and the energetic support it received from Secretary of the Interior Smith.

September 26, 1862: At several [cabinet] meetings of late the subject of deporting the colored race has been discussed. Indeed for months, almost from the commencement of this administration, it has been at times considered. More than a year ago it was thrust on me by Thompson and others in connection with the Chiriquí Grant. Speculators used it as a means of disposing of that grant to our Government. The President, encouraged by Blair and Smith, was disposed to favor it. Blair is honest and disinterested; perhaps Smith is so, yet I have not been favorably impressed with his zeal in behalf of the Chiriquí Association. As early as May, 1861, a great pressure was made upon me to enter into a coal contract with this company. The President was earnest in the matter. Smith, with the Thompsons [Ambrose and his son], urged and stimulated him, and they were as importunate with me as the President. I spent two or three hours on different days looking over the papers – titles, maps, reports, and evidence – and came to the conclusion that there *was* fraud and cheat in the affair. It appeared to be a swindling speculation.

---

[10] For an exceptionally illuminating account of the lead-up to the issuance of the preliminary Emancipation Proclamation, the interval between it and the final Proclamation's promulgation on January 1, 1863, and the varied reactions to both measures, see Louis P. Masur, *Lincoln's Hundred Days: The Emancipation Proclamation and the War for the Union* (Cambridge, Mass.: Harvard University Press, 2012).

Told the President I had no confidence in it, and asked to be excused from its further consideration. The papers were then referred to Smith to investigate and report. After a month or two he reported strongly in favor of the scheme, and advised that the Navy Department should make an immediate contract for the coal before foreign governments got hold of it .... The President was quite earnest in its favor, but I objected and desired to be excused from any participation in it. Two or three times it has been revived, but I have crowded off action. Chase gave me assistance on one occasion, and the scheme was dropped until this question of deporting colored persons came up, when Smith again brought forward Thompson's Chiriquí Grant. He made a skillful and taking report, embracing both coal and negroes. Each was to assist the other. The negroes were to be transported to Chiriquí to mine coal for the Navy, and the Secretary of the Navy was to make an immediate advance of $50,000 for coal not yet mined – nor laborers obtained to mine it, nor any satisfactory information or proof that there was decent coal to be mined.[11] I respectfully declined adopting his views. Chase and Stanton sustained me, and Mr. Bates to an extent. Blair, who first favored it, cooled off, as the question was discussed, but the President and Smith were persistent.

It came out that the governments and rival parties in Central America denied the legality of the Chiriquí Grant – declared it was a bogus sale. The President concluded he ought to be better satisfied on this point, and would send out [an] agent. At this stage of the case Senator [Samuel C.] Pomeroy [a Kansas Republican] appeared and took upon himself a negro emigrating colonization scheme. Would himself go out and take with him a cargo of negroes, and hunt up a place for them – all professedly in the cause of humanity.

On Tuesday last the President brought forward the subject and desired the members of the Cabinet to each take it into serious consideration. He thought a treaty could be made to advantage, and territory secured to which the negroes could be sent. Several governments had signified their willingness to receive them. Mr. Seward said some were willing to take them without expense to us.

Mr. Blair made a long argumentative statement in favor of deportation. It would be necessary to rid the country of its black population, and some place must be found for them. He is strongly for deportation, has given the subject much thought, but yet seems to have no matured system which he can recommend. Mr. Bates was for compulsory deportation.

---

[11] A subsequent investigation found that Chiriquí Strip coal, if placed in a confined space such as the hold of a ship, was prone to ignite by spontaneous combustion.

The negro would not go voluntarily, had great local attachments and no enterprise. The President objected unequivocally to compulsion. Their emigration must be voluntary and without expense to themselves. Great Britain, Denmark, and perhaps other powers would take them [in their western hemisphere colonies]. I remarked there was no necessity for a treaty. Any person who desired to leave the country could do so now, whether white or black, and it was best to leave it so – a voluntary system; the emigrant who chose to leave our shores could and would go where there were the best inducements.

These remarks seemed to strike Seward, who, I perceive, has been in consultation with the President and some of the foreign ministers, and on his motion the subject was postponed, with an understanding it would be taken up to-day. Mr. Bates had a very well prepared paper which he read, expressing his views. Little was said by any one else except Seward, who followed up my suggestions. But the President is not satisfied; says he wants a treaty. Smith says the Senate would never ratify a treaty conferring any power, and advised that Seward should make a contract.

October 7, 1862: There was an indisposition to press the subject of negro emigration to Chiriquí at the meeting of the Cabinet, against the wishes and remonstrances of the States of Central America.

Thus ended the Chiriquí colonization scheme. It did not, however, end Lincoln's interest in colonization, although Welles does not mention it in his diary. On December 31, 1862 (the day before the final Emancipation Proclamation was issued), he contracted with another promoter, Bernard Kock, to colonize up to 5,000 African Americans on the Île á Vache, a small island off the coast of Haiti. Using funds provided by two New York investors, Kock in April 1863 transported some 450 black men, women, and children to the island, where they supposedly would raise Sea Island cotton. Conditions on the island were wretched, however, and within a few months many of the colonists had died of deprivation or disease, and some others had fled to the Haitian mainland. In February 1864, the adminis- tration sent a ship to return the surviving colonists to the United States.[12]

---

[12] Historians differ over whether the primary motive for Lincoln's interest in colonization was political expediency, racial prejudice, or a humanitarian belief that black Americans could never attain equality in the U.S. and thus would be better off somewhere that was free of the intense racism pervading American society. For an insightful analysis of this complex issue, see Eric Foner, "Lincoln and Colonization," in Eric Foner, ed., *Our Lincoln: New Perspectives on Lincoln and His World* (New York: W. W. Norton, 2008), pp. 135 – 166. Although Lincoln never mentioned colonization in public after issuing the final Emancipation Proclamation, recent scholarship has shown that he continued to pursue the idea for at least another year, and perhaps longer. See Phillip W.

* * * * * * *

In the Emancipation Proclamation, Lincoln, invoking discretionary authority Congress had given him in July 1862, announced that blacks would henceforth be enlisted as soldiers. About 180,000 of them served in the army – nine percent of all Union enlisted men. In contrast, as early as October 1861, Welles, with Lincoln's tacit approval, was authorizing some naval officers to enlist African American sailors. Ultimately, they accounted for about 15 percent of all the enlisted men who served in the navy during the war.[13]

January 10, 1863: The President sent for Stanton and myself; wished us to consult and do what we could for the employment of the contrabands, and as the Rebels threatened to kill all caught with arms in their hands, to employ them where they would not be liable to be captured. On the ships he thought they were well cared for, and suggested to Stanton that they could perform garrison duty at Memphis, Columbus [Kentucky], and other places and let the [white] soldiers go on more active service.

May 26, 1863: There was a sharp controversy between Chase and Blair on the subject of the Fugitive Slave Law, as attempted to be executed on one Hall here in the district. Both were earnest, Blair for executing the law, Chase for permitting the man to enter the service of the United States instead of being remanded into slavery. The President said this was one of those questions that always embarrassed him. It reminded him of a man in Illinois who was in debt and terribly annoyed by a pressing creditor, until finally the debtor assumed [i.e., pretended] to be crazy whenever the creditor broached the subject. "I," said the President, "have on more than one occasion, in this room, when beset by extremists on this question, been compelled to appear to be very mad. I think," he continued, "none of you will ever dispose of this subject without getting mad."

June 6, 1863: The Irish element is dissatisfied with the service, and there is an unconquerable prejudice on the part of many whites against black soldiers. But all our increased military strength now comes from the negroes.[14]

Magness and Sebastian N. Page, *Colonization After Emancipation: Lincoln and the Movement for Black Resettlement* (Columbia: University of Missouri Press, 2011).

[13] Symonds, *Lincoln and His Admirals*, p. 165.

[14] By early 1863, voluntary enlistments in the Union army by whites had fallen sharply, prompting Congress to enact a conscription law in March that took effect in July. During this period, the large number of black volunteers helped make up the slack.

✳ ✳ ✳ ✳ ✳ ✳ ✳

August 13, 1863: [In a conversation with Chase] I said that no slave who had left his Rebel master could be restored, but that an immediate, universal, unconditional sweep, were the Rebellion crushed, might be injurious to both the slave and his owner, involving industrial and social difficulties and disturbances and that these embarrassments required deliberate, wise thought and consideration. The Proclamation of Emancipation was justifiable as a military necessity against Rebel enemies, who were making use of these slaves to destroy our national existence; it *was* in self-defense and for our own preservation, the first law of nature. But were the Rebellion suppressed, the disposition of the slavery question was, in my view, one of the most delicate and important that had ever devolved on those who administrated the government. Were all the Slave States involved in the Rebellion, the case would be different, for then all would fare alike. The only solution which I could perceive was for the Border States to pass emancipation laws. The Federal Government could not interfere with them; it had and could with the rebellious States. They had made war for slavery, had appealed to arms, and must abide the result. But we must be careful, in our zeal on this subject, not to destroy the great framework of our governmental system. The States had rights which must be respected, the General Government limitations beyond which it must not pass.

August 19, 1863: What is to be done with the slaves and slavery? Were slavery out of the way, there would seem to be no serious obstacle to the reestablishment of the Union. But the cause which was made the pretext of the Civil War will not be readily given up by the [southern] masses, who have been duped and misled by their leaders, and who have so large an interest at stake, without a further struggle.

August 22, 1863: Slavery has received its death-blow. The seeds which have been sown by this war will germinate, were peace restored to-morrow and the States reunited with the rotten institution in each of them. What is to be the effect of the Proclamation, and what will be the exact status of the slaves and the slaveowners, were the States now to resume their position, I am not prepared to say. The courts would adjudicate the questions; there would be legislative action in Congress and in the States also; there would be sense and practical wisdom on the part of intelligent and candid men who are not carried away by prejudice, fanaticism, and wild theories. No slave who has left a Rebel master, or has served under the flag, can ever be forced into involuntary servitude.

The constitutional relations of the States have not been changed by the Rebellion, but the personal condition of every Rebel is affected. The two are not identical. The rights of the States are unimpaired; the rights of those who have participated in the Rebellion have been forfeited.

✵ ✵ ✵ ✵ ✵ ✵ ✵

On April 12, 1864, a 1500-man Confederate cavalry force commanded by General Nathan Bedford Forrest attacked the Union garrison at Fort Pillow on the Mississippi River about 50 miles north of Memphis. It was defended by fewer than 600 troops, half of them African Americans, the other half white Tennessee loyalists. Shortly after the fort fell, northern press reports, citing interviews with survivors, stated that the victorious rebels had shot and killed a large number of black soldiers who had surrendered or had thrown down their weapons and were trying to surrender. The Fort Pillow massacre, as it came to be called, aroused outrage in the North – outrage not diminished when Forrest publicly denied that his men had killed any Union soldiers except in combat. In response to the public furor, two cabinet meetings were devoted to discussing how the Lincoln administration should respond.[15]

May 3, 1864: At the Cabinet meeting the President requested each member to give him an opinion as to what course the Government should pursue in relation to the recent massacre at Fort Pillow. The committee from Congress who have visited the scene returned yesterday and will soon report. All the reported horrors are said to be verified. The President wishes to be prepared to act as soon as the subject is brought to his notice officially and hence [seeks] Cabinet advice in advance.

The subject is one of great responsibility and great embarrassment, especially before we are in possession of the facts and evidence of the committee. There must be something in these terrible reports, but I distrust Congressional committees. They exaggerate.

---

[15] For the remainder of the war and long thereafter debate raged, largely along North-South lines, about whether there had indeed been a massacre at Fort Pillow. Today, most historians believe there was a massacre, but it is uncertain whether Forrest ordered it or rebel soldiers, outraged at the sight of blacks in uniform, acted on their own initiative. John Cimprich, "The Fort Pillow Massacre: Assessing the Evidence," in John David Smith, ed., *Black Soldiers in Blue: African American Troops in the Civil War Era* (Chapel Hill: University of North Carolina Press, 2002), pp. 150 – 168, provides a careful analysis of the conflicting claims about what occurred. Also see Cimprich, *Fort Pillow, A Civil War Massacre, and Public Memory* (Baton Rouge: Louisiana State University Press, 2005).

May 5, 1864: I have written a letter to the President in relation to the Fort Pillow massacre, but it is not satisfactory to me, nor can I make it so without the evidence of what was done, nor am I certain that even then I could come to a conclusion on so grave and important a question. The idea of retaliation – killing man for man – which is the popular noisy demand, is barbarous, and I cannot assent to or advise it. The leading officers should be held accountable and punished, but how? The policy of killing negro soldiers after they have surrendered must not be permitted, and the Rebel leaders should be called upon to avow or disavow it. But how is this to be done? Shall we go to Jeff Davis and his government, or apply to General Lee? If they will give us no answer, or declare they will kill the negroes, or justify Forrest, shall we take innocent Rebel officers as hostages? The whole subject is beset with difficulties. I cannot yield to any inhuman scheme of retaliation. Must wait the publication of the testimony.

May 6, 1864: At the Cabinet-meeting each of the members read his opinion. There had, I think, been some concert between Seward and Stanton and probably Chase; that is, they had talked on the subject, although there was no coincidence of views on all respects. Although I was dissatisfied with my own, it was as well as most others.

Between Mr. Bates and Mr. Blair a suggestion came out that met my views better than anything that had previously been offered. It is that the President should by proclamation declare the officers who had command at the massacre outlaws, and require any of our officers who may capture them, to detain them in custody and not exchange them, but hold them to punishment. The thought was not very distinctly enunciated. In a conversation that followed the reading of our papers, I expressed myself favorable to this new suggestion, which relieved the subject of much of the difficulty. It avoids communication with the Rebel authorities. Takes the matter in our own hands. We get rid of the barbarity of retaliation.

Stanton fell in with my suggestion, so far as to propose that, should Forrest, or [General James] Chalmers [Forrest's second in command], or any officer conspicuous in this butchery be captured, he should be turned over for trial for the murders at Fort Pillow. I sat beside Chase and mentioned to him some of the advantages of this course, and he said it made a favorable impression. I urged him to say so, for it appeared to me that the President and Seward did not appreciate it.

Neither during nor after the war was any Confederate officer or enlisted man charged with a crime in connection with the Fort Pillow massacre.

* * * * * * *

January 31, 1865: The vote was taken to-day in the House on the Constitutional Amendment abolishing slavery, which was carried 119 to 56.[16] It is a step towards the reestablishment of the Union in its integrity, yet it will be a shock to the framework of Southern society. But that has already been sadly shattered by their own inconsiderate and calamitous course. When, however, the cause, or assignable cause for the Rebellion is utterly extinguished, the States can and will resume their original position, acting each for itself. How soon the people in those States will arrive at right conclusions on this subject cannot now be determined.

[16] The Senate had approved the amendment by the required two-thirds vote in April of 1864, but two months later a vote in the House fell short of two-thirds. When the House reconsidered the measure in the second session of the 38th Congress, the two-thirds margin was attained, with two votes to spare, because enough Democrats and conservative border-state Unionists either switched their vote to "aye" or absented themselves from the balloting. Ratification of the amendment by the requisite three-fourths of the states was completed in December 1865.

Chapter 2

CABINET PROBLEMS AND CABINET CRISIS

This chapter deals with two interrelated topics. Section I contains a selection of Welles's numerous complaints that Lincoln failed to make fuller, more-regular use of the cabinet as a consultative and advisory body, a failing he usually blamed on Secretary of State Seward at least much as on the president. The second section reproduces Welles's detailed account of the cabinet crisis of December 1862, when a caucus of Republican senators, believing Seward was reluctant about emancipation and a drag on the administration and the war effort, tried to force Lincoln to oust him from the cabinet.

I

In the following excerpt Welles discusses at length what he sees as the fundamental problem with the cabinet's functioning and how the problem originated during the early weeks of the administration. He emphasizes Seward's desire to be the administration's dominant force – a kind of prime minister or premier. Viewed in the light of modern Lincoln scholarship, Welles can be faulted for overstating Seward's influence on the president and failing to understand Lincoln's skill at protecting his power and prerogatives.[1] (Significantly, in some of his post-war writings, Welles himself took issue with claims that Seward had dominated the

---

[1] Many historians have emphasized Lincoln's exceptional skill at protecting his presidential prerogatives and maintaining the initiative on virtually every important issue he confronted. A good overview of the topic is William E. Gienapp, "Abraham Lincoln and Presidential Leadership," in James M. McPherson, ed., *"We Cannot Escape History": Lincoln and the Last Best Hope of Earth* (Urbana and Chicago: University of Illinois Press, 1995), pp. 63-85.

administration.[2]) It is also possible that Welles's criticisms of Seward, in both this and other chapters, reflect jealousy that Seward had established an unusually close personal relationship with the president – much closer than any other cabinet member.

September 16, 1862: At the Executive Mansion, the Secretary of State informed us there was to be no Cabinet meeting. He was authorized by the President to communicate the fact. Smith said it would be as well, perhaps, to postpone the Cabinet meetings indefinitely – there seemed no use latterly for our coming together. Others expressed corresponding opinions. Seward turned off, a little annoyed.

An unfavorable impression is getting abroad in regard to the President and the Administration, not without reason, perhaps, and which prompted Smith and others to express their minds freely. There is really very little of a government there at this time, so far as most of the Cabinet is concerned. Seward spends more or less of each day with the President, and absorbs his attention, and influences his action. . . . The President has, I believe, sincere respect and regard for each and every member of the Cabinet, but Seward seeks and has outstanding influence, which is not always wisely used. The President would do better without him, were he to follow his own instincts, and were he to consult all his advisers in council, he would find his own opinions confirmed. No one attempts to obtrude himself, or warn the President, or suggest to him that others than S. be consulted on some of the important measures of which they are not informed until they see them in operation, or hear of them from others. Chase is much chafed by these things, and endeavors, and to some extent succeeds, in also getting beside the President, and obtaining knowledge of what is going forward. But this only excites and stimulates Seward, who has the inside track and means to keep it. The President is unsuspicious – readily gives his confidence, but only one of his Cabinet has manifested a disposition to monopolize it. But important measures are sometimes checked almost as soon as introduced, and, without any consultation, or without being again brought forward, are disposed of, only the Secretary of State having had a view, or ear, or eye of the matter. . . . With greater leisure than most of the Cabinet officers, unless it be Smith of the Interior, he runs to the President two or three times a day, gets his ear, gives him his tongue, makes himself interesting, and artfully contrives to dispose of measures without [cabinet] action or give them direction independent of his associates. . . .

_____

[2] These writings are discussed in the Afterword.

I have administered the Navy Department almost entirely independent of Cabinet consultation, and I may say almost without direction of the President, who not only gives me his confidence but intrusts all naval matters to me. This has not been my wish. Though glad to have his confidence, I should prefer that every important naval movement should pass a Cabinet review. Today, for instance, [Charles] Wilkes was given the appointment of Acting Rear Admiral, and I have sent him off to cruise in the West Indies [in quest of Confederate commerce raiders]. All this has been done without Cabinet consultation, or advice with anyone except Seward and the President. . . . My instructions to our naval officers – commanders of squadrons or single ships – cruising on our blockade duty, have never been submitted to the Cabinet, though I have communicated them freely to each [member]. . . .

So in regard to each and all the Departments; if I have known of their regulations and instructions, much of it has not been in Cabinet consultations. Seward beyond any and all others is responsible for this state of things. It has given him individual power, but at the expense of good administration. . . .

In the early days of the Administration all the Cabinet officers were absorbed by labors and efforts to make themselves familiar with their duties, so as rightly to discharge them. Those duties were more onerous and trying with the great rupture that was going on in the Government, avowedly to destroy it, than had ever been experienced by their predecessors.

Whilst the other members of the Cabinet were thus absorbed in preparing for impending disaster, the Secretary of State spent a considerable portion of every day with the President, instructing him, relating interesting details of occurrences in the Senate, and inculcating his political notions. I think he has no very profound or sincere convictions. Cabinet meetings, which should, at that exciting and interesting period, have been daily, were infrequent, irregular, and without system. The Secretary of State notified his associates when the President desired a meeting of the heads of Departments. It seemed unadvisable to the Premier – as he liked to be called and considered – that the members should meet often, and they did not. Consequently there was very little concerted action.

Each head of a Department took up and managed the affairs which devolved upon him as he best could, without much knowledge of the transactions of his associates, but as each consulted with the President, the Premier, from daily, almost hourly, intercourse with him, continued to ascertain the doings of each and all, while imparting but little of his own course to any. Great events of a general character began to impel the members to assemble. . . . The conduct of affairs was awkward and embarrassing, and after a few weeks the members, without preconcert, expressed a wish to be better advised on affairs of government for which they were measurably responsible to the country. They advised meetings on stated days for general and current affairs, and when there was occasion, special calls would be made. The Secretary of State alone dissented, hesitated, doubted, objected, thought it inexpedient, said all had so much to do that we could not spare the time; but the President was pleased with the suggestion, and concurred with the rest of the Cabinet. [It was agreed that the cabinet would regularly meet at noon every Tuesday and Friday, with special meetings called at other times as needed.]

The form of proceeding was discussed. Mr. Seward thought that would take care of itself. Some suggestions were made in regard to important appointments which had been made by each head of Department, the Secretary of State taking the lead in selecting high officials without general consultation. There seemed an understanding between the Secretaries of State and Treasury, who had charge of the most important appointments, of which the President was perhaps cognizant. Chase had extensive patronage, Seward appointments of character. The two arranged that each should make his own selection of subordinates. These two men had political aspirations which did not extend to their associates. . . . Chase thought he was fortifying himself by this arrangement, but it was one of the mistakes of his life.

Without going farther into details, the effect of these proceedings in those early days was to dwarf the President and elevate the Secretary of State. The latter also belittled the sphere of his associates so far as he could. Many of the important measures, particularly of his own Department, he managed to predispose of, or contrived to have determined, independent of the Cabinet. . . .

Between Seward and Chase there is perpetual rivalry and mutual dislike. Each is ambitious. Both had capacity. Seward is dexterous; Chase is strong. Seward makes constant mistakes, but recovers with a facility that is wonderful and often without injury to himself; Chase commits fewer blunders, but perseveres in them when made, often to his own serious detriment.

April 17, 1863: But little was before the Cabinet, which of late can hardly be called a council. Each Department conducts and manages its own affairs, informing the President to the extent it pleases. Seward encourages this state of things. He has less active duties than the rest of us, and watches and waits on the President daily, and gathers from him the doings of his associates and often influences indirectly their measures and movements, while he communicates very little, especially of that which he does not wish them to know.

June 30, 1863: The President did not join us to-day in Cabinet. He was with the Secretary of War and General [in Chief Henry] Halleck, and sent word there would be no meeting. This is wrong, but I know no remedy. At such a time as this, it would seem there should be free, full, and constant intercourse and interchange of views, and combined effort. The Government should not be carried on in the War or State Departments, nor ought there be an attempt of that kind.[3]

September 29, 1863: No matter of special importance; nothing but current business in Cabinet. Seward and Stanton were not present. The latter seems to make it a point recently not to attend. Others, therefore, run to him. I will not. Military operations are of late managed at the War Department, irrespective of the rest of the Cabinet. . . . The President spends much of his time there. Seward and Chase make daily visitations to Stanton, sometimes two or three times daily. I have not the time, nor do I want the privilege, though I doubtless could have it for Stanton treats me respectfully and with as much confidence as he does any one when I approach him, except Seward. But I cannot run to the War Department and pay court. Chase does this, complains because he is compelled to do it, and then . . . becomes reconciled.

December 31, 1863: The Cabinet, if a little discordant in some of its elements, has been united as regards him [Lincoln]. Chase has perhaps some aspirations for the place of Chief Executive. Seward has, I think, surrendered any expectation for the present, and shows wisdom in giving the President a fair support. Blair and Bates are earnest friends of the President, and so, I think, is Usher.[4] Stanton is insincere, but will, I have no doubt, act with Seward under present circumstances.

March 25, 1864: Chase . . . remarked [at today's cabinet meeting] that nothing could be expected where there were no Cabinet consultations and

---

[3] Welles wrote this entry on the eve of the Battle of Gettysburg. It is questionable whether Lincoln should have spent his time in a general discussion with the cabinet instead of stationing himself at the War Department to keep close tabs on the developing military situation in Pennsylvania.

[4] John Usher became secretary of the interior on January 1, 1863, following Caleb Smith's resignation to become a federal judge. Usher had been the assistant secretary since March of 1862.

no concerted action. Stanton and the President were in consultation at the time in a corner of the room. This is no unfrequent occurrence between the two at our meetings, and is certainly inconsiderate and in exceeding bad taste.

April 22, 1864: Neither Seward nor Chase nor Stanton was at the Cabinet meeting to-day. For some time Chase has been disinclined to be present and evidently for a purpose. When sometimes with him, he takes occasion to allude to the Administration as departmental – as not having council, not acting in concert. There is much truth in it, and his example and conduct contribute to it. Seward is more responsible than any one, however, although he is generally present. Stanton does not care usually to come, for the President is much of his time at the War Department, and what is said or done is communicated by the President, who is fond of telling as well as of hearing what is new. Three or four times daily the President goes to the War Department and into the telegraph office to look over communications.

April 26, 1864: Neither Chase nor Blair were at the Cabinet to-day, nor was Stanton. The course of these men is reprehensible, and yet the President, I am sorry to say, does not reprove but rather encourages it by bringing forward no important measure connected with either.

July 25, 1864: Blair is sore and vexed because the President makes a confidant and adviser of Seward, without consulting the rest of the Cabinet. I told him this had been the policy from the beginning. Seward and Chase had each striven for the position of Special Executive Counsel; that it had apparently been divided between them, but Seward had outgeneraled or outintrigued Chase. The latter was often consulted when others were not, but often he was not aware of things which were intrusted to Seward and managed by him.

August 2, 1864: Stanton dislikes to meet Blair in council, knowing that B. dislikes and really despises him. Seward and Stanton move together in all matters. . . . Both mouse about the President, who, in his intense curiosity, interest and inquisitiveness, spends much of his time at the War Department, watching the telegraph. Of course, opportunities like these are not lost by Stanton.

II

*Pessimism pervaded Washington, and much of the Union, as 1862 neared its
end. The war effort seemed to be stalled. Then on December 13th, the Army of
the Potomac suffered a devastating defeat at Fredericksburg, Virginia, sustaining
some 12,600 casualties to the Confederates' approximately 5300. A perception
was widespread that the Lincoln administration lacked energy and a sense of
direction and was so riven by internal strife as to be virtually paralyzed. Treasury Secretary Chase had done much to foster this perception by privately telling
various Republican senators that the administration was weak and confused, that
Lincoln rarely consulted the cabinet about important issues, and that the cabinet
was too divided to agree on important policy questions. Chase placed most of the
blame on Seward, portraying him as only halfhearted in his support of the war
effort and as a conservative who was hostile to emancipation and exercised an
excessive, even controlling influence on Lincoln. It was against this backdrop
that the cabinet crisis of December 1862 played out. Welles's diary entries for
December 19th through the 23rd provide a detailed, generally accurate account of
the crisis. They also reveal the help Welles gave Lincoln in resolving the crisis.*

*This episode was a critical moment in Lincoln's presidency. If the caucus of Repub-
lican senators had succeeded in forcing him to remove Seward, it would have
made him appear weak in the eyes of supporters and opponents alike, encouraged
additional legislative encroachments on his executive authority, and upset the
balance in the cabinet between conservative, moderate, and radical Republicans.*

December 19, 1862: Soon after reaching the Department this A.M., I received a note from Nicolay, the President's secretary, requesting me to
attend a special Cabinet meeting at half-past ten. All the members were
punctually there except Seward.

The President desired that what he had to communicate should not
be the subject of conversation elsewhere, and proceeded to inform us that
on Wednesday evening [December 17th], about six o'clock, Senator Preston
King [of New York] and F. W. Seward [Seward's son, who was the assistant secretary of state] came into his room, each bearing a communication.
That which Mr. King presented was the resignation of the Secretary of
State, and Mr. F. W. Seward handed in his own. Mr. King then informed
the President that at a Republican caucus held that day a pointed and
positive opposition had shown itself against the Secretary of State, which
terminated in a unanimous expression, with one exception, against him
and a wish for his removal. The feeling finally shaped itself into resolutions of a general character, and the appointment of a committee of nine

to bear them to the President, and to communicate to him the sentiments of the Republican Senators. Mr. King, the former colleague and the friend of Mr. Seward, being also from the same State, felt it to be a duty to inform the Secretary at once of what had occurred. On receiving this information, Mr. Seward immediately tendered his resignation. Mr. King suggested it would be well for the committee to wait upon the President at an early moment, and, the President agreeing with him, Mr. King on Wednesday morning notified Judge [Jacob] Collamer [senator from Vermont], the chairman, who sent word to the President that they would call at the Executive Mansion at any hour after six that evening, and the President sent word he would receive them at seven.[5]

The committee came at the time specified, and the President says the evening was spent in a pretty free and animated conversation. No opposition was manifested towards any other member of the Cabinet than Mr. Seward. Some not very friendly feelings were shown towards one or two others, but no wish that any one should leave but the Secretary of State. Him they charged, if not with infidelity, with indifference, with want of earnestness in the War, with want of sympathy with the country in this great struggle, and with many things objectionable, and especially with a too great ascendency and control of the President and measures of administration. This, he said, was the point and pith of their complaint.

The President in reply to the committee stated how this movement shocked and grieved him; that the Cabinet he had selected in view of impending difficulties and of all the responsibilities upon him; that the members and himself had gone on harmoniously, whatever had been their previous party feelings and associations; that there had never been serious disagreements, though there had been differences; that in the overwhelming troubles of the country, which had borne heavily upon him, he had been sustained and consoled by the good feeling and the mutual and unselfish confidence and zeal that pervaded the Cabinet. . . .

[Lincoln] said this movement was uncalled for, that there was no such charge, admitting all that was said, as should break up or overthrow a Cabinet, nor was it possible for him to go on with a total abandonment of old friends. . . .

The President requested that we should, with him, meet the committee. This did not receive the approval of Mr. Chase, who said he had no knowledge whatever of the movement, or the resignation, until since he had entered the room. Mr. Bates knew of no good that would come

---

[5] Welles's reference to "Wednesday morning" is in error. Senator Collamer sent Lincoln a request for a meeting the morning of Thursday, the 18th, and it was held that evening.

of an interview. I stated that I could see no harm in it, and if the President wished it, I thought it a duty for us to attend. Mr. Blair thought it would be well for us to be present, and finally all acquiesced. The President named half-past seven this evening.

December 20, 1862: At the meeting last evening there were present of the committee Senators Collamer, Fessenden, Harris, Trumbull, Grimes, Howard, Sumner, and Pomeroy. Wade was absent. The President and all the Cabinet but Seward were present. The subject was opened by the President, who read the [Senate caucus's] resolutions and stated the substance of his interviews with the committee – their object and purpose. He spoke of the unity of his Cabinet, and how, though they could not be expected to think and speak alike on all subjects, all had acquiesced in measures when once decided. The necessities of the times, he said, had prevented frequent and long sessions of the Cabinet, and the submission of every question at the meetings.

Secretary Chase indorsed the President's statement fully and entirely, but regretted that there was not a more full and thorough consideration and canvass of every important measure in open Cabinet.[6]

Senator Collamer . . . succeeded the President and calmly and fairly presented the views of the committee and of those whom they represented. They wanted united counsels, combined wisdom, and energetic action. If there is truth in the maxim that in a multitude of counselors there is safety, it might be well that those advisers who were near the President and selected by him, and all of whom were more or less responsible, should be consulted on the great questions which affected the national welfare, and that the ear of the Executive should be open to all and that he should have the minds of all.

Senator Fessenden [of Maine] was skillful but not a little tart; felt, it could be seen, more than he cared to say; wanted the whole Cabinet to consider and decide great questions, and that no one should absorb the whole Executive. Spoke of a remark which he had heard from J.Q. Adams on the floor of Congress in regard to a measure of his administration. Mr. Adams said the measure was adopted against his wishes and opinion, but

---

[6] Chase faced a painful dilemma: either show himself to be disloyal to the president by disputing what Lincoln had said, or else discredit himself with the senators, to whom he had told a much different story. By endorsing Lincoln's statement about the cabinet's unity and its members' unanimous support of decisions once taken, Chase dismayed the senators, whose case against Seward relied heavily on information provided by Chase. When other senators later asked Senator Collamer to explain the discrepancy, Collamer replied, "He lied." Quoted in David Donald, *Lincoln* (New York: Simon & Schuster, 1995), p. 405.

he was outvoted by Mr. Clay and others [in his cabinet]. He wished an administration so conducted.

Grimes [of Iowa], Sumner [of Massachusetts], and Trumbull [of Illinois] were pointed, emphatic, and unequivocal in their hostility to Mr. Seward; each was unrelenting and unforgiving. Blair spoke earnestly and well. Sustained the President, and dissented most decidedly from the idea of a plural Executive; claimed that the President was accountable for his administration, might ask opinions or not of either and as many as he pleased, of all or none, of his Cabinet. Mr. Bates took much the same view.

The President managed his own case, speaking freely, and showed great tact and ability, provided such a subject were a proper one for such a meeting and discussion. I have no doubt he considered it most judicious to conciliate the Senators with respectful deference, whatever may have been his opinion of their interference. When he closed his remarks, he said it would be a gratification to him if each member of the committee would state whether he now thought it advisable to dismiss Mr. Seward, and whether his exclusion would strengthen or weaken the Administration and the Union cause in their respective States. Grimes, Trumbull, and Sumner, who had expressed themselves decidedly against the continuance of Mr. Seward in the Cabinet, indicated no change of opinion. Collamer and Fessenden declined committing themselves on the subject – were not prepared to answer the questions. Senator Harris [of New York] felt it a duty to say that while many of the friends of the Administration would be gratified, others would feel deeply wounded, and the effect of Mr. Seward's retirement would, on the whole, be calamitous in the State of New York. Pomeroy of Kansas said, personally, he believed the withdrawal of Mr. Seward would be a good movement and he sincerely wished it might take place. Howard of Michigan declined answering the question.

During the discussion, the [annual] volume of diplomatic correspondence [for 1861], recently published, was alluded to; some letters denounced as unwise and impolitic were specified, one of which, a confidential dispatch to Mr. Adams, was read.[7] If it was unwise to write, it was certainly injudicious and indiscreet to publish such a document. Mr. Seward has genius and talent – no one better knows it than himself – but he is often wanting in true wisdom, sound judgment, and discreet statesmanship. The committee believe that he thinks more of the glorification of Seward than the welfare of the country. He wishes the glorification of

---

[7] This probably was a letter Seward sent to Charles Francis Adams, the American minister to Great Britain, in 1861 that equated northern abolitionists with fire-eating southern secessionists.

both, and believes he is the man to accomplish it, but has unwittingly and unwarily begotten and brought upon himself a vast amount of distrust and hostility on the part of Senators, by his endeavors to impress them and others with the belief that he is the Administration. It is a mistake; the Senators have measured and know him.

It was nearly midnight when we left the President; and it could not be otherwise than that all my wakeful moments should be absorbed with a subject which, time and circumstances considered, was of grave importance to the Administration and the country. A Senatorial combination to dictate to the President in regard to his political family in the height of a civil war which threatens the existence of the Republic cannot be permitted to succeed, even if the person to whom they object were as obnoxious as they represent. After fully canvassing the subject in all its phases, my mind was clear as to the course which it was my duty to pursue, and what I believed was the President's duty also.

My first movement this morning was to call on the President as soon as I supposed he could have breakfasted. . . . I informed the President I had pondered the events of yesterday and last evening, and felt it incumbent on me to advise him not to accept the resignation of Mr. Seward; that if there were objections, real or imaginary, against Mr. Seward, the time, manner, and circumstances – the occasion, and the method of presenting what the Senators considered objections – were all inappropriate and wrong; that no party or faction should be permitted to dictate to the President in regard to his Cabinet; that if would be of evil example and fraught with incalculable injury to the Government and country; that neither the legislative department, nor the Senate branch of it, should be allowed to encroach on the Executive prerogatives and rights; that it devolved on him, and was his duty to assert and maintain the rights and independence of the Executive; that he ought not, against his own convictions, to yield one iota of the authority intrusted to him on the demand of either branch of Congress or of both combined, or to any party, whatever might be its views and intentions; that Mr. Seward had his infirmities and errors; that he and I differed on many things, as did other members of the Cabinet; that he was disposed to step beyond his own legitimate bounds and not duly respect the rights of his associates, but these were matters that did not call for Senatorial interference. In short, I considered it for the true interest of the country, now as in the future, that this scheme should be defeated; that, so believing, I had at the earliest moment given him my conclusions.

The President was much gratified; said the whole thing had struck him as it had me, and if carried out as the Senators prescribed, the whole Government must cave in. It could not stand, could not hold water; the bottom would be out.

I added that, having expressed my wish that he would not accept Mr. Seward's resignation, I thought it equally important that Seward should not press its acceptance. In this he also concurred, and asked if I had seen Seward. I replied I had not, my first duty was with him, and, having ascertained that we agreed, I would now go over and see him. He earnestly desired me to do so.

I went immediately to Seward's house. Stanton was with him. Seward was excited, talking vehemently to Stanton of the course pursued and the results that must follow if the scheme succeeded; told Stanton he (Stanton) would be the next victim. . . . As Seward and myself then entered into conversation, he related what the President had already communicated – how Preston King had come to him, he wrote his resignation at once, and so did Fred, etc., etc. In the mean time Stanton rose, and remarking he had much to do, and, as Governor S. had been over this matter with him, he would leave.

I then stated my interview with the President, my advice that the President must not accept, nor he press, his resignation. Seward was greatly pleased with my views; said he had but one course before him when the doings of the Senators were communicated, but that if the President and country required of him any duty in this emergency he did not feel at liberty to refuse it. He spoke of his long political experience; dwelt on his own sagacity and his great services; feels deeply this movement, which was wholly unexpected; tries to suppress any exhibition of personal grievance or disappointment, but is painfully wounded, mortified, and chagrined. I told him I should return and report to the President our interview and that he acquiesced. He said he had no objections, but he thought the subject should be disposed of one way or the other at once. He is disappointed, I see, that the President did not promptly refuse to consider his resignation, and dismiss, or refuse to parley with, the committee.

When I returned to the White House, Chase and Stanton were in the President's office, but he was absent. A few words were interchanged on the great topic in hand. I was very emphatic in my opposition to the acceptance of Seward's resignation. Neither gave me a direct answer or an opinion on the subject, though I think both wished to be understood as acquiescing.

When the President came in . . . his first address was to me, asking if I "had seen the man." I replied that I had, and that he assented to my views. He then turned to Chase and said, "I sent for you, for this matter is giving me great trouble."

Chase said he had been painfully affected by the meeting last evening, which was a total surprise to him, and, after some not very explicit remarks as to how he was affected, informed the President he had prepared his resignation. "Where is it?" said the President quickly, his eye lighting up in a moment. "I brought it with me," said Chase, taking the paper from his pocket; "I wrote it this morning." "Let me have it," said the President, reaching his long arm and fingers towards C., who held on, seemingly reluctant to part with the letter, which was sealed, and which he apparently hesitated to surrender. Something further he wished to say, but the President was eager and did not perceive it, but took the letter.

"This," said he, looking towards me with a triumphal laugh, "cuts the Gordian knot." An air of satisfaction spread over his countenance such as I have not seen for some time. "I can dispose of this subject now," he added, as he turned on his chair; "I see my way clear."

Chase sat by Stanton, fronting the fire; the President beside the fire, his face towards them, Stanton nearest him. I was on the sofa near the east window. While the President was reading the note, which was brief, Chase turned round and looked towards me, a little perplexed. He would, I think, have been better satisfied could this interview with the President have been without the presence of others, or at least if I was away. The President was so delighted that he saw not how others were affected.

"Mr. President," said Stanton with solemnity, "I informed you day before yesterday that I was ready to tender you my resignation. I wish you, sir, to consider my resignation at this time in your possession."

"You may go to your Department," said the President; "I don't want yours. This," holding out Chase's letter, "is all I want; this relieves me; my way is clear; the trouble is ended. I will detain neither of you longer." We all rose to leave, but Stanton held back as we reached the door. Chase and myself came downstairs together. He was moody and taciturn. Some one stopped him on the lower stairs and I passed on, but C. was not a minute behind me, and before I reached the Department, Stanton came staving along.

Preston King called at my house this evening and gave me particulars of what had been said and done at the caucuses of the Republican Senators – of the surprise he felt when he found the hostility so universal against Seward, and that some of the calmest and most considerate Senators were the most decided; stated the course pursued by himself, which was frank, friendly, and manly. He was greatly pleased with my course, of which he had been informed by Seward and the President in part; and I gave him some facts which they did not. Blair tells me that his father's views correspond with mine, and the approval of F. P. Blair and Preston King gives me assurance that I am right. . . .

I am inclined to think that Chase, Stanton, and Caleb Smith have each participated [in the movement against Seward], if not directly, by expressions of discontent to their Senatorial confidants. Chase and Smith, I know, are a good deal dissatisfied with Seward and have not hesitated to make known their feelings in some quarters. With Stanton I have little intimacy. He came into the Cabinet under Seward's wing, and he knows it, but Stanton is, by nature, an intriguer, courts favor, is not faithful in his friendships, is given to cliquism. His obligations to Seward would not deter him from raising a breeze against Seward to favor himself. Chase and Seward entered the Cabinet as rivals, and have so continued. There was an effort by Seward's friends [prior to Lincoln's inauguration] to exclude Chase from the Treasury; the President did not yield to it, but it is obvious that Seward's more pleasant nature and skill have enabled him to get to windward of Chase in administrative management, and the latter feels it. Transactions take place of a general character, not unfrequently, of which Chase and others are not advised until they are made public. Often the fact reaches them through the papers. Seward has not exhibited shrewdness in this. It may have afforded him a temporary triumph as regarded Chase, and he doubtless flatters himself that it strengthens a belief which he desires should prevail that he is the "power behind the throne greater than the throne itself," that he really is the Executive. The result of all this has been the alienation of a large portion of his old friends without getting new ones, and finally this appointment of the committee which asked his removal. The objections urged are the points on which Chase is most sensitive.

For two or three months Stanton has evinced a growing opposition to Seward, with whom he was, at first, intimate and to whom he was much devoted. I have observed that, as he became alienated towards Seward, his friendship for Chase increased.

My differences with Seward I have settled with him in the day and time of their occurrences. They have not been many, but they have been troublesome and annoying because they were meddlesome and disturbing. He gets behind me, tampers with my subordinates, and interferes injuriously and ignorantly in naval matters. I have not made these matters subjects of complaint outside. . . .

In his intercourse with his colleagues, save the rivalry between himself and Chase and the supercilious arrogance which he sometimes displays, [Seward] has been courteous, affable, and, I think, anxious to preserve harmony in the Cabinet. I have seen no effort to get up combinations for himself personally, or against others. He supposed himself immensely popular at the moment when friends were estranged, and was as surprised as myself when he learned the Senatorial movement for his overthrow.

December 23, 1862: It was announced yesterday morning that the President had requested Mr. Seward and Mr. Chase to withdraw their resignations and resume their duties. This took the public by surprise. Chase's resignation was scarcely known, and his friends, particularly those in the late movement [to oust Seward], were a little disgusted when they found that he and Seward were in the same category.[8]

Seward's influence has often been anything but salutary. Not that he was evil inclined, but he is meddlesome and has no fixed principles or policy. Chase has chafed under Seward's management, yet has tried to conceal any exhibition of irritated feelings. Seward, assuming to be helmsman, has, while affecting superiority, tried to be soothing and conciliating. The President feels that he is under obligations to each, and that both are serviceable. He is friendly to both. He is fond of Seward. He respects Chase. Seward comforts him; Chase he deems a necessity.

Chastened by the cabinet crisis, Seward henceforth meddled less in the affairs of other departments and abandoned the pretense of being a kind of premier within the administration. In the immediate aftermath of the crisis, Lincoln, who seems also to have been somewhat chastened, took pains to consult with the cabinet more often. But as is evident from the 1863 and 1864 excerpts in Section I of this chapter, it wasn't long before Welles was again complaining in his diary that the president neglected the cabinet, that attendance at cabinet meetings was poor, that individual department heads were acting on their own without consulting their colleagues (or even keeping them informed about their actions), and that Seward was still exerting undue influence.

---

[8] Shortly after the crisis was resolved, Lincoln pointed up the crucial importance of having both Seward's and Chase's resignations in hand by remarking that, "I can ride on now, I've got a pumpkin in each end of my bag." Quoted in William Gienapp, *Abraham Lincoln and Civil War America: A Biography* (New York: Oxford University Press, 2002), p. 123. In a conversation with his assistant private secretary, John Hay, ten months later, Lincoln expressed pride in his adept handling of the crisis. "I do not now see how it could have been done better," he said. "I am sure it was right. If I had yielded to that storm & dismissed Seward the thing would all have slumped over one way & we should have been left with a scanty handful of supporters. When Chase sent in his resignation I saw that the game was in my own hands & I put it through." Michael Burlingame and John R. Turner Ettlinger, eds., *Inside Lincoln's White House: The Complete Civil War Diary of John Hay* (Carbondale and Edwardsville: Southern Illinois University Press, 1997), p. 104.

Chapter 3

WELLES ON LINCOLN

The first section of this chapter presents some of Welles's judgments about Lincoln as president – judgments in which admiration and commendation are leavened with criticism. The excerpts in Section II illustrate Lincoln's sense of humor, his knack for making a serious point by telling an amusing story, his compassion (some would say soft-heartedness), and his accessibility to members of the general public.

I

Chapter 1 [undated, p. 25 of the published diary]: President Lincoln never shunned any responsibility and often declared that he, and not his Cabinet, was in fault for errors imputed to them.

September 16, 1862: The President has good sense, intelligence, and an excellent heart, but is sadly perplexed and distressed by events. He distrusts his own administrative ability and experience, and I think Seward encourages this distrust. . . .

On September 24, 1862, just two days after issuing the preliminary Emancipation Proclamation, Lincoln, without consulting the cabinet, issued a proclamation suspending the writ of habeas corpus *in cases of civilians arrested and detained by the military for acts that allegedly impeded the war effort or otherwise aided the rebellion. This prevented such detainees from petitioning a judge to determine whether their arrest was warranted and if the judge determined that it was not, ordering their release. The following entry reflects Welles's longstanding concern about the potential abuse of power by the central government.*

September 25, 1862: The President has issued a proclamation on martial law – suspension of *habeas corpus* he terms it, meaning, of course, a suspension of the privilege of *habeas corpus*. Of this proclamation I knew nothing until I saw it in the papers, and am not sorry that I did not. I question the utility of a multiplicity of proclamations striking deep on great questions.

July 7, 1863: The president . . . said he had spoken to Halleck and urged that the right tone and spirit should be infused into officers and men, and that General Meade especially should be reminded of his (the President's) wishes and expectations [that Meade would vigorously pursue Lee's battered army as it retreated from Gettysburg.] But General Halleck gave him a short and curt reply, showing that he did not participate and sympathize in this feeling, and, said the President, "I drop the subject."

This is the President's error. His own convictions and conclusions are infinitely superior to Halleck's – even in military operations more sensible and more correct always – but yet he says, "It being strictly a military question, it is proper I should defer to Halleck, whom I have called here to counsel, advise, and direct in these matters, where he is an expert." I questioned whether he should be considered an expert. I look upon Halleck as a pretty good critic of other men's deeds and acts, but as incapable of originating or directing military operations. . . .

[Shortly after returning] to the Navy Department I was handed a dispatch from Admiral [David Dixon] Porter [commander of the Mississippi River Squadron], communicating the fall of Vicksburg on the fourth of July. . . . I immediately returned to the Executive Mansion. The President was detailing certain points relative to Grant's movements on the map to Chase and two or three others, when I gave him the tidings. Putting down the map, he rose at once, said we would drop these topics, and "I myself will telegraph this news to General Meade." He rose and seized his hat, but suddenly stopped, his countenance beaming with joy; he caught my hand, and, throwing his arm around me, exclaimed: "What can we do for the Secretary of the Navy for this glorious intelligence? He is always giving us good news.[1] I cannot, in words, tell you my joy over this result. It is great, Mr. Welles, it is great!"

We walked across the lawn together. "This," said he, "will relieve [General Nathaniel] Banks [who was besieging Port Hudson, Louisiana,

---

[1] Other naval "good news" Lincoln probably had in mind included Admiral Du Pont's seizure of Port Royal Sound, South Carolina, in November 1861 and of Fort Pulaski in Georgia the following April, Flag Officer (later Admiral) Andrew Hull Foote's capture of Fort Henry on the Tennessee River in February 1862, and Admiral Farragut's successful campaign to take New Orleans in April 1862.

about 200 miles south of Vicksburg.] It will inspire Meade." The opportunity I thought a good one to request him to insist upon his own views, to enforce them, not only on Meade but on Halleck.

Following the New York draft riot in July 1863, New York Governor Horatio Seymour, a Democrat, wanted Lincoln to postpone the draft until its constitutionality had been tested before the Supreme Court. Welles comments on the issue in the two ensuing excerpts.

August 7, 1863: The President read us a letter received from Horatio Seymour . . . on the subject of the draft, which he asks may be postponed. The letter is a party, political document, filled with perverted statements, and apologizing for and diverting attention from his mob.

The President also read his reply [refusing to suspend the draft], which is manly, vigorous, and decisive. He did not permit himself to be drawn away on frivolous and remote issues, which was obviously the intent of Seymour.

August 12, 1863: The President has a brief reply to Governor Seymour's rejoinder, which is very well. Stanton said to me he wished the President would stop letter-writing, for which he has a liking. I might not disagree with Stanton as regards some of the correspondence alluded to, but I think the President has been more successful with Seymour than some others. His . . . letters and writings are generally unpretending and abound in good sense.

One of the more vexing and persistent problems Lincoln faced was the conflict between the conservative Unionist and the radical Unionist political factions in Missouri, which often seemed more interested in battling one another politically than in defeating the Confederacy. In the following excerpt, Welles comments on one of Lincoln's several attempts to encourage them to cooperate.

October 16, 1863: The President read to the Cabinet his letter to the Missouri radicals and also a letter to General [John C.] Schofield [commander of the military district of Missouri, who Lincoln hoped could act the peacemaker between the two factions]. Both exhibit shrewdness and good sense, on a difficult and troublesome subject. There is no cause for dissension among the friends of the Administration in Missouri, and the President does not commit himself to either party in this controversy, but, like some of us, has little respect for the wild vagaries of the unjust and extreme radical portion.

December 31, 1863: The President has well maintained his position, and under trying circumstances acquitted himself in a manner that will be better appreciated in the future than now. He sometimes fails to discriminate rightly between true and false friends, and has been the victim of the prejudices and duplicity of others.

January 8, 1864: The President's estimate of character is very correct, and he frequently divests himself of partiality with a readiness that has surprised me.

February 3, 1864: Almost daily we have some indications of Presidential aspirations and incipient operations of the campaign. The President does not conceal the interest he takes, and yet I perceive nothing unfair or intrusive. He is sometimes deceived by heartless intriguers who impose upon him. Some appointments have been secured by mischievous men, which would never have been made had he known the facts. In some respects he is a singular man and not fully understood. He has great shrewdness, but sometimes his assertion or management is greatly astray and seldom aids him. When he . . . relies on his own right intentions and good common sense, he is strongest. So in regard to his friends whom he to a considerable extent distrusts, and yet confides in his opponents. A great and almost inexcusable error for a man in his position.

During the war, Lincoln made numerous visits to the Army of the Potomac to consult with its senior officers and to convey his and the country's gratitude to the troops. In the following two excerpts about Lincoln's visit to see the recently appointed general in chief of the Union armies, Ulysses S. Grant, near Petersburg, Virginia, Welles expresses seemingly contradictory views of such presidential "excursions."

June 20, 1864: The President in his intense anxiety has made up his mind to visit General Grant at his headquarters, and left this P.M. at five. Mr. [Gustavus V.] Fox [assistant secretary of the navy] has gone with him, and not unlikely favored and encouraged the President in this step, which I do not approve. It has been my policy to discourage the President in these excursions. Some of the Cabinet favored them. . . .

He can do no good. It can hardly be otherwise than to do harm, even if no accident befalls him. Better for him and the country that he should remain at his post here.

June 24, 1864: The President was in very good spirits at the Cabinet. His journey has done him good, physically, and strengthened him mentally and inspired confidence in the General and army.

On June 29, 1864, Secretary of the Treasury Chase, unhappy that Lincoln refused to appoint his choice to the position of assistant treasurer in New York City, submitted his resignation. He expected this would force the president to back down – a tactic he had successfully employed before. But this time, Lincoln accepted the resignation. Welles, who had always abhorred paper money not convertible to specie (i.e., gold) and thus took a very dim view of the government's issuance of non-convertible greenback currency to help fund the war effort, was dismayed at the apparent ignorance of monetary policy that Lincoln exhibited in seeking Chase's replacement.

July 1, 1864: [Former] Governor [David] Tod [of Ohio] has declined the position of Secretary of the Treasury. It does not surprise me. Senator [William Pitt] Fessenden [of Maine] has been appointed, who will, it is said, accept, which does surprise me. I doubt if his health will permit him to bear the burden. He has abilities; is of the same school as Chase. Has been Chairman of the Committee of Finance during Chase's administration of the Treasury, and . . . a supporter of his policy. Yet I have had an impression that Fessenden is an improvement upon Chase, and I trust he is.

But the President's course is a riddle. Tod is a hardmoney man; Fessenden has pressed through Congress the paper [money] system of Chase. One day Tod is selected; on his refusal, Fessenden is brought forward. This can in no other way be reconciled than in the President's want of knowledge of the subject. His attention never has been given to the subject. He seems not aware that within twenty-four hours he has swung to opposite extremes.

August 31, 1864: It is an infirmity of the President that he permits the little newsmongers [reporters] to come around him and be intimate, and in this he is encouraged by Seward, who does the same, and even courts the corrupt and the vicious, which the President does not. He has great inquisitiveness. Likes to hear all the political gossip as much as Seward. But the President is honest, sincere, and confiding – traits which are not so prominent in some by whom he is surrounded.

March 23, 1865: The President has gone to the front, chiefly to get rid of the throng [of favor-seekers] that is pressing upon him. . . . He makes his office much more laborious than he should. Does not generalize and takes upon himself questions that properly belong to the Departments, often causing derangement and irregularity. The more he yields, the greater the pressure upon him. It has now become such that he is compelled to flee and there is no doubt he is much worn down; besides he wishes the War terminated, and, to this end that severe terms shall not be exacted of the Rebels.

II

Reacting to the first sally of the Confederate ironclad Virginia (*née* Merrimack) *against the Union fleet in Hampton Roads, Virginia, in March 1862, a panicky Secretary of War Stanton ordered that 60 barges be filled with stone and sunk at Kettle Bottom Shoals in the Potomac River to prevent the deep-draft rebel warship from steaming up the river to bombard Washington. Welles adamantly opposed the idea. He argued that the Confederates would risk using their prized ironclad only in the relative safety of the deep waters of Hampton Roads, that in any event the water was too shallow at Kettle Bottom Shoals for it to cross, and that sinking the barges there would prevent Union vessels from going down the river to the Chesapeake Bay to support General George B. McClellan's forthcoming Peninsula Campaign to take Richmond (see Chapter 5). Lincoln decided that the barges would be loaded and moved to Kettle Bottom Shoals, but they were not to be sunk unless the* Virginia *actually entered the river. Events proved Welles was right, and it gave rise to the following humorous anecdote.*

Chapter 1 *[undated, p. 67, of the published diary]* Some weeks later, when the President, with Stanton and some others, was going down the river in a steamer, the long line of boats on the Maryland side near the Kettle Bottom Shoals attracted attention, and someone inquired concerning them. "Oh," said the President, "that is Stanton's navy. That is the fleet concerning which he and Mr. Welles became so excited in my room. Welles was incensed and opposed the scheme, and it seems Neptune was right. Stanton's navy is as useless as the paps of a man to a sucking child. There may be some show to amuse the child, but they are good for nothing for service."

The following episode occurred as Robert E. Lee's Army of Northern Virginia was preparing to cross the Potomac River into Maryland in the campaign that culminated in the Battle of Gettysburg (July 1 – 3, 1863). At the time, there was much confusion in Washington about Lee's whereabouts and intentions.

June 17, 1863: Had a telegram at ten last night from Mr. [Samuel] Felton, President of the Philadelphia & Baltimore Railroad, requesting that a gunboat might be sent to Havre de Grace [Maryland] to protect the Company's ferryboat and property. Says he has information that the Rebels intend going down the river to seize it.

I went forthwith to the War Department to ascertain whether there was really any such alarming necessity, for it seemed to me, from all I had been able to learn, that it was a panic invocation. Found the President and Stanton at the War Department, jubilant over intelligence just received that no Rebels had reached Carlisle, as had been reported, and it was believed they had not even entered Pennsylvania. . . . Soon a messenger came in from General [Robert] Schenck, who declares no Rebels have crossed the Potomac, that the stragglers and baggage-trains of [General Robert] Milroy had run away in affright, and squads of them, on different parallel roads, had alarmed each other, and each fled in terror with all speed to Harrisburg. This alone was asserted to be the basis of the great panic which had alarmed Pennsylvania and the country. . . .[2]

The President was in excellent humor. He said this flight would be a capital joke for Orpheus C. Kerr to get hold of. He could give scope to his imagination over the terror of broken squads of panic-stricken teamsters, frightened at each other and alarming all Pennsylvania. [Quartermaster General Montgomery] Meigs . . . inquired who this person (Orpheus C. Kerr) was. "Why," said the President, "have you not read those papers? They are in two volumes; any one who has not read them must be a heathen." He said he had enjoyed them greatly, except when they attempted to play their wit on him, which did not strike him as very successful, but rather disgusted him. "Now the hits that are given to you, Mr. Welles, or to Chase, I can enjoy, but I dare say they may have disgusted you while I was laughing at them."[3]

January 8, 1864: To-day at the Executive Mansion. Only Usher with myself was present, and no business transacted. Mr. Hudson of Massachusetts, formerly Member of Congress, was with the President. Conversation was general, with anecdotes as usual. These are usually very appropriate

---

[2] On June 14th, Milroy, who commanded the garrison at Winchester, Virginia, was forced to evacuate the town by elements of General Richard S. Ewell's corps of Lee's army and suffered heavy losses as he tried to withdraw to the relative safety of Harper's Ferry. It was during this retreat that the reported incident involving stragglers and Milroy's baggage trains apparently occurred.

[3] Orpheus C. Kerr, which is a pun on "office seeker," was the pen name of humorist Robert Henry Newell.

and instructive, conveying much truth in few words, well, if not always elegantly, told.

The "Dominican question" referred to in the following excerpt arose in response to Spain's attempt to re-colonize the Dominican Republic, a predominantly black nation that had been fully independent since 1844. In 1863, Spain invaded the country at the invitation of a political faction that expected to enhance its power if the country rejoined the Spanish colonial empire. This triggered the "War of Restoration" against the Spanish forces. It continued until 1865, when the invaders withdrew.

February 2, 1864: But little of importance was done at the Cabinet meeting . . . . Seward was embarrassed about the Dominican question. To move either way threatened difficulty. On one side Spain [which the administration did not want to alienate], on the other side the negro [i.e., the black insurgents fighting to evict the Spanish forces, who enjoyed considerable popular sympathy in the North]. The President remarked that the dilemma reminded him of the interview between two negroes, one of whom was a preacher endeavoring to admonish and enlighten the other. "There are," said Josh, the preacher, "two roads for you, Joe. Be careful which you take. One ob dem leads straight to hell, de odder go right to damnation." Joe opened his eyes under the impressive eloquence and awful future and exclaimed, "Josh, take which road you please; I go troo de wood." "I am not disposed to take any new trouble," said the President, "just at this time, and shall neither go for Spain nor the negro in this matter, but shall take to the woods."[4]

January 7, 1864: The case of R. Law tried by court martial, which has been in my hands for a month nearly, was disposed of to-day. The court found him guilty . . . and sentenced him to be dismissed from the Navy, but recommended him to clemency. Proposed to the President three years' suspension, the first six months without pay. This to be the general order, but if, at the expiration of six or eight months, it was thought best to remit the remainder of the punishment, it could be done. "Look over the subject carefully," said the President, "and make the case as light as possible on

---

[4] Lincoln's attempt to mimic African American dialect was a common practice among white Americans in the 19th Century, but is generally regarded as offensive today. In his book *Lincoln and Seward* (New York: Sheldon & Co., 1874), p. 184, Welles recounted this story but added that Lincoln concluded by declaring, "We shall maintain an honest and strict neutrality." (The circumstances that led Welles to write this book are discussed in the Afterword.)

his father's account, who is an old friend of mine, and I shall be glad to do all that you can recommend."

December **24, 1864**: Called on the President to commute the punishment of a person [presumably a navy seaman] condemned to be hung. He at once assented and is always disposed to mitigate punishment, and to grant favors. Sometimes this is a weakness. As a matter of duty and friendship I mentioned to him the case of Laura Jones, a young lady who was residing in Richmond and there engaged to be married but came up three years ago to attend her sick mother and had been unable to pass through the lines and return. I briefly stated her case and handed a letter from her to Mrs. Welles that he might read. It was a touching appeal from the poor girl, who says truly the years of her youth are passing away. I knew if the President read the letter, Laura would get the pass. I therefore only mentioned some of the general facts. He at once said he would give her a pass. I told him her sympathies were with the Secessionists, and it would be better he should read her own statement. But he declined and said he would let her go; the war had depopulated the country and prevented marriages enough, and if he could do a kindness of this sort he was disposed to, unless I advised otherwise. He wrote a pass and handed [it to] me.

February **19, 1864**: As I went into the Cabinet meeting a fair, plump lady pressed forward and insisted she must see the President – only for a moment – wanted nothing. The President directed that she should be admitted. She said her name was Holmes, that she belonged in Dubuque, Iowa, was passing East and came from Baltimore expressly to have a look at President Lincoln. "Well, in the matter of looking at one another," said the President, "I have altogether the advantage." She wished his autograph, and was a special admirer and enthusiastic.

Chapter 4

Taking the Measure of Men

One of the conspicuous features of Welles's diary is his blunt, often highly critical characterizations of his cabinet colleagues and other politically influential figures. The excerpts in Section I of this chapter are about cabinet members. The focus is on Secretaries Seward, Stanton, and Chase, but brief comments about Postmaster General Montgomery Blair are also included.[1] Section II consists of Welles's opinions of six other prominent public men.

I

Seward

September 16, 1862: The qualities of Seward are almost the precise opposite of the President. He is obtrusive, never reserved or diffident of his own powers, is assuming and presuming, meddlesome, unreliable and uncertain, ready to exercise authority always, never doubting his right until challenged; and then he becomes timid, doubtful, distrustful, and inventive of schemes to extricate himself, or to change his position. He is not particularly scrupulous in accomplishing an end, nor so mindful of what is due to others as would be expected of one who aims to be courteous towards equals. The President he treats with a familiarity bordering on disrespect, but the President, though he observes this, never so receives it but treats it as a weakness in one to whom he attributes qualities essential to statesmanship, and whose pliability and ready shrewdness he finds convenient.

---

[1] Additional diary passages characterizing Seward, Stanton, and Chase appear in several other chapters.

August 4, 1863: Little done at Cabinet. Seward undertook to talk wise in relation to Commander Collins and the "Mont Blanc" [a blockade-runner whose seizure the British protested – see Chapter 6], but really betrayed inexcusable ignorance of the subject of prize and prize courts, and admiralty law. . . .

May 20, 1864: The recent arrest of a Spaniard (Arguellis) who was in New York, and who was abducted [and sent to Cuba, a Spanish colony, for prosecution], it is said, by certain officials under instructions or by direction of the Secretary of State is exciting inquiry. Arguellis is accused of having, in some way, participated in the slave trade. But if the assertion be true, we have no extradition treaty with Spain, and I am therefore surprised at the proceeding. There is such hostility to the slave trade that a great wrong may perhaps be perpetrated with impunity and without scrutiny, but I hope not. Nothing has been said in Cabinet on the subject, nor do I know anything in regard to it, except what I see in the papers.

Mr. Seward sometimes does strange things, and I am inclined to believe he has committed one of those freaks which make me constantly apprehensive of his acts. He knows that slavery is odious and all concerned in slave traffic are distrusted, and has improved the occasion to exercise arbitrary power, expecting to win popular applause by doing an illegal act. Constitutional limitations are to him unnecessary restraints.[2]

September 27, 1864: The President has been made to believe that the order [authorizing a Texas Unionist to export cotton through the blockade] was essential; the Secretary of State has so presented the subject to him that he probably thought it a duty. There are times when I can hardly persuade myself that the President's natural sagacity has been so duped, but his confidence in Seward is great, although he must know him to be, I will not say a trickster, because of his position and our association, but [too] over-cunning to be strictly honest. And when I say this, I do not apply to him dishonesty in money transactions when dealing with men, or the government perhaps but political cheating, deceiving, wrong administration. He knows this scheme to bring out cotton was a fraud, and hence, instead of

---

[2] Welles raised this issue at the June 6th cabinet meeting, suggesting that in the absence of an extradition treaty with Spain, the seizure of Arguellis and his transport to Cuba may have violated New York's law against kidnapping. Seward replied that although there was no extradition treaty, the U.S. government could still choose to turn him over to the Spanish authorities as an act of comity between the two nations. Welles was unconvinced, but let the matter drop. Seward had probably acted as he did in hopes of gaining favor with the Spanish government regarding American efforts to curb blockade-runners' use of Cuba as a base of operations.

coming directly to me, who have charge of the blockade, or bringing the question before the Cabinet in a frank and honorable manner, there is this secret, roundabout proceeding, so characteristic of the Secretary of State.[3]

January 30, 1865: [Seward] has queer fancies for a statesman. He told me last week that he had looked in no book on international law or admiralty law since he entered on the duties of his present office. His thoughts, he says, come to the same conclusions as the writers and students. In administrating the government he seems to have little idea of constitutional and legal restraints, but acts as if the ruler was omnipotent. Hence he has involved himself in constant difficulties.[4]

STANTON

September 12, 1862: In his dislike of Stanton, [Montgomery] Blair is sincere, but in his detestation he may fail to allow Stanton qualities that he really possesses. Stanton is no favorite of mine. But he has energy and application. I doubt his sincerity always. He wants no general to overtop him, is jealous of others in any position who have influence and popular regard; but he has cunning and skill to suppress his feelings. Is, in short, a hypocrite, a moral coward, while affecting to be, and to a certain extent being, brusque, and over-valiant in words. . . .

Stanton's appointment to the War Department was a strange one. I was never a favorite of Seward, and Stanton, knowing his creator, sympathized with him. For several months after his appointment, he exhibited some of his unhappy traits in regard to myself. He has from the first been filled with panics and alarms, in which I have not sympathized; and I have sometimes exhibited little respect for his mercurial flights and sensational disturbances. He saw on more than one occasion that I was cool when he was excited, and he well knew that I neither admired his policy nor indorsed his views. Of course we were courteously civil, but reserved and distant. In the course of events there was a change. The Navy and my course was in favor, while my mercurial colleague was denounced. His deportment changed, and we have since moved along harmoniously at

---

[3] Welles's objection to this order led Lincoln to revoke it.

[4] On April 23, 1863, Senator Charles A. Sumner (see Section II, below) had said much the same thing, commenting, as Welles recorded it in his diary, that Seward "knows nothing of international law and is wanting in common sense, treats grave questions lightly and without comprehending their importance and bearings."

least. He is impulsive, not administrative; has quickness, rashness, when he has nothing to fear; is more violent than vigorous, more demonstrative than discriminating, more vain than wise; is arrogant and domineering towards those in subordinate positions if they will submit to his insolence, but is a sycophant and intriguer in deportment and language with those whom he fears. He has more force and greater capacity than [his predecessor Simon] Cameron; but the qualities I have mentioned and his uneasy, restless nature make him an unfit man in many respects for the War Department in times like these.

July 8, 1863: The rejoicing in regard to Vicksburg [which surrendered to Grant's forces on July 4th] is immense. Admiral Porter's brief dispatch to me was promptly transmitted over the whole country, and led, everywhere, to spontaneous gatherings, firing of guns, ringing of bells, and general gratification and gladness. . . . [5] The whole country is joyous. I am told, however, that Stanton is excessively angry because Admiral Porter heralded the news to me in advance of General Grant to the War Department. The telegraph office is in the War Department Building, which has a censorship over all that passes or is received. Everything goes under the Secretary's eye, and he craves to announce all important information. In these matters he takes as deep an interest as in army movements which decide the welfare of the country.

October 1, 1864: Stanton has been for the departmental system always.[6] Pressing, violent, and impatient, and intolerant, intriguing and tyrannical, he is exceedingly offensive in his manners, deportment, and many of his acts.

CHASE

Early in the war, Welles's view of Chase was largely positive. (It will be recalled that he had favored Chase for the presidential nomination in 1860 and voted for him on all three ballots at the Republican national convention.) But over time, he

---

[5] Acting Rear Admiral David Dixon Porter's report to Welles of this great victory reached Washington before General Grant's report to Stanton did, and as was seen in Chapter 3, Welles immediately carried the news to Lincoln.

[6] By "departmental system" Welles meant one in which each cabinet member operated his department with near-total autonomy and opposed general cabinet discussion of matters falling in his bailiwick – the exact opposite of Welles's view of the cabinet's proper role.

became much more critical of the treasury secretary. Among the reasons Welles's opinion changed were Chase's role in precipitating the December 1862 cabinet crisis, his overweening ambition to become president, and his advocacy of financial policies (especially the issuance of paper currency not convertible to specie) that Welles deplored.

October 10, 1862: The currency and financial questions will soon be as troublesome as the management of the armies. In making Treasury notes or irredeemable paper of any kind a legal tender, and in flooding the country with inconvertible paper money down to a dollar and fractional parts of a dollar, the Secretary of the Treasury may obtain momentary ease and comfort, but woe and misery will follow to the country. Mr. Chase has a good deal of ability, but has never made finance his study. His general ideas appear to be crudely sound, but he does not act upon them, and his principal and most active and persistent advisers are of a bad school.

February 15, 1864: The movements of parties and partisans are becoming distinct. I think there are indications that Chase intends to press his pretensions as a candidate [for president], and much of the Treasury machinery and the special agencies have that end in view. This is to be regretted. It appears to me that the whole effort is a forced one and can result in no good to himself, but may embarrass the Administration. The extreme radicals are turning their attention to him and also to Fremont. As between the two, Chase is incomparably the most talented and capable, and yet I have little confidence in his financial ability, nor do I trust his political principles. The President, I think, fears Chase, and he also respects him.

February 22, 1864: A circular, "strictly private," signed by Senator Pomeroy [a radical Republican from Kansas] and in favor of Mr. Chase for President, has been detected and published. Its recoil will be more dangerous, I apprehend, than its projectile. That is, it will damage Chase more than Lincoln. The effect on the two men themselves will not be serious. Both of them desire the position, and it is not surprising; it certainly is not in the President, who would be gratified with an indorsement. Were I to advise Chase, it would be not to aspire for the position, especially not as a competitor with the man who has given him his confidence, and with whom he has acted in the administration of the government at a most eventful period. The President well understands Chase's wish, and is somewhat hurt that he should press forward under the circumstances. Chase tries to have it thought that he is indifferent and scarcely cognizant of what is doing in his behalf, but no one of his partisans is so well posted as Chase himself.[7]

June 25, 1864: The Treasury management is terrible, ruinous. Navy requisitions are wantonly withheld for weeks, to the injury and ruin of the contractor. In the end the government will suffer greatly, for persons will not deal with the government at ordinary current rates. The pay of the sailors and workmen is delayed until they are almost mutinous and riotous. There is no justifiable excuse for this neglect. But Mr. Chase, having committed blunders in his issues [of paper currency], is now desirous of retiring certain paper, and avails himself of funds of creditors on naval account to accomplish this. It is most unjust. The money honestly due to government creditors should not be withheld for Treasury schemes, or to retrieve its mistakes.

I am daily more dissatisfied with the Treasury management. Everything is growing worse. Chase has not the sagacity, knowledge, or ability of a financier. He is a man of expedients, and will break down the government. There is no one to check him. The President surrendered the finances to his management entirely. Other members of the Cabinet are not consulted. Any dissent from, or doubts even, of his measures is considered as a declaration of hostility and an embarrassment of his administration. I believe I am the only one who has expressed an opinion that questioned his policy, and that expression was mild and kindly uttered. Blair said about as much and both [of us] were lectured by Chase. But he knew not then, nor does he know now, the elementary principles of finance and currency. Congress surrenders to his capricious and superficial qualities as pliantly as the President and the Cabinet. If they do not legalize his projects, the Treasury is to be closed, and under a threat, or something approaching a threat, his schemes are sanctioned, and laws are made to carry them into effect; but woe awaits the country in consequence.

June 30, 1864: The retirement [i.e., resignation] of Chase appears to give relief rather than otherwise, which surprises me. I had thought it might create a shock for a brief period, though I did not fear that it would be lasting. I look upon it as a blessing. The country could not go on a great while longer under his management, which has been one of expedients and of no fixed principles, or profound and correct financial knowledge.

---

[7] Shortly after the so-called Pomeroy circular was made public, a discomfited Chase announced he was no longer seeking the Republican presidential nomination, though he continued to hope the party would turn to him when the national nominating convention met in early June.

It is understood that a disagreement between himself and the President in relation to the appointment of Assistant Treasurer at New York was the cause of his leaving. I think likely that was the occasion of his tendering his resignation, and I have little doubt he was greatly surprised that it was accepted. He may not admit this, but it is none the less true, I apprehend. Yet there were some circumstances to favor his going – there is a financial gulf ahead.

August 5, 1864: I was with the President on Wednesday [the 3ʳᵈ] when Governor Morgan [former governor of New York, now in the Senate] was there, and the President produced the correspondence that had passed between himself and Chase at the time C. resigned. It was characteristic. I do not think it was wholly unexpected to either, and yet both were a little surprised. The President had made up his mind that he would not be again overridden in his own appointments. Chase felt he must enforce his determinations, which he had always successfully carried out. In coming to the conclusion that a separation must take place, the President was prompted by some, and sustained by all, his Cabinet without an exception. Chase's retirement has offended nobody, and has gratified almost everybody.

August 25, 1864: I hear little of Chase, though I doubt not that his [presidential] aspirations are unextinguished. That he is disappointed because his retirement made so little sensation and has been so readily acquiesced in, I have no doubt and I have heard that he had written a friend here to the effect that it was expedient, under the circumstances, to support Lincoln, although he had many dislikes to the man and his policy. But I am assured he has an expectation, sometimes amounting to confidence, that Fremont [running on a third-party ticket – see Section II] will be withdrawn and that there will be union and harmony. I can believe most of this. Chase has a good deal of intellect and knows the path where duty points, and in his calmer moments, resolves to pursue it. But with a mind of considerable resources, he has great weaknesses that constantly impair all his strength. He has inordinate ambition, intense selfishness, and insufferable vanity. These traits impair his moral courage; they make him a sycophant with the truly great, and arrogant towards the humble. The society of the former he courts, for he has mental acquirement and appreciation, but his political surroundings are the mean, the abject, the adulators who pander to his weaknesses. That he is irresolute and wavering, his instinctive sagacity prompting him rightly, but his selfish and vain ambition turning him to error, is unquestionably true. I have little doubt, however, that he will, eventually, when satisfied that his aspirations are not to be gratified, support the reelection of the President. Am not certain it is not already so arranged.

As Welles anticipated, Chase did eventually endorse Lincoln for reelection and even campaigned for him. Once reelected, Lincoln nominated the former treasury secretary to be chief justice of the Supreme Court. Welles, who had recommended Montgomery Blair for the position, was dubious about the appointment.

December 6, 1864: I hope the selection may prove a good one. I would not have advised it, because I have apprehensions on that subject. Chase has mental power and resources, but he is ambitious and restless, prone to intrigue and subtle management. If he applies himself strictly and faithfully to his duties, he may succeed on the bench, although his mind, I fear, is not so much judicial as ministerial. He will be likely to use the place for political advancement and thereby endanger confidence in the court. He wants moral courage and frankness, is fond of adulation, and is a sycophant. I hope the President may have no occasion to regret his selection.

BLAIR

Montgomery Blair was Welles's best friend among cabinet members, and the one he respected most. He had been acquainted with the postmaster general's father, the wealthy and influential journalist-politician Francis Preston Blair, Sr., since the 1830s.

December 23, 1862: On important questions, Blair is as potent with the President as either [Seward or Chase], and sometimes I think equal to both. With some egotism, Blair has great good sense, a better knowledge and estimate of military men than either or both the others, and, I think, is possessed of more solid, reliable administrative ability.

September 23, 1864 [the day Blair resigned at Lincoln's request]: In parting with Blair the President parts with a true friend, and he leaves no adviser so able, sagacious. Honest, truthful, and sincere, he has been wise, discriminating, and correct.[8]

---

[8] Blair, who was commonly viewed as the most conservative member of the cabinet, had made many enemies among moderate and especially radical Republicans. Lincoln asked for Blair's resignation to mollify them and perhaps as a *quid pro quo for* Fremont's withdrawal from the presidential race.

II

SENATOR SUMNER

Charles A. Sumner of Massachusetts was among the most radical Republicans in the Senate – militant champion of not only emancipation but also racial equality. Harvard educated and exceptionally cosmopolitan, he chaired the Senate Foreign Relations Committee and was particularly valuable to the Lincoln administration because of his knowledge of British politics and his *correspondence with Richard Cobden and John Bright, two Liberal members of Parliament who were warm supporters of the Union. Despite fundamental differences in background and outlook, Lincoln and Sumner established a generally good personal and political relationship.[9] Welles and Sumner also differed on many issues, but they too got along well and often lined up together against Seward on foreign policy questions (see Chapter 6). Many of Sumner's contemporaries viewed him in stark black-or-white terms. Welles's characterization of him is noteworthy for instead depicting him in shades of gray.*

January 2, 1864: Senator Sumner called on Saturday as usual. After disposing of some little matters of business, he spoke of the President and the election. He says the President is moving for a reelection, and has, he knows, spoken to several persons on the subject very explicitly. I told him the President had exchanged no word with me on the subject, but that I had taken for granted he would be a candidate, that I thought all Presidents had entertained dreams of that nature, and that my impressions are that a pretty strong current is setting in his favor. To this Sumner made no response, affirmatively or negatively. I think his present thoughts are in another direction, but not very decidedly so. Neither of us cared to press the other. Whether he had in view to sound me I was uncertain, and am still.

In many respects Sumner is deficient as a party leader, though he has talents, acquirements, sincerity, and patriotism, with much philanthropy. He is theoretical rather than practical. He is credulous to weakness with those who are his friends; and has not the suspicions and jealousies that are too common with men of his position. Towards the slaveholders he is implacable, and is ready to go to extremes to break up not only the system

---

[9] Sumner and Mrs. Lincoln formed a particularly close friendship, and the handsome bachelor sometimes escorted her to social and cultural events when the president was unable to attend.

of bondage, but the political fabric in all the rebellious States. His theorizing propensities and the resentments that follow from deep personal injuries work together in his warfare against that domineering oligarchy which has inflicted great calamities on our country.[10]

As Chairman of the Committee on Foreign Relations, his services at this time are invaluable. He is in many respects the opposite of Seward and, on international law and the science of government, is vastly the superior of the Secretary of State. But the latter has versatility of genius and unsurpassed pliability, so that he can readily adapt himself to whatever may seem expedient. Sumner acts from fixed principles but honest convictions, investigating questions in which he is interested elaborately, and bringing great knowledge and authorities to his support. Seward can have no great deference for principles of any kind and his convictions change without hesitation if deemed expedient. . . .

Sumner has not the arts that are the chief stock in trade . . . of some tolerably successful politicians, and he is often the victim of cunning fellows of greatly inferior capacity who use him. When Senator Dixon of Connecticut desired, and was intriguing for, a reelection to the Senate, he contrived to get a *quasi* indorsement from Sumner in a general letter, which was used effectually to defeat Sumner's best friends in Connecticut and injure the cause nearest his heart. [For more on Dixon, see Chapter 7.] Too late Sumner regrets his error, but will repeat it when a cunning mind shall need to practice the deception. He can stand firm and immovable on great questions, but is swayed by little social appeals to his kindness. His knowledge of men is imperfect and unreliable, and hence, while he will always have position with his party he will never be the trusted leader.

Senator Hale

John P. Hale, a radical Republican from New Hampshire, chaired the Senate Naval Affairs Committee and used it as a platform from which regularly to assail the Navy Department and Welles's administration of it. Not one to suffer fools gladly and deeming Hale a fool (among other things!), Welles wrote numerous diary entries about him, employing some of the most scathing – and occasionally

---

[10] Welles is alluding to the severe beating South Carolina Congressman Preston Brooks inflicted on Sumner on May 22, 1856, as he sat at his desk on the floor of the Senate. Brooks was retaliating for Sumner's harsh personal criticism of Brooks's elderly relative and fellow South Carolinian, Senator Andrew P. Butler, in a speech on May 19th and 20th. Sumner's injuries were such that he did not return to the Senate until 1859.

amusing – prose that appears in the wartime portion of the diary. The following excerpts illustrate Welles's animus toward Hale.

September 25, 1862: The real character of J. P. Hale is exhibited in a single transaction. He wrote me an impertinent and dictatorial letter which I received on Wednesday morning, admonishing me not to violate law in the appointment of midshipmen. Learning from my answer that I was making these appointments notwithstanding his warning and protest, he had the superlative meanness to call on Assistant Secretary Fox, and request him, if I was actually making the appointments which he declares to be illegal, to procure on his (Hale's) application the appointment of a New Hampshire lad for whom he felt an interest. This is after his supercilious letter to me, and one equally supercilious to Fox, in which he buttoned up his virtue to the throat and said he would never acquiesce in such a violation of the law. Oh, John P. Hale, how transparent is thy virtue! Long speeches, loud professions, Scriptural quotations, funny anecdotes, vehement denunciations avail not to cover thy nakedness, which is very bald.

July 27, 1863: Had a strange letter from Senator John P. Hale, protesting against the appointment of Commodore [G. J.] Van Brunt to the command of the Portsmouth Navy Yard, because he and V. B. are not on friendly terms. He wishes me to become a party to a personal controversy and to do injustice to an officer for the reason that he and that officer are not in cordial relations. The pretensions and arrogance of Senators become amazing, and this man, or Senator, would carry his private personal disagreement into public official action. Such are his ideas of propriety and Senatorial privilege and power that he would not only prostitute public duty to gratify his puerile resentment, but he would have the Department debased into an instrument to minister to his malignity. [Welles goes on to say that he had never intended to make Van Brunt commander of the Portsmouth navy yard, but if he had, Hale's objection would not have deterred him from doing so.]

June 6, 1864: I rejoice at it [the New Hampshire legislature's decision not to reelect Hale to another term], for he is worthless, a profligate politician, a poor Senator, an indifferent statesman, not without talents, though destitute of industry. He has some humor, is fond of scandal, delights in defaming, and is reckless of truth in his assaults. The country will sustain no loss from his retirement. As chairman of the Naval Committee and the organ of communication between the Navy Department and the Senate, he has rendered no service, but has been a constant embarrassment and obstruction. During the whole of this civil war, when all our energies and efforts were exerted in the cause of the Union and the country, no assistance, no word of encouragement even, has ever come to the Department from John P. Hale. But constant assaults, insinuations, and pronounced, if not willful and deliberate, misrepresentations have emanated from him . . . . I am glad that his factious conduct is not indorsed by his State, and that the buffoon and vilifier will not be in a position to do further injury.[11]

Horatio Seymour

Seymour was elected governor of New York in November 1862. Like other Democratic regulars (as distinct from War Democrats, who gave the administration almost unqualified support, and Peace, or Copperhead, Democrats, who were straight-out foes of the war), he was lukewarm about the war effort, and his opposition to the 1863 draft law caused serious problems for the Lincoln administration. Although defeated for reelection in 1864, he was the Democratic nominee for president in 1868.

September 27, 1862: Seymour, the Democratic [gubernatorial] candidate, has smartness, but not firm, honest principles. He is an inveterate place-hunter, fond of office and not always choice of means in obtaining it. More of a party man than patriot.

January 10, 1863: The great problem which is being solved in these days seems to be scarcely realized by our public and really great men. It is sad to witness in this period of calamity, when the nation is struggling for existence, and the cause of good government and civil liberty is at stake, the spirit of party overpowering patriotism. The Governors in several of the States have presented their messages during the week. Tod of Ohio exhibits a manly, wholesome, and vigorous tone, others also do well, but the jesuitical and heartless insincerity of Seymour is devoid of true statesmanship, and a discredit to the position he occupies. Unhallowed partisan and personal aspirations are moving springs with him. That such a man, at such a time, should have been elected to such a place does no credit to popular intelligence and public virtue.

---

[11] After Hale's term ended, Lincoln nominated him to be U. S. minister to Spain, a position for which Welles judged him to be "eminently unfit." Diary, March 11, 1865.

HORACE GREELEY

As editor of the New York Tribune, *the eccentric and unpredictable Greeley was the country's most famous newspaperman. Early in the war, he pressed Lincoln to emancipate the slaves and ardently backed the war effort. By 1864, however, he was so appalled by the war's terrible cost in blood and treasure that he began advocating peace, seemingly at almost any price. In July, he convinced himself that Confederate agents operating in Canada were authorized to negotiate a peaceful settlement and he urged Lincoln to make an overture to them. Though highly skeptical, Lincoln commissioned a reluctant Greeley to sound out the supposed peace commissioners himself. Greeley met with one of them at Niagara Falls, Canada, and learned that they were not empowered to negotiate for peace. At this meeting, Greeley delivered a "To Whom It May Concern" letter in which Lincoln set forth two preconditions for peace: the restoration of the Union and the rebel states' abandonment of slavery. When the Confederates made the letter public, many Democratic politicians and editors, letting the wish father the thought, claimed it showed that the Union could be restored without further bloodshed if only Lincoln would drop his stubborn insistence on emancipation. This claim resonated with a war-weary northern public, and for a time appeared to jeopardize Lincoln's prospects for reelection. The so-called Niagara peace initiative forms the backdrop to the following three excerpts about Greeley.*

July 22, 1864: At the Cabinet meeting the President read his correspondence with Horace Greeley on the subject of peace propositions from George Saunders [a Kentuckian who sometimes worked for the Confederate government and was acquainted with the Confederate agents] and others at Niagara Falls.[12] The President has acquitted himself very well – if he was to engage in the matter at all – but I am sorry that he permits himself, in this irregular way, to be induced to engage in correspondence with irresponsible parties like Saunders and [Clement C.] Clay [one of the Confederate agents] or scheming busybodies like Greeley. There is no doubt that the President and the whole Administration are misrepresented and misunderstood on the subject of peace, and Greeley is one of those who has done and is doing great harm and injustice in this matter. In this instance he was evidently anxious to thrust himself forward as an actor, and yet when once engaged he began to be alarmed; he failed to honestly and frankly communicate the President's first letters [to the rebel agents], as was his duty, but sent a letter of his own, which was not true and correct, and found himself involved in the meshes of his own frail net.

---

[12] The correct spelling is Sanders.

August 13, 1864: The *Tribune* is owned by a company which really desired to give a fair support to the Administration, but Greeley, the editor, is erratic, unreliable, without stability, an enemy of the Administration, a creature of sentiment or impulse, not of reason nor principle. Having gone to extremes in the measures that fermented and brought on this war, he would now go to extremes to quell it. I am prepared to see him acquiesce in a division of the Union, or the continuance of slavery, to accomplish his personal party schemes. There are no men or measures to which he will adhere faithfully.[13]

August 19, 1864: [At the cabinet meeting] Blair inquired about the Niagara peace correspondence. The President went over the particulars. Had sent the whole correspondence to Greeley for publication, excepting one or two passages in Greeley's letters which spoke of a bankrupted country and awful calamities. But Greeley had replied he would not consent to any suppression of his letters or any part of them; and the President remarked that, though G. had put him in a false attitude, he thought it better he should bear it [i.e., being criticized for letting the correspondence go unpublished], than that the country should be distressed by such a howl, from such a person, on such an occasion. Concerning Greeley . . . he said to-day that Greeley is an old shoe – good for nothing now, whatever he has been. "In early life, and with few mechanics and but little means in the West, we used," said he, "to make our shoes last a great while with much mending, and sometimes, when far gone, we found the leather so rotten the stitches would not hold. Greeley is so rotten that nothing can be done with him. He is not truthful – the stitches all tear out."

JOHN C. FREMONT

Fremont won fame as "The Pathfinder" in the 1840s for a series of army expeditions he led exploring large parts of the trans-Mississippi West; he was also instrumental in seizing California for the United States during the Mexican-American War. Fremont was well-connected politically by virtue of his marriage to the very talented and ambitious Jessie Benton, the daughter of Thomas Hart Benton of Missouri, one of Andrew Jackson's closest allies and a powerful figure in the Democratic Party for three decades, most of them as a U.S. senator. Fremont became

---

[13] This harsh judgment notwithstanding, when the self-styled "Liberal Republicans" and the Democratic Party jointly nominated Greeley for president in 1872, Welles supported his candidacy.

a free-soil Democrat and in 1856 was the Republican presidential nominee. His background made it virtually inevitable he would be commissioned a major general early in the war. But he proved ineffective in two successive commands, and in June 1862 he refused to serve under John Pope in the newly created (and short-lived) Army of Virginia. Fremont then moved to New York City and expected soon to be summoned to a new command. Lincoln had taken his measure, however, and despite lobbying by Fremont's admirers, the summons never came. At the end of May 1864, a mixed bag of dissidents and malcontents nominated him to challenge Lincoln's reelection from the left. He might have taken enough votes from Lincoln to enable the Democratic candidate, George B. McClellan, to win. But under strong pressure, Fremont withdrew from the race on September 22nd.[14]

June 1, 1864: We have to-day the results of a meeting of strange odds and ends of parties, and factions, and disappointed and aspiring individuals at Cleveland. Fremont is nominated as their candidate for President and John Cochrane for Vice-President. . . .

I very earnestly supported Fremont in 1856. He was then put forward as the representative of the principles for which we were contending, and I have no reason to give that he was not faithful to the cause. He was, however, as soon as nominated, surrounded, to a great extent, by bad men, in whom no good man had confidence. His bearing was very well so far as he appeared before the public. I saw that he was anxious to be elected but not offensively so; he was not obtrusive, but, on the contrary, reserved and retiring. In nothing did he show extraordinary ability or character, but my conclusions were that his real traits were undeveloped. But he did not grow upon me as reserved men usually do. . . .

Fremont has gained no reputation during the War. In power his surroundings are awful. Reckless, improvident, wasteful, pompous, purposeless, vain, and incompetent. In his explorations, however, he showed endurance, and he had the reputation of attaching his men to him. His journals were readable, but I have been told they were prepared and mostly written by Colonel Benton. On all occasions he puts on airs, is ambitious, and would not serve under men of superior military capacity and experience. Fremont first and country after. For a long time he has been in foolish intrigues for the Presidency. . . .

---

[14] For an informative account of the 1864 presidential race, including Fremont's abortive candidacy, see David E. Long, *The Jewel of Liberty: Abraham Lincoln's Re-Election and the End of Slavery* (Mechanicsburg, Pa.: Stackpole Books, 1994).

PRESTON KING

Welles tended to be critical even of men he liked and respected. But he did occa-
sionally express a positive view unalloyed by criticism, as is evident in his char-
acterization of his longtime friend Preston King. Born in upstate New York, King
entered politics as a dedicated Jacksonian Democrat, just as Welles did. A member
of the House of Representatives in the mid 1840s, he was an ardent advocate of
the Wilmot Proviso. After a two-year hiatus, he was again elected to Congress in
1848, this time on the Free-Soil Party ticket, and reelected in 1850. After passage
of the Kansas-Nebraska Act, he moved to the fledgling Republican Party and in
1857 was elected to the Senate. He failed of reelection in 1863.

February 13, 1864: Had a pleasant half-hour interview with Preston King,
who made a special call to see me. Few men are his equal for sagacity,
comprehensiveness, sound judgment, and fearlessness of purpose. Such
statesmen do honor to their State and country. His loss to the Senate cannot be supplied. I like his successor, [Edward] Morgan [also a Republican],
who has good sense and will make a good Senator, but he cannot make
King's place good. I know not who can. Why are the services of such men
set aside by small politicians? But King is making himself useful, and has
come to Washington from patriotic motives to advise with our legislators
and statesmen, and to cheer and encourage the soldiers.

I sometimes think he is more true to principles than I am myself.[15]
Speaking of Fernando Wood [a notorious Copperhead Congressman from
New York City], we each expressed a common and general sentiment of
surprise and disgust that any district could elect such a Representative.
But the whole city of New York is alike leprous and rotten. This brought
the question, how can such a place be regenerated and purified? What is
the remedy? While I expressed a reluctant conviction, which is gradu-
ally coming over me, that in such a vicious community, the system of free
suffrage was abased, and it was becoming a problem whether there should
not be an outside movement, or some restriction on voting to correct the
evil, King maintained the old faith and would let the evil correct itself. If
factious or partisan violence will go so far as to elect men like Wood or
Brooks [another New York Copperhead Congressman]; if men of property
and character will prostitute themselves to vote for them and consent to
have their city misgoverned and themselves misrepresented, let them take
the consequences. The evil will correct itself. After they have disgraced

---

[15] Given Welles's belief that he himself was unswervingly devoted to principle, coming
from him this was high praise indeed.

themselves sufficiently and loaded themselves with taxes and debt, they will finally rouse to a sense of duty, and retrieve the city from misrule and bad management. Such is the reasoning of Preston King.

When King committed suicide in late November 1865, Welles penned a lengthy tribute in his diary that credited him with "boldly meeting the arrogant and imperious slaveholding oligarchy and organizing the party which eventually overthrew them." Welles also noted that 25 years earlier, King "was in the Retreat for the Insane in Hartford, and there I knew him," adding that it was a recurrence of the old "malady" that had led him to take his own life. (Diary, December 1, 1865).

Chapter 5

GENERALS AND ADMIRALS AT WAR

Welles's characterizations of senior army and navy officers were just as candid and often as caustic as his comments about his cabinet colleagues and other prominent civilians. This chapter focuses on his views of Generals George B. McClellan, Henry W. Halleck, George G. Meade, Ulysses S. Grant, and William T. Sherman (Section I) and of Admirals Samuel F. Du Pont, David G. Farragut, and David Dixon Porter (Section II). Included are opinions Lincoln expressed about several of these officers and Welles recorded. The entries about McClellan and Meade also provide an insider's perspective on Antietam and Gettysburg, two of the war's most important battles.

I

McCLELLAN

This lengthy set of excerpts sheds light on the rise and fall of George Brinton McClellan, who was the subject of intense controversy during the war and to some extent remains so today. Most historians are critical of his tactics and strategy; and they portray him as deficient in such qualities essential to military success as self-confidence, tenacity, and moral courage.[1] However, when he was summoned to Washington to take command of the nascent Army of the Potomac following the embarrassing Union defeat at the first Battle of Bull Run (Manassas) on July 21, 1861, he was widely hailed as the savior of the Union. The scion of a prominent Philadelphia family who graduated second in the West Point Class of 1846,

---

[1] McClellan is not without defenders among historians, however. See, for example, Ethan S. Rafuse, *McClellan's War: The Failure of Moderation in the Struggle for the Union* (Bloomington: Indiana University Press, 2005).

McClellan was adept at training his mostly raw troops, instilling discipline in them, and bolstering their morale. But to the growing displeasure of Lincoln, cabinet members, Congressional Republicans, and much of the press, he repeatedly delayed the start of offensive operations. Not until mid March 1862 did he finally get under way. His 100,000-man army was transported down the Potomac River and Chesapeake Bay to Fortress Monroe on the tip of the peninsula between the York and James Rivers. From there he planned to move up the peninsula to take Richmond. Although the plan had merit, it ultimately failed. This was partly because of McClellan's excessive caution, tactical errors, gross exaggeration of the size of the enemy army, and distaste for hard fighting; it was also partly because during the campaign's climactic Seven Days Battles (June 25th – July 1st), the opposing forces were commanded by Robert E. Lee.

On August 3rd, McClellan was ordered to abandon the Peninsula Campaign and bring his army to the Washington area. He did so slowly and grudgingly, but by the middle of August, the last Union troops were on their way northward. He was directed to send many of them to reinforce General John Pope's recently created Army of Virginia, which would soon begin an overland offensive against Lee's army. He did so reluctantly, feeling nothing but contempt for Pope. At the time it was widely believed, as it is by many historians, that his balkiness in forwarding the troops contributed to Pope's defeat at the second Battle of Bull Run at the end of August. McClellan's conduct prompted Stanton and Chase to press hard for his dismissal. But Lincoln chose, instead, to put him in charge of Washington's defenses, and after the Army of Virginia had been absorbed into the Army of the Potomac, restored him to command. McClellan's immediate task was to repel Lee's invasion of western Maryland, which culminated at the Battle of Antietam on September 17th. In these excerpts Welles provides a generally well-informed account of the circumstances leading to McClellan's ultimate downfall and offers astute observations about his shortcomings.

August 31, 1862: For the last two or three days there has been fighting at the front and army movements of interest. McClellan with most of his army arrived at Alexandria [across the Potomac from Washington] a week or more ago, but inertness, inactivity, and sluggishness seem to prevail. Some of the troops have gone forward to join Pope, who has been beyond Manassas, where he has encountered Stonewall Jackson and the Rebel forces for the last three days in a severe struggle.

　　The energy and rapid movements of the Rebels are in such striking contrast with that of some of our own officers that I shall not be seriously surprised at any sudden dash from them. . . .

Yesterday, Saturday, P.M., when [I was] about leaving the Department, Chase called on me with a protest signed by himself and Stanton, against continuing McClellan in command and demanding his immediate dismissal. . . . I told him I was not prepared to sign the document; that I preferred another method of meeting the question; that if asked by the President, and even if not asked, I was prepared to express my opinion, which, as he knew, had long been averse to McClellan and was much aggravated from what I had recently learned at the War Department; that I did not choose to denounce McC. for incapacity, or declare him a traitor, but I would say, and it was perhaps my duty to say, that I believed his withdrawal was demanded and that even his dismissal would be a blessing to the country.

Chase said that was not sufficient, that the time had arrived when the Cabinet must act with energy and promptitude, for either the Government or McClellan must go down. . . .

I proposed that there should be a general consultation with the President. He objected to this until the document was signed, which should be done at once.

This method of getting signatures without an interchange of views with those who were associated in council was repugnant to my idea of duty and right. . . . I informed C. that I should desire to advise with them [other cabinet members] in so important a matter; that I was disinclined to sign the paper; did not like the proceeding; that I could not, though I wished McClellan removed after what I had heard, and should have no hesitation in saying so at the proper time and place and in what I considered the right way. . . .[2]

Met, by invitation, a few friends last evening at Baron Gerolt's.[3] . . . Feeling anxious concerning affairs in front, I excused myself to go to the War Department . . . . Found Stanton and Caleb Smith alone in the Secretary's room. The conduct of McClellan was soon taken up. . . . Stanton . . . [stated] his inability to procure any satisfactory information from McClellan, who had no plan and no system. Said this vague, indefinite uncertainty was oppressive. That near the close of January [1862] he pressed this subject on the President, who issued the order to him [Stanton] and myself for an advance on the 22nd of February. McClellan began at once to interpose objections, yet did nothing, but talked always vaguely and

---

[2] When describing this encounter with Chase in *Lincoln and Seward,* p. 193, Welles added that the president "had selected his Cabinet to consult and advise with, not to conspire against him."

[3] Gerolt was the Prussian minister to the United States.

indefinitely and of various matters except those immediately in hand. The President insisted on, and ordered, a forward movement. Then McClellan informed them he intended a demonstration on the upper waters of the Potomac, and boats for a [pontoon] bridge were prepared with great labor and expense. He went up there and telegraphed back that two or three officers had done admirably in preparing the bridge and he wished them to be brevetted.[4] The whole thing was absurd, eventuated in nothing, and he was ordered back.

The President then commanded that the army should proceed to Richmond. McClellan delayed, hesitated, said he must go by way of the Peninsula, would take transports at Annapolis. In order that he should have no excuse, but without any faith in his plan, Stanton said he ordered transports and supplies to Annapolis. The President, in the mean time, urged and pressed a forward movement towards Manassas. Spoke of its results – the evacuation by the Rebels, who fled before the General came, who did not pursue them but came back to Washington. The transports were then ordered round to the Potomac, where the troops were shipped to Fortress Monroe. The plans – the number of troops to proceed, the number that was to remain – Stanton recounted. These arrangements were somewhat deranged by the sudden raid of Jackson towards Winchester [Virginia], which withdrew [General] Banks from Manassas, leaving no force between Washington and the Rebel army at Gordonsville. He [Lincoln] then ordered [General Irvin] McDowell and his division, also [General William] Franklin's, to remain. . . . McClellan had made the withholding of this necessary force to protect the seat of government his excuse for not being more rapid and effective – was constantly complaining. The President wrote him how, by his arrangement, only 18,000 troops, remnants and odd parcels, were left to protect the Capital. Still McClellan was everlastingly complaining and underrating his forces; said he had but 96,000, when his own returns showed he had 123,000. But, to stop his complaints and urge him forward, the President finally, on the 10th of June, sent him [General George] McCall and his division, with which he promised to proceed at once to Richmond, but did not until finally attacked [by Lee on June 26th].

McClellan's excuse for going by way of the Peninsula was that he might have good roads and dry ground, but his complaints were unceasing, after he got there, of bad roads, water, and swamps.

---

[4] See Chapter 7, note 21, for an explanation of brevet promotions.

When finally ordered to withdraw from James River [to the vicinity of Washington], he delayed obeying the order for thirteen days, and never did comply until General [Ambrose] Burnside was sent to supersede him if he did not move.

Since his arrival at Alexandria, Stanton says, only delay and embarrassment had governed him. General Halleck had, among other things, ordered General Franklin's division to go forward promptly to support Pope at Manassas. When Franklin got as far as Annandale he was stopped by McClellan, against orders. McClellan's excuse was he thought Franklin might be in danger if he proceeded farther. For twenty-four hours that large force remained stationary, hearing the whole time the guns of the battle that was raging in front. In consequence of this delay by command of McClellan, against specific orders, he [Stanton] apprehended, our army would be compelled to fall back. . . .

Stanton . . . said he understood from Chase that I declined to sign the protest which he had drawn up against McClellan's continuance in command, and asked if I did not think we ought to get rid of him. I told him I might not differ with him on that point . . . but that I disliked the method and manner of proceeding, that it was discourteous and disrespectful to the President. . . . [Stanton said] he could not and would not submit to a continuance of this state of things. . . . He said General Pope telegraphed to McClellan for supplies; the latter informed P. they were at Alexandria, and if P. would send an escort he could have them. A general fighting, on the field of battle, to send to a general in the rear and in repose an escort! . . .

We hear, this Sunday morning, that our army has fallen back to Centreville [after its defeat at Second Bull Run]. Pope writes in pretty good spirits that we have lost no guns, etc. The Rebels were largely reinforced, while our troops, detained at Annandale by McClellan's orders, did not arrive to support our wearied and exhausted men. McClellan telegraphs that he hears "Pope is badly cut up."

September 1, 1862: I was satisfied there was a fixed determination to remove, and if possible disgrace, McClellan. Chase frankly stated . . . that he deliberately believed McClellan ought to be shot, and should, were he President, be brought to summary punishment. I told him he was aware my faith in McClellan's energy and reliability was shaken nine months ago; that as early as last December I had, as he would recollect, expressed my disappointment in the man and stated to him specially, as the friend and indorser of McClellan, my misgivings in order that he might remove my doubts or confirm them. His indifference and neglect, his failure in the many instances to fulfill his promises, when the Rebels were erecting batteries on the west bank of the Potomac to close the navigation of the river, had forfeited my confidence in his efficiency and reliability. But at that time McClellan was a general favorite, and neither he (Chase) nor any one heeded my doubts and apprehensions.

A few weeks after the navigation of the river was first obstructed by the Rebel batteries last November, I made known to the President and Cabinet how I was put off by General McClellan with frivolous and unsatisfactory answers, until I ceased conversing with him on the subject. To me it seemed he had no plan or policy of his own, or any realizing sense of the condition of affairs. He was occupied with reviews and dress-parades – perhaps with drills and discipline, but was regardless of the political aspect of the question, the effect of the closing of the only avenue from the National Capital to the ocean and the embarrassment which would follow to the Government itself. Though deprecating his course and calling his attention to it, I did not think, as Chase now says he does, and as I hear others say, that he was imbecile, a coward, a traitor; but it was notorious that he hesitated, doubted, had not self-reliance – innate moral courage, and was wanting, in my opinion, in several of the essential requisites of a general in chief command.

September 2, 1862: At Cabinet meeting . . . it was stated that Pope . . . was falling back, intending to retreat within the Washington intrenchments on the opposite side of the [Potomac] river. . . . Those who have favored Pope are disturbed and disappointed. The general conviction is that he is a failure here, and there is a belief and admission on all hands that he has not been seconded and sustained as he should have been by several generals. Personal jealousies and professional rivalries, the bane and curse of all armies, have entered deeply into ours.

The President was called out for a short time and while he was absent Stanton said he was informed McClellan had been ordered to take command of the forces in Washington. General surprise was expressed. When the President came in he said he had done what seemed to him best. Halleck had proposed it.[5] McClellan knows this whole ground – his specialty is to defend – he is a good engineer, all admit; there is no better organizer – he can be trusted to act on the defensive; but having the "slows," he is good for nothing for an onward movement. . . . There was

---

[5] In *Lincoln and Seward*, p. 196, Welles wrote that Lincoln said Halleck had "fully approved" of putting McClellan in command of Washington's defense, not that Halleck had proposed it.

a more disturbed and desponding feeling than I have ever witnessed in council and the President was extremely distressed. There was a general conversation as regarded the infirmities of McClellan, but it was claimed he had beyond any officer the confidence of the army. Though deficient in the positive qualities which are necessary for an energetic commander, his organizing powers could be temporarily available till the troops could rally.

September 3, 1862: The army has no head. . . . McClellan is an intelligent engineer, but not a commander. To attack or advance with energy and power is not in his reading or studies, nor is it in his nature or disposition to advance. I sometimes fear his heart is not in the cause, yet I do not entertain the thought that he is unfaithful. The study of military operations interests and amuses him. He likes show, parade, and power. Wishes to outgeneral the Rebels, but not to kill and destroy them. In a conversation which I had with him in May last . . . he said he desired of all things to capture Charleston; he would demolish and annihilate the city. He detested, he said, both South Carolina and Massachusetts, and should rejoice to see both States extinguished. Both were and always had been ultra and mischievous, and he could not tell which he hated most. These were the remarks of the General-in-Chief at the head of our armies then in the field, and when as large a proportion of his troops were from Massachusetts as from any State in the Union, while as large a proportion of those opposed, who were fighting the Union, were from South Carolina as from any State. He was leading the men of Massachusetts against the men of South Carolina, yet he, the General, detests them alike.[6]

I cannot relieve my mind from the belief that to him, in a great degree, and to his example, influence, and conduct are to be attributed some portion of our late reverses – more than to any other person on either side. His reluctance to move or have others move, his inactivity, his detention of Franklin, his omission to send forward supplies unless Pope would send a cavalry escort from the battlefield, and the tone of his dispatches, all show a moody state of feeling. The treatment which he and the generals associated with him have received, in the selection of Pope, was injudicious,

---

[6] Welles's reference to McClellan as "General-in-Chief" at the time of their conversation in May 1862 is incorrect. Lincoln had appointed McClellan to that position on November 1, 1861, but relieved him of it on March 11, 1862, because he wanted McClellan to concentrate all of his attention on the forthcoming Peninsula Campaign. Lincoln left the position vacant until July 11th, when he named Henry Halleck to it. Had the Peninsula Campaign succeeded, the president probably would have rewarded McClellan by reappointing him general in chief instead of summoning Halleck from the west to take the position..

impolitic, wrong perhaps, but is no justification for their withholding one tithe of strength in a great emergency, where the lives of their countrymen and the welfare of the country were in danger. The soldiers he has commanded are doubtless attached to him. They have been trained to it, and he has kindly cared for them while under him. They have imbibed the prejudices of these officers, and the officers have, I fear, manifested a spirit more factious than patriotic. I have thought they have reason to complain, at the proper time, but not on the field of battle, that a young officer of no high reputation [i.e., Pope] should be brought from a Western Department and placed over them. . . .

September 6, 1862: We have information that the Rebels have crossed the Potomac in considerable force, with a view of invading Maryland and pushing on into Pennsylvania. Our army is passing north. This evening some twenty or thirty thousand passed my house within three hours. There was design in having them come up through H Street, and pass by McClellan's house, which they cheered lustily, instead of passing by the White House and honoring the President. . . .

McClellan's partisans have the ascendency in the army, though he has lost the confidence of the country, chiefly from delays, or what the President aptly terms the "slows."

September 7, 1862: When I started to come away [from visiting the War Department], Chase came also, and as we came down stairs asked me to walk with him to the President's. As we crossed the lawn, he said with feeling, everything was going wrong. He feared the country was ruined. McClellan was having everything his own way, as he (Chase) feared he would if decisive measures were not promptly taken for his dismissal. It was the reward for perfidy. My refusal to sign the paper he had prepared was fraught with great evil to the country. I replied that I viewed that matter differently. . . . I agreed he wanted decision, that he hesitated to strike, had behaved badly in the late trouble, but I did not believe he was unfaithful and destitute of patriotism. But aside from McClellan, and the fact that it would, with the feeling which pervaded the army, have been an impolitic step to dismiss him, the proposed combination in the Cabinet would have been wrong to the President. . . .

From what I have seen and heard within the last few days, the more highly do I appreciate the President's judgment and sagacity in the stand he made, and the course he took. . . .

In a brief talk with him as we were walking together on Friday [the 5th], the President said with much emphasis: "I must have McClellan to reorganize the army and bring it out of chaos. But there has been a design, a purpose in breaking down Pope, without regard of consequences to the country. It is shocking to see and know this; but there is no remedy at present, McClellan has the army with him."

My convictions are with the President that McClellan and his generals are this day stronger than the Administration with a considerable portion of the Army of the Potomac. It is not so in the country, where McClellan has lost favor.

September 8, 1862: [The president] expressed himself very decidedly concerning the management or mismanagement of the army. Said, "We had the enemy in the hollow of our hands on Friday, if our generals, who are vexed with Pope, had done their duty.[7] All our present difficulties and reverses have been brought upon us by these quarrels of the generals." These were, I think, his very words. . . .

In a conversation this morning with Chase, he said it was a doubtful matter whether my declining to sign the paper against McClellan was productive of good or harm. If I had done it, he said, McClellan would have been disposed of and not now in command, but the condition of the army was such under his long manipulation that it might have been hazardous at this juncture to have dismissed him. I assured him I had seen no moment yet when I regretted my decision, and my opinion of McClellan had undergone no change. He has military capacity and acquirements, but he makes no decision, delays, hesitates, vacillates – will, I fear, do nothing affirmative. His conduct during late events aggravates his indecision and is wholly unjustifiable and inexcusable.

But I will not prophesy what he will do in his present command. He has a great opportunity, and I hope and pray he may improve it. The President says truly he has the "slows," but he can gather the army together better than any other man. Let us give him credit when he deserves it.

September 12, 1862: "The officers and soldiers," the President said, "were pleased with the selection [of McClellan to continue in command]. . . . McC. has great powers of organization and discipline; he comprehends and can arrange combinations better than any of our generals, and there his usefulness ends. He can't go ahead – he can't strike a blow. . . ."

---

[7] Lincoln was referring not to the immediately preceding Friday (September 5th), when there was no significant fighting in Virginia, but to Friday, August 29th, the opening day of the second Battle of Bull Run.

September 13, 1862: The country is very desponding and much disheartened. There is a growing distrust of the Administration and of its ability and power to conduct the war. The new appointment of McC. has impaired public confidence and yet it has inspired strength and vigor in the army. Officers and soldiers appear to be united in his favor and willing to follow his lead. It has now been almost a week since he left Washington, yet he has not overtaken the enemy . . . . I am not without hopes that his late experience and the strong pressure of public opinion will rouse him to thorough work.

September 15, 1862: Some rumors yesterday and more direct information to-day are cheering to the Union cause. McClellan telegraphs a victory, defeat of the enemy with loss of 15,000 men, and that "General Lee admits they are badly whipped." To whom Lee made this confession so that it should be brought straight to McC. and telegraphed here does not appear.[8]

September 18, 1862 [*the day after the Battle of Antietam*]: We have authentic news that a long and sanguinary battle has been fought. McClellan telegraphs that the fight between the two armies was for fourteen hours. The Rebels must have been in strong position to have maintained such a fight against our large army. He also telegraphs that our loss is heavy, particularly in generals, but gives neither names nor results. His dispatches are seldom clear or satisfactory. "Behaved splendidly," "performed handsomely," but what was accomplished is never told and our anxiety is intense.

September 19, 1862: Nothing from the army, except that, instead of following up the victory, attacking and capturing the Rebels, they, after a day's armistice, are rapidly escaping across the river. McClellan says they are crossing and that [General Alfred] Pleasanton is after them. Oh dear![9]

September 20, 1862: Nothing conclusive from the army. The Rebels have crossed the river without being hurt or seriously molested – much in

---

[8] The enemy casualty toll of 15,000 that McClellan reported was wildly off the mark for any battle fought during the run-up to the Battle of Antietam. Even in that battle – the bloodiest one-day engagement of the war – Confederate casualties fell more than a thousand shy of 15,000. (Union casualties numbered about 12,500.)

[9] Welles's plaintive "Oh dear" probably reflected his awareness that Pleasanton commanded McClellan's cavalry, which had a mediocre record and was too small a force to inflict serious damage on Lee's retreating army. In the end, McClellan never undertook significant offensive action against Lee's battered forces, despite Lincoln's repeated promptings.

character with the general management of the war. Little is said on the subject. . . . There is no abatement of hostility to McClellan.

September 23, 1862: No news from the army. The Rebels appear to be moving back into Virginia in their own time and way, to select their own resting place, and to do, in short, pretty much as they please. Am sad, sick, sorrowful over this state of things, but see no remedy without change of officers.

September 26, 1862: It is now almost a fortnight since the battle near Sharpsburg [Antietam]. The Rebels have recrossed the Potomac, but our army is doing nothing.

October 11, 1862: We have word which seems reliable that [J.E.B.] Stuart's Rebel cavalry have been to Chambersburg [Pennsylvania] in the rear of McClellan, while he was absent in Philadelphia stopping at the Continental Hotel. I hope neither statement is true. But am apprehensive that both may be correct.

October 13, 1862: We have the mortifying intelligence that the Rebel cavalry rode entirely around our great Army of the Potomac, crossing the river above it, pushing on in the rear beyond the Pennsylvania line into the Cumberland Valley, then east and south, recrossing the Potomac below McClellan and our troops, near the mouth of the Monocacy. This is the second time this feat has been performed by J. E. B. Stuart around McClellan's army. The first was on the Peninsula. It is humiliating, disgraceful.

In this raid the Rebels have possessed themselves of a good deal of plunder, reclothed their men from our stores, run off a thousand horses, fat cattle, etc., etc. . . . McClellan had returned from Philadelphia with his wife, a most estimable and charming lady who cannot have been gratified with this exhibit of her husband's public duties. . . . His opponents will triumph in this evidence of alleged inertness and imbecility.

October 18, 1862: It is just five weeks since the Battle of Antietam, and the army is quiet, reposing in camp. The country groans, but nothing is done. Certainly the confidence of the people must give way under this fatuous inaction.

December 3, 1862 [*This was Welles's first diary entry since November 4th. In it he reviews some of the major events occurring during that month-long hiatus.*]: A change of the commander of the Army of the Potomac has taken place.

[McClellan was relieved on November 7th.] McClellan is ordered to Trenton [his personal residence], and Burnside succeeds him.

HALLECK

Henry W. Halleck was often referred to as "Old Brains" because he had written an influential book, Elements of Military Art and Science *(1846), and other works of military history and theory. After serving eight months as commander of the Military Department of Missouri, he was brought east and appointed general in chief of all Union armies on July 11, 1862. He held the position until Lincoln named Grant to succeed him on March 10, 1864, at which time Halleck became the army's chief of staff under Grant. Welles's judgments of Halleck were consistently severe.*

September 10, 1862: General Halleck is nominally General-in-Chief and discharging many of the important functions of the War Department. . . . He has intellect and considerable acquirements, but his mind is heavy and irresolute, and he appears to me to possess but little original military talent.

November 4, 1862: Mr. Bates quietly suggested that Halleck should take command of the army [the Army of the Potomac] in person. But the President said, and all the Cabinet concurred in the opinion, that H. would be an indifferent general in the field, that he shrank from responsibility in his present position, that he is a moral coward, worth but little except as a critic, though intelligent and educated.

January 5, 1863: Halleck is heavy-headed; wants sagacity, readiness, courage, and heart. . . . In all military matters he seems destitute of resources, skill, or capacity. He is more tardy and irresolute than McClellan. . . .

June 2, 1863: There was some discussion of affairs at Vicksburg. The importance of capturing that stronghold and opening the navigation of the river is appreciated by all, and confidence is expressed in Grant [whose army had been besieging the city since May 23rd], but it seems that not enough was doing. The President said Halleck declares he can furnish no additional troops. As yet I have seen nothing to admire in the military management of General Halleck. . . . At this time when the resources of the nation should be called out and activity pervade all military operations, he sits back in his chair, doing comparatively nothing.

June 16, 1863: Halleck sits, and smokes, and swears, and scratches his arm . . . but exhibits little military capacity or intelligence; is obfusticated, muddy, uncertain, stupid as to what is doing or to be done.[10]

July 16, 1863: In this whole summer's campaign I have been unable to see, hear, or obtain evidence of power, or will, or talent, or originality on the part of General Halleck. He has suggested nothing, decided nothing, done nothing but scold and smoke. Is it possible the energies of the nation should be wasted by such a man?

September 26, 1863: General Halleck has earnestly and constantly smoked cigars and rubbed his arms, while the Rebels have been vigorously concentrating their forces to overwhelm [General William] Rosecrans. We all, except General Halleck, know that Longstreet with 20,000 men has gone from Lee's army somewhere. The information does not seem to have reached Halleck; if it has he has taken no measures in regard to it. Not a recruit was sent to Rosecrans, who held the key that controlled the Rebel centre, and of which they must dispossess him or their cause is endangered. H. has never seemed to realize the importance of that position – nor, I am sorry to say, of any other.[11]

MEADE

George G. Meade, an 1835 graduate of West Point, was promoted from captain in the regular army to brigadier general of volunteers in August 1861. He rose from brigade commander to command of a division and then of a corps and was

---

[10] At the time Welles wrote this comment, Lee and the Army of Northern Virginia were well started on the invasion that culminated in the Battle of Gettysburg.

[11] Shortly after Rosecrans's Army of the Cumberland occupied Chattanooga on September 9, 1863, it pushed into north Georgia in pursuit of Braxton Bragg's Army of Tennessee, which Rosecrans mistakenly believed was in retreat. At the ensuing Battle of Chickamauga (September 19th and 20th), the federal army suffered a costly defeat and had to withdraw into Chattanooga, where Bragg besieged it. Bragg's victory was made possible in part because he had been reinforced by 12,000 men (not the 20,000 Welles mentions) sent from Lee's army. On Stanton's initiative, General Joseph Hooker was dispatched with two corps (20,000 men) from the Army of the Potomac to help break the siege; another 17,000 troops, commanded by General William T. Sherman, were summoned from Mississippi. And Grant, who was now in command of the entire theater of operations, replaced Rosecrans with General George Thomas. In late November, the reinforced federals routed Bragg's army in the battles of Lookout Mountain and Missionary Ridge, forcing it to fall back all the way to Dalton, Georgia. With Chattanooga now firmly in Union hands, the stage was set for Sherman to launch his campaign to take Atlanta the following spring.

promoted to major general in December 1862. On June 27, 1863, four days before the Battle of Gettysburg began, Lincoln put him in command of the Army of the Potomac, replacing "Fighting Joe" Hooker, who had lost the Battle of Chancellorsville the previous May. Meade's victory in the turning-point Gettysburg battle ensured him a prominent place in the annals of the Civil War. There continues to be controversy, however, over whether he could have crushed Lee's defeated army had he vigorously pursued it in the days following the battle. The failure to follow up the victory has often been attributed to an excess of caution on the part of Meade or many of his subordinate generals. But a plausible argument can be made that the Army of the Potomac was so disorganized and exhausted by three days of intense fighting that it was incapable of mounting an effective pursuit of Lee.

Meade remained at the head of the Army of the Potomac to the war's end. After Grant became general in chief in March 1864, he chose to accompany Meade's army during the long campaign to defeat Lee and take Richmond that began in May and ended with Lee's surrender the following April. Thus Meade's responsibilities were reduced to tactical and administrative matters while Grant took over strategic planning and decision-making. Most of the ensuing excerpts focus on Gettysburg and its aftermath and they highlight Welles's belief, which Lincoln shared, that by not following up his Gettysburg victory, Meade missed an extraordinary opportunity to deal the Army of Northern Virginia a mortal blow.

June 28, 1863: His brother officers speak well of [Meade], but he is considered rather a "smooth bore" than a rifle.[12]

June 29, 1863: Great apprehension prevails. The change of commanders is thus far well received. No regret is expressed that Hooker has been relieved . . . . Meade has not so much character as such a command requires. He is, however, kindly favored – will be well supported, have the best wishes of all, but does not inspire immediate confidence. A little time may improve this, and give him name and fame.

July 4, 1863: Dispatches . . . state that Lee with his army commenced a retreat this a.m. at three o'clock. Our army is waiting for supplies to come up before following. A little of the old infirmity. [Darius] Couch [commanding the Pennsylvania militia] is said to be dilatory. Has not yet left Harrisburg. His force has not pushed forward with alacrity. Meade

---

[12] During the Civil War the traditional smoothbore musket was largely replaced by rifled shoulder arms, which were much superior to smoothbores in both range and accuracy. So characterizing Meade as a "smooth bore" was hardly high praise.

sent him word, "the sound of my guns should have prompted your move-ment." Lee and the Rebels may escape in consequence.

Although Lee's defeated army began its retreat from Gettysburg the night of July 3ʳᵈ – 4ᵗʰ, the rain-swollen upper Potomac River prevented most of it from returning to Virginia until the 13ᵗʰ. Lincoln hoped Meade would capture Lee's army before the river fell enough for it to cross.

July 7, 1863: The President said this morning, with a countenance indi-cating sadness and despondency, that Meade still lingered at Gettysburg, when he should have been at Hagerstown [Maryland] or near the Potomac, to cut off the retreating army of Lee. . . . He feared the old idea of driving the Rebels out of Pennsylvania and Maryland, instead of capturing them, was still prevalent among the officers.

July 14, 1863: [Learning as the cabinet assembled that Lee had either crossed the Potomac back to Virginia or was about to do so] the President said he did not believe we could take up anything in Cabinet to-day. Prob-ably none of us were in a right frame of mind for deliberation; he was not. He wanted to see General Halleck at once. Stanton left abruptly. I retired slowly. The President hurried and overtook me. We walked together across the lawn and stopped and conversed a few moments at the gate. He said, with a voice and countenance which I shall never forget, that he had dreaded yet expected this – that there has seemed to him for a full week a determi-nation that Lee should escape with his force and plunder – "and that, my God, is the last of this Army of the Potomac. There is bad faith somewhere. Meade has been pressed and urged, but only one of his generals was for an immediate attack, was ready to pounce on Lee – the rest held back. What does it mean, Mr. Welles? Great God! what does it mean?"

July 15, 1863: Lee's army has recrossed the Potomac, unmolested, carrying off all its artillery and the property stolen in Pennsylvania. When I ask why such an escape was permitted, I am told that the generals opposed an attack. What generals? None are named. Meade is in command there; Halleck is General-in-Chief here. They should be held responsible.

July 17, 1863: Some remarks [at today's cabinet meeting] on the great error of General Meade in permitting Lee and the Rebel army with all their plunder to escape led the President to say he would not yet give up that officer. "He has committed," said the President, "a terrible mistake, but we will try him farther." No one expressed his approval, but Seward said,

"Excepting the escape of Lee, Meade has shown ability." It was evident that the retention of Meade had been decided.

July 18, 1863: Had Meade done his duty, we should have witnessed a speedy change throughout the South. It is a misfortune that the command of the army had not been in stronger hands, and that he had not a more competent superior than Halleck. The late infirm action will cause a postponement of the end. Lee has been allowed to retreat unmolested with his army and guns, and the immense plunder which the Rebels have pillaged. The generals have succeeded in prolonging the war.

July 24, 1863: [At today's cabinet meeting] some inquiry was made in regard to army movements and Meade in particular, but no definite information was communicated. Meade is watching the enemy as fast as he can since he let them slip and get away from him. . . . Meade is unequal to his position, cannot grasp and direct so large a force, would do better with a smaller force and more limited field, or as a second under an abler general.

July 26, 1863: The President agreed with me fully [that more troops should be sent to General Quincy Gillmore, who was engaged in a combined effort with Admiral John Dahlgren's naval squadron to take Charleston], but said he knew not where the troops could come from, unless from the Army of the Potomac, but if they were going to fight they would want all their men. I asked if he really believed Meade was going to have a battle. He looked at me earnestly for a moment and said: "Well, to be candid, I have no faith that Meade will attack Lee – nothing looks like it to me. I believe he can never have another as good opportunity as that which he trifled away. Everything since has dragged with him. No, I don't believe he is going to fight."

September 21, 1863: I asked [Lincoln] what Meade was doing with his immense army and Lee's skeleton and depleted show in front.[13] He said he could not learn that Meade was doing anything, or wanted to do any thing. "It is," said he, "the same old story of this Army of the Potomac. Imbecility, inefficiency – don't want to *do* – is defending the Capital. I inquired of Meade," said he, "what force was in front. Meade replied he thought there were 40,000 infantry. I replied he might have said 50,000, and if Lee with 50,000 could defend their capital against our 90,0000 – and if defense is all our armies are to do – we might, I thought, detach 50,000 from his

---

[13] This is an allusion to Lee's dispatch of 12,000 men to reinforce Bragg's army in the Chattanooga area.

command, and thus leave him with 40,000 to defend us. Oh," groaned the President, "it is terrible, terrible, this weakness, this indifference of our Potomac generals, with such armies of good and brave men."

"Why," said I, "not rid yourself of Meade, who may be a good man and a good officer but is not a great general, certainly is not the man for the position he occupies? The escape of Lee with his army across Potomac has distressed me almost beyond any occurrence of the War. And the impression made upon me in the personal interview shortly afterward was not what I wished, had inspired no confidence."

The President assented to all I said, but "What can I do," he asked, "with such generals as we have? Who among them is any better than Meade? To sweep away the whole of them from the chief command would cause a shock, and be likely to lead to combinations and troubles greater than we now have. I see all the difficulties as you do. They oppress me."

GRANT AND SHERMAN

Ulysses S. Grant and William Tecumseh Sherman, who graduated from West Point in 1843 and 1840, respectively, were to be the Union's two most successful generals, even though neither of them was in the army when the Civil War broke out. (Sherman resigned his commission in 1853, as Grant did the following year.) Welles wrote relatively little about either of them in his wartime diary. Perhaps this is because Grant operated in the western theater, far from Washington, for all but the last 13 months of the war, and the same was true of Sherman for almost the entire war.[14]

June 2, 1864: There is intense anxiety in relation to the Army of the Potomac. Great confidence is felt in Grant, but the immense slaughter of our brave men chills and sickens us all. The hospitals are crowded with the thousands of mutilated and dying heroes who have poured out their blood for the Union cause. Lee has returned to the vicinity of Richmond.[15]

The next two excerpts refer to a fiasco on July 30th. After a month of surreptitious tunneling by soldiers who had been coal miners, a large quantity of explosives was

---

[14] Welles had much more to say about Grant in the portion of the diary covering Andrew Johnson's presidency.

[15] When later editing the diary, Welles added to this sentence "overpowered by numbers, beaten but hardly defeated." Between the Battle of the Wilderness (May 5th and 6th) and the unsuccessful June 18th assault on the rebel defenses at Petersburg, a period of almost constant fighting, Union casualties numbered between 60,000 and 65,000.

detonated directly beneath a section of the Confederate defensive line at Petersburg. The blast, which killed over 250 rebels and caused hundreds more to flee, created a long, wide, and deep gap in the Confederate line – what came to be called "the Crater." Union troops, many of them African Americans, rushed forward to attack the enemy position. But instead of going around the Crater, many soldiers entered it and became trapped. Recovering from the initial shock, the rebels rallied and soon were gunning down numerous bluecoats as they struggled desperately to climb out of the Crater. Many of the black soldiers were killed while trying to surrender. In the end, this failed attack cost some 4,000 Union casualties compared to the enemy's approximately 1500.

August 2, 1864: The explosion and assault at Petersburg on Saturday last appears to have been badly managed. The results were bad and the effect has been disheartening in the extreme. There must have been some defect or weakness on the part of some one or more. I have been waiting to get the facts, but do not yet get them to my satisfaction. It is stated in some of the letters written that lots were cast as to which corps [actually, which division of the 9th Corps] and which officers should lead in the assault. I fear there may be truth in the report, but if so, and Grant was in it or cognizant of it, my confidence in him would be impaired. I should not be surprised to learn that Meade committed such an act . . . . But I shall be reluctant to believe this of Grant. He may, however, have given the matter over to Meade, who has done this. Admiral Porter [see Section II, below] has always said there was something wanting in Grant, which Sherman could always supply, and vice versa as regards Sherman, but that the two together made a very perfect general officer and they ought never to be separated. If Grant is confiding in Meade, as he did Sherman, Grant will make a failure, I fear, for Meade is not Sherman, nor the equal of Sherman . . . . [I have] an awakening apprehension that Grant is not equal to the position assigned him. God grant that I may be mistaken, for the slaughtered thousands of my countrymen who poured out their rich blood for three months on the soil of Virginia from the Wilderness to Petersburg under his generalship can never be atoned in this world or the next if he is a failure.

August 5, 1864: I told Blair as we left the Executive Mansion to-day that I felt depressed in consequence of the result at Petersburg, beyond what I ought from the fight itself, in consequence of impaired confidence in Grant. He tried to encourage me and partially succeeded. I do not distrust or depreciate General G.; but think he needs a better second in command, a more competent executive officer than General Meade, and he should have known that fact earlier. The worth of our generals is often purchased at too great a cost of blood and treasure.

February 21, 1865: General Sherman is proving himself a great general, and his movements from Chattanooga to the present demonstrate his ability as an officer.[16] He has greater resources, a more prolific mind, than Grant, and perhaps as much tenacity.

April 7, 1865 [two days before Lee's surrender at Appomattox]: In the closing up of this Rebellion, General Grant has proved himself a man of undoubted military talent and genius.[17] Those who have doubted and hesitated must concede him great capacity as a general. His final demonstrations and movements have been masterly. The persistency which he has exhibited is as much to be admired as any quality in his character. He is, however, too regardless of life.

II

One of the three admirals treated here, Samuel F. Du Pont, was very successful early in the war. But he later fell out of favor with Welles and was kept on the sidelines during the final two years of the conflict. By contrast, Welles's views of David Dixon Porter and especially David G. Farragut were largely positive from start to finish.

Du Pont

Samuel F. Du Pont became the war's first naval hero when in November 1861 he led a successful expedition to take Port Royal Sound on the South Carolina coast between Charleston and Savannah, Georgia. A much-needed supply base was

---

[16] Starting out from Chattanooga on May 7, 1864, Sherman took Atlanta on September 2nd; on November 16th he began his "March to the Sea," occupying Savannah on December 21st; on January 19, 1865, he began a movement into South Carolina, through which his troops cut a particularly destructive swath before crossing into North Carolina on March 7th, where they generally conducted themselves with considerably more restraint than they had shown in the birthplace of secession.

[17] When revising the diary, Welles retained the statement that Grant "has proved himself a man of military talent," but he crossed out "and genius." He then proceeded to write that Grant is "slow and destitute of genius." This fundamental change from what he had originally written almost certainly resulted from the intense animus Welles came to feel toward Grant because of their deep differences during Reconstruction.

established there for Du Pont's South Atlantic Blockading Squadron. His victory lifted northern morale, which had suffered under the impact of the defeat at the first Battle of Bull Run and McClellan's lack of movement. Over the next several months, Du Pont's forces established further lodgments along the South Atlantic coast and in April 1862 took Fort Pulaski at the mouth of the Savannah River, making it difficult for blockade-runners to enter or leave the city of Savannah. He was promoted in July 1862 from captain and flag officer to rear admiral (then the navy's highest rank). The bloom came off the rose, however, when he failed at his next major assignment.

In the fall of 1862, the administration decided to initiate a campaign to take Charleston, which as the place where the war started had great symbolic (though only limited strategic) significance. Welles and Assistant Secretary Gustavus V. Fox envisioned a fleet of the new Passaic-class monitors, which were larger and more heavily armed than the original USS Monitor, steaming past Charleston's formidable outer defenses, including Fort Sumter, entering the inner harbor, and demanding that the city and the forts surrender, or else Charleston would be bombarded. Du Pont had misgivings about this plan. He preferred that army troops land on Morris Island at the mouth of the harbor, besiege its main defensive installation, and once it surrendered, shell Fort Sumter into submission. Only then would his warships enter the harbor. Du Pont's preferred approach may well have stood a better chance of success than the Welles-Fox scheme. But Welles and Fox rejected it, wanting all of the laurels for the navy, with the army's role limited to providing occupation troops once Charleston fell to Du Pont's warships. Lincoln also disliked it, because it reminded him of McClellan's prolonged – and unnecessary – siege of Yorktown at the start of the Peninsula Campaign. In any case, Du Pont, not wanting to look weak and uncooperative in the eyes of his superiors, failed clearly and forcefully to explain to them why he believed their plan was unlikely to succeed. Instead, he dragged his feet, sent Washington a steady stream of complaints about supplies, and insisted that he needed more than the five monitors earmarked for the operation. (Ultimately, he received seven monitors, plus the New Ironsides, a 50-gun ironclad frigate, and the Keokuk, an experimental vessel with only very thin iron cladding.)

On April 7, 1863, Du Pont finally set the operation in motion. But instead of running by Charleston's outer fortifications, his ironclads engaged them. They did relatively little harm, but sustained significant damage themselves (although only one ship, the Keokuk, sank as a result of gunfire from the enemy batteries.) After about two hours, Du Pont called a halt; and soon thereafter he decided it would be ill-advised to try again. In his report to Welles, he blamed the lack of success on the monitors' unsuitability for this kind of offensive action. In June Welles removed

Du Pont from command, as the admiral had said he should do if the secretary could find a better man for the job. Controversy over the failed operation persisted well into 1864, as Du Pont sought vindication. But his failure at Charleston effectively ended his career. The ensuing excerpts trace the evolution of Welles's opinion of Du Pont and reveal the Navy Secretary's slant on the Charleston episode.

October 2, 1862: Admiral Du Pont arrived to-day; looks hale and hearty – is a skillful and sagacious officer. Has a fine address, is a courtier with perhaps too much finesse and management, resorts too much to extraneous and subordinate influences to accomplish what he might easily attain directly, and, like many naval officers [is] given to the formation of cliques . . . . It is well that the officers should not only respect but have an attachment to their commanders, but not at the expense of true patriotism and the service. But all that I have yet seen is excusable. Certainly, while he continues to do his duty so well, I shall make no controversy with him.

March 12, 1863: Had a letter from Chief Engineer Stimers last night.[18] Says the attack on Charleston will be delayed; suggests it will be made the first week in April. . . . The delay, hesitation, uncertainty in the Army of the Potomac over again. Du Pont is getting as prudent as McClellan – is very careful – all dash, energy, and force are softened under the great responsibility. He has a reputation to preserve instead of one to make.

Stimers arrived this morning and read to me the minutes of a council held on board the Wabash [Du Pont's flagship]. The army officers were present, and it is plain they were a drawback on naval operations. Talk of beginning the attack on Charleston by an assault on the sand-batteries at the mouth of the harbor instead of running past them. Of obstructions and torpedos [underwater mines] little is known, but great apprehensions are entertained. Stimers is sent up to get more ironclads and more [mortar] rafts. The President came in, and the whole subject was recounted. His views and mine are alike. To delay for the objects stated till April will be to postpone till May. Expressed ourselves very decidedly, and told Stimers to hurry back.

April 9, 1863: A yearning, craving desire for tidings from Charleston, but the day has passed without a word. . . .

---

[18] Alban Stimers was involved in overseeing the construction of some of the monitors and was an enthusiastic proponent of their use in the Charleston operation. "Chief Engineer" was the rank he held, as did other experienced navy engineers. It does not mean that he was at the head of all navy engineers. (See Chapter 6 for additional information about Stimers.)

A desperate stand will be made at Charleston, and their defenses are formidable. Delay has given them time and warning, and they have improved them. They know also that there is no city so culpable, or against which there is such intense animosity. We shall not get the place, if we get it on this first trial, without great sacrifice. There are fifty-two steamers for the work and the most formidable ironclad force that ever went into battle. These great and long-delayed preparations weigh heavily upon me. As a general thing, such immense expeditions are failures. Providence delights to humble man in his might and prostrate his strength. For months my confidence has not increased, and now that the conflict is upon us, my disquietude is greater still. I have hope and trust in Du Pont, in the glorious band of officers that are with him, and in the iron bulwarks we have furnished as well as in a righteous cause.

The President, who has often a sort of intuitive sagacity, has spoken discouragingly of operations at Charleston. . . . Du Pont's dispatches and movements have not inspired him with faith; they remind him, he says, of McClellan. . . . I do not believe the monitors impregnable under the concentrated fire and immense weight of metal that can be thrown upon them, but it can hardly be otherwise than that some, probably most of them, will pass [Fort Sumter].

April 12, 1863: An intense and anxious feeling on all hands respecting Charleston. . . . Between 2 and 3 P.M. Commander Rhind of the Keokuk, Upshur, and Lieutenant Forrest called at my house with dispatches from Du Pont. They were not very full or satisfactory – contained no details. He has no idea of taking Charleston by the Navy. . . . He has been coming to that conclusion for months, though he has not said so. The result of this demonstration, though not a success, is not conclusive. The monitor vessels have proved their resisting power, and, but for [the underwater] obstructions, could have passed the forts and gone to the wharves of Charleston. This in itself is a great achievement. . . .

Du Pont has been allowed to decide for himself in regard to proceedings, has selected, and had, the best officers and vessels in the service, and his force is in every respect picked and chosen. Perhaps I have erred in not giving him orders. Possibly the fact that he was assured that all was confided to him depressed and oppressed him with the responsibility, and has prevented him from telling me freely and without reserve his doubts, apprehensions. I have for some time felt that he wanted the confidence that is essential to success.

April 20, 1863: Received Admiral Du Pont's detailed report with those of his officers. The document is not such as I should have expected from him a short time ago, but matters of late prevent me from feeling any disappointment. . . . The tone and views of the sub-reports have the ring, or want of ring, of the Admiral in command. . . . A pall is thrown over all. Nothing has been done, and it is the recommendation of all, from the Admiral down, that no effort be made to do anything.

I am by no means confident that we are acting wisely in expending so much strength and effort on Charleston, a place of little strategic importance, but it is lamentable to witness the tone, language, want of vitality and vigor, and want of zeal among so many of the best officers of the service. I cannot be mistaken as to the source and cause. A magnetic power in the head [i.e., Du Pont], which should have inspired and stimulated them, is wanting; they have been discouraged instead of encouraged, depressed not strengthened.

April 30, 1863: Had a long, studied, complaining letter from Admiral Du Pont, of some twenty pages, in explanation and refutation of a letter in the *Baltimore American*, which criticizes and censures his conduct at Charleston. The dispatch is no credit to Du Pont, who could be better employed. He is evidently thinking much more of Du Pont than of the service or the country. I fear he can be no longer useful in his present command, and am mortified and vexed that I did not earlier detect his vanity and weakness. . . . All Du Pont's letters since the 8th show that he had no heart, no confidence, no zeal in his work – that he went into the fight with a predetermined conviction that it would not be a success – that he is prejudiced against the monitor class of vessels, and would attribute to them his failure, but that he has no taste for rough, close fighting.

May 14, 1863: Du Pont is morbidly sensitive, and to vindicate himself wants to publish every defect and weakness of the ironclads and to disparage them, regardless of its effect in inspiring the Rebels to resist them, and impairing the confidence of our own men in their invulnerability.

June 3, 1863: Wrote Du Pont that [Andrew Hull] Foote would relieve him.[19]

---

[19] Foote, an old friend of Welles's, died of kidney failure on June 26th, shortly before he was to have taken over from Du Pont as commander of the South Atlantic Blockading Squadron. (For more on Foote, see Chapter 8.) Welles then gave the post to Admiral John A. Dahlgren, albeit with misgivings since Dahlgren had virtually no sea-going experience and many naval officers resented the close relationship he had established with Lincoln as commandant of the Washington Navy Yard and head of the Bureau of Ordnance.

I think he anticipates it and perhaps wants it to take place. He makes no suggestions, gives no advice, presents no opinion, says he will obey orders.... I perceive he is preparing for a controversy with the Department – laying out the ground, getting his officers committed – and he has many strong friends in Congress and elsewhere. He has been well and kindly treated by the Department.

October 31, 1863: I was getting materials and preparing the outlines for my Annual Report, when I received a communication from Du Pont, deliberately prepared, and with evident malicious intent, at his home near Wilmington, complaining of "harsh language," "wounding words," and "injurious imputations" in my letters and dispatches relative to his failure on the 7th of April. I am conscious of no such wrong as he attributes to me. Though grieved and disappointed in what took place, I felt no resentment to call out such denunciations, nor could he have had any such opinion in the day and time of those occurrences, or he would then have made his complaint. But the correspondence closed last June – he has been for months in Delaware, nursing discontent and chafing under disappointed ambition. His mind, as [Captain Percival] Drayton reports, has become morbid. He was for a time the great naval hero, but Farragut has eclipsed him. He has seen Farragut toasted and complimented, dined and extolled by our countrymen and by foreigners, until his envy and vexation could no longer be repressed. He therefore reviews the past, and, too proud to acknowledge or admit errors, faults, or infirmities, he assails me, who have been his friend, and declares he must again place on the files of the Department his indignant refutation of my charges. He specifies no charges, quotes no language, mentions no exceptional remark. I have treated him gently, for I respect his acquirements, though I dislike his intrigues. He doubtless thought I should refuse to receive and place on file his unjust complaint, and I at first hesitated whether to do so.

Du Pont has ability, pride, and intrigue, but he has not the great essentials of a naval commander. . . . Thinks of himself more than of the country and the service. . . . He is not made for such terrific encounters as that of Farragut at New Orleans, and as are necessary to resist Sumter and capture Charleston. He has too much pride to be a coward – would sooner die than show the white feather – but the innate moral courage of Farragut or John Rodgers[20] is not his. He feels his infirmity, and knows that

---

[20] John Rodgers, whose father had distinguished himself as a naval officer during the War of 1812, led the James River flotilla during McClellan's Peninsula Campaign and commanded several monitors later in the war. Both Welles and Lincoln greatly admired him.

I perceive it. But it is a weakness for which I did not reproach him, or use harsh language. I pitied him.

A month after Du Pont's removal from command, his successor, Admiral John A. Dahlgren, and Major General Quincy Gillmore mounted a combined army-navy operation against Charleston that resembled the approach Du Pont had favored. After long and bloody fighting, Morris Island was captured and heavy shelling severely damaged Fort Sumter, although an attempt to take it by assault in early September failed. Despite continued pressure during the next 16 months, Charleston held out until February 17, 1865. However, with the federals holding Morris Island and a large naval presence in and around the entry to the harbor, blockade-running into and out of Charleston diminished from the fall of 1863 onward and by late 1864 had come to an almost complete halt.[21]

PORTER

David Dixon Porter was part of the third generation of Porters to serve in the navy. His grandfather and a great uncle both commanded warships during the American Revolution. His father was a hero of the War of 1812, and an uncle served with distinction in that conflict, too. David's three brothers also became naval officers. Moreover, David Farragut, the war's preeminent naval officer, was Porter's foster brother, his father having adopted Farragut as a child. Porter entered the navy as a midshipman in 1829 at age 16 and held the rank of lieutenant at the outbreak of the war. He was promoted to commander a few days after the fall of Fort Sumter. In April 1862, he was in charge of a task force of mortar-carrying schooners that participated in Farragut's successful campaign to take New Orleans. When Porter assumed command of the Mississippi River Squadron in the fall of that year (at age 49), the rank of acting rear admiral came with it. He gained fame (and promotion to rear admiral) for the crucial role he played in support of Grant's successful campaign to take Vicksburg. In the fall of 1864 he was given command of the North Atlantic Blockading Squadron. In the ensuing excerpts, Welles traces the arc of Porter's career and offers astute, generally favorable comments about him.[22] Soon after Welles's departure from the Navy Department in March 1869, however, he became highly critical of the policies Porter, by then the navy's top uniformed officer, was pursuing.

---

[21] For an informative account of the protracted struggle to take Charleston, see Craig L. Symonds, *The Civil War at Sea* (New York: Oxford University Press, 2012), Chapter 5.

[22] Richard S. West, Jr. argues that because Welles was unusually adept at character analysis he was able to identify junior officers, such as David Porter, who merited promotion ahead of more-senior officers having less potential for leadership. West, *Gideon Welles: Lincoln's Navy Department* (Indianapolis: Bobbs-Merrill, 1943), pp 205 – 207.

October 1, 1862: Relieved Davis and appointed D. D. Porter to the Western Flotilla, which is hereafter to be called a squadron.[23] Porter is but a Commander, but has stirring and positive qualities, is fertile in resources, has great energy, excessive and sometimes unscrupulous ambition, is impressed with and boastful of his own powers, given to exaggeration in everything relating to himself – a Porter infirmity – is not generous to older and superior living officers, whom he is ready to traduce, but is kind and patronizing to juniors and inferiors. Is given to cliquism but is brave and daring like all his family. He has not the high moral qualities of Foote to organize the flotilla, and is not considered a fortunate officer; has not what sailors admire, "luck," and it is a question how he will succeed. His selection will be unsatisfactory to many, but his field of operation is peculiar, and a young and active officer is required for the duty.

October 10, 1862: D. D. Porter left Wednesday to take command of the Mississippi Squadron, with the appointment of Acting [Rear] Admiral. This is an experiment, and the results not entirely certain. Many officers of the Navy who are his seniors will be dissatisfied, while his juniors will be stimulated. The river naval service is unique. Foote performed wonders and dissipated many prejudices. The army has fallen in love with the gunboats and wants them in every creek. . . . Porter is destitute of some of the best qualities of Foote, but excels him perhaps in others. The service requires great energy, great activity, abundant resources. Porter is full of each, but is reckless, improvident, and too assuming.

March 17, 1863: The accounts from Porter, above Vicksburg, are not satisfactory. He is fertile in expedients, some of which are costly without adequate results. His dispatches are full of verbosity, and the mail which brings them also brings ludicrous letters and caricatures to Heap, a [Navy Department] clerk who is his brother-in-law, filled with laughable and burlesque accounts of amusing and ridiculous proceedings. These may be excusable as a means of amusement to keep up his spirits and those of his men, but I should be glad to witness, or hear of something more substantial and of energies employed in what is really useful. Porter has capabilities and I am expecting much of him, but he is by no means an Admiral Foote.

---

[23] Charles H. Davis replaced Andrew H. Foote as head of the Western Flotilla in early May 1862 when Foote was forced to take a leave of absence because a painful leg wound sustained in February during his and Grant's combined campaign to take Fort Donelson on the Cumberland River in Tennessee had failed to heal, and also because he was mentally exhausted from overwork.

On April 16th, just a month after Welles penned the above criticism, Porter, in a daring nighttime venture, successfully led 10 of his warships and three army transports southward past the guns of Vicksburg, with the loss of only one of the transports. A fleet of army barges and transports followed six nights later. Meanwhile, Grant was marching two of his three corps down the west bank of the Mississippi past Vicksburg to a position further south, where he rendezvoused with Porter. On April 30th, Porter began escorting the troops across the river to Bruinsburg, on the river's east bank, about 35 miles below Vicksburg. In the first half of May, Grant won four major battles south and east of Vicksburg. After two failed attempts to take the city by assault (on May 19th and 22nd), his forces began a siege on May 23rd that led to its surrender on July 4th. During the siege, Porter's warships regularly bombarded the city and prevented aid reaching it from across the river. Afterwards, Grant warmly praised Porter for his contributions to the campaign, which together with Meade's concurrent victory at Gettysburg, marked a turning point in the war.

July 11, 1863: Wrote a congratulatory letter to Porter on the fall of Vicksburg. Called on the President and advised that Porter should be made a rear admiral. He assented very cheerfully, though his estimate of Porter is not so high as mine. Stanton denies him any merit; speaks of him as a gas-bag, who makes a great fuss and claims credit that belongs to others. Chase, Seward, and Blair agree with me that Porter has done good service.[24]

The navy had long wanted to mount a combined operation with the army against Wilmington, North Carolina, one of the Confederacy's main blockade-running ports. But it wasn't until late summer of 1864 that the army leadership became receptive to the idea. The key to sealing off Wilmington was to capture the formidable Fort Fisher, which guarded the waterway leading to the city. The navy's part in the joint operation would be under the direction of the commander of the North Atlantic Blockading Squadron, at the time Acting Rear Admiral Samuel Phillips Lee. Welles deemed Lee ill-suited for the task and intended to replace him with Admiral Farragut.[25] But Farragut begged off, citing poor health and the need for an extended period of shore leave to recuperate. Welles then decided to send Admiral Lee west to take over Porter's squadron on the Mississippi and bring Porter east to assume command of the blockading squadron and lead the navy's part of the Wilmington operation.

---

[24] When later revising the diary, Welles added: "I am aware of his infirmities. He is selfish, presuming, and wasteful, but is brave and energetic."

[25] Grant, who as general in chief would have to approve army participation in the Fort Fisher operation, also thought Lee was the wrong man for the job and might have vetoed army involvement had Lee not been replaced with someone Grant trusted, as he did Porter.

September 13, 1864: Admiral Porter is probably the best man for the service, but it will cut Lee to the quick. Porter is young, and his rapid promotion has placed him in rank beyond those who were once his seniors, some of whom it might be well to have in this expedition. But again personal considerations must yield to the public necessities. I think Porter must perform this duty.

September 17, 1864: Talked over the subject of Wilmington, examined its localities, and considered the position of things fully with Porter and Fox. . . .

Porter has preferred retaining the Mississippi Squadron, but repeated what he has heretofore said – that he had been treated kindly by the Department, and if I ordered him to go over Niagara Falls in an iron pot he should obey the order.

October 6, 1864: Admiral Porter has arrived from Cairo [Illinois] and proceeds to-morrow to Hampton Roads to take command of the North Atlantic Squadron. It is with reluctance that he comes into this transfer, but yet he breathes not an objection. I should not have mentioned the circumstance but for the fact that many put a false construction upon it.[26] He will have a difficult task to perform and not the thanks he will deserve, I fear, if successful, but curses if he fails.

The initial assault on Fort Fisher in late December was unsuccessful. This was mainly because of the ineptitude of Benjamin Butler, the politician-turned-general who commanded the army contingent in the combined operation. But Porter also bore some of the blame, since the large flotilla he commanded was less effective in bombarding the fort than expected. A second attempt in mid January 1865 succeeded. This was partly because Grant had replaced Butler with General Alfred H. Terry, a non-professional but very competent officer from Connecticut, and partly because Porter did a much better job of positioning his warships and directing their fire.[27] Once the fort was in federal hands, there was no urgent need to occupy Wilmington, which the army didn't do until February 22nd, just hours after its Confederate defenders had decamped.

---

[26] Welles is alluding to the likelihood that Porter's many critics would interpret this move as another instance of his supposedly ruthless and unrelenting scheming to get ahead.

[27] Although Terry's pre-war military experience had been limited to service in the state militia, his wartime record as an officer of volunteer troops was sufficiently impressive that he was accepted into the small regular (i.e., standing) army at the war's end and spent the remainder of his active life as a professional soldier, ultimately attaining the rank of major general.

FARRAGUT

David Farragut, who for most of the war commanded the West Gulf Blockading Squadron, won his reputation as the Civil War's greatest naval officer largely because of two high-risk expeditions he led, both of them in his flagship, the USS Hartford, a steam-powered, propeller-driven sloop of war. The first expedition, in April 1862, took New Orleans, the Confederacy's largest port, which naval historian William M. Fowler, Jr., regards as probably the navy's most important achievement during the war because it closed Confederate access to the sea via the Mississippi River.[28] The second, in August 1864, secured control of Mobile Bay, thus closing the city of Mobile to blockade-runners. As Farragut's 17 warships fought their way past the two forts guarding the entrance to the bay, one of them sank almost instantly when it hit an underwater mine, creating uncertainty among the captains of other ships about whether to proceed. At this critical moment Farragut supposedly called out the immortal words, "Damn the torpedoes! Full speed ahead!" (Actually, he probably said, "Four bells!" – a signal to the engine room to lay on full power.) The below excerpts show the high regard both Welles and Lincoln had for Farragut.[29]

January 28, 1863: Farragut has prompt, energetic, excellent qualities, but no fondness for written details. Does but one thing at a time, but does that strong and well. Is better fitted to lead an expedition through danger and difficulty than to command an extensive blockade; is a good officer in a great emergency, will more willingly take great risks in order to obtain great results than any officer in high position in either naval or military service, and, unlike most of them, prefers that others should tell the story of his well-doing rather than relate it himself.

September 21, 1863: Alluding to the failures of the generals, particularly those who commanded the armies of the Potomac, [Lincoln] thought the selections, if unfortunate, were not imputable entirely to him. The

---

[28] William M. Fowler, Jr., *Under Two Flags: The American Navy in the Civil War* (New York: W. W. Norton, 1990), p. 126.

[29] New Orleans and Mobile Bay were not Farragut's only significant naval actions. In March 1863, for example, he led seven ships up the Mississippi in an attempt to run past heavily fortified Port Hudson, Louisiana. Only the *Hartford* and the *Albatross* made it, four of the other ships being forced to turn back and a fifth blowing up under relentless Confederate fire. But those two were enough to disrupt the passage of enemy supplies across the river that helped sustain Vicksburg and Port Hudson. Then starting in May, a dozen of Farragut's warships bombarded Port Hudson in support of the army's siege of the town, which surrendered on July 8th, four days after Grant took Vicksburg. Port Hudson's fall removed the last obstacle to Union control of the river's entire length.

An August Morning with Farragut, The Battle of Mobile Bay, August 5, 1864, oil painting by William H. Overend (1883). The USS *Hartford* engages the CSS *Tennessee*, with Farragut in the rigging in order to see above the smoke of battle. Source: The Wadsworth Atheneum Museum of Art, Hartford, CT/Art Resource, NY.

Generals-in-Chief and the Secretary of War should, he said, know the men better than he. The Navy Department had given him no trouble in this respect; perhaps naval training was more uniform and equal than the military. I thought not; that we had our troubles, but they were less conspicuous. In the selection of Farragut and Porter, I thought we had been particularly fortunate; and Du Pont had merit also. He thought there had not been, take it all in all, so good an appointment in either branch of the service as Farragut, whom he did not know or recollect when I gave him command. Du Pont he classed, and has often, with McClellan, but Porter he considers a busy schemer, bold but not of high qualities as a chief. For some reason he has not so high an appreciation of Porter as I think he deserves, but no man surpasses Farragut with him.

August 9, 1864: News of Farragut's having passed Forts Morgan and Gaines [at the entrance to Mobile Bay] was received last night, and sent a thrill of joy through all true hearts.[30]

September 2, 1864 [*Today Welles received Farragut's dispatch on the surrender of Fort Morgan, which completed the conquest of Mobile Bay.*]: Some of the Administration presses and leaders have undertaken to censure me for slighting Du Pont. Not one of them awards me any credit for selecting Farragut. Yet it was a great responsibility, and until he had proved himself worthy of my choice, I felt it.

The contrast between Farragut and Du Pont is marked. No one can now hesitate to say which is the real hero; yet three years ago it would have been different. Farragut is earnest, unselfish, devoted to the country and the service. He sees to every movement, forms his line of battle with care and skill, puts himself at the head, carries out his plan, if there is difficulty leads the way, dashes by forts and overcomes obstructions. Du Pont, as we saw at Sumter [i.e., the abortive April 7, 1863 attempt to take Charleston], puts himself in the most formidable vessel, has no order of battle, leads the way only until he gets within cannon-shot range, then stops, says his ship would not steer well, declines, however, to go into any other, but signals to them to go forward without any plan of battle, does not enjoin upon them to dash by the forts; they are stopped under the guns of [Forts] Sumter and Moultrie, and are battered for an hour, a sufficient length of time to have

---

[30] The victory at Mobile Bay and Sherman's occupation of Atlanta on September 2nd went far to dispel the mood of defeatism that had gripped the northern public after Grant's Overland Campaign, with its unprecedented casualty toll, ended in stalemate around Petersburg. Without these two victories, it is possible Lincoln would not have been reelected.

gone to Charleston wharves, and then they are signalled to turn about and come back to the Admiral out of harm's way.

When I appointed Du Pont to command a squadron, I met the public expectation. All but a few naval officers . . . approved and applauded so judicious an appointment. But no cheerful response was made to the appointment of Farragut. Some naval officers said he was a daring, dashing fellow, but they doubted his discretion and ability to command a squadron judiciously. Members of Congress inquired who he was . . . and questioned whether I was not making a mistake, for he was a Southern man and had a Southern wife. Neither the President nor any member of the Cabinet knew him, or knew of him except, perhaps, Seward. . . .

Farragut became a marked man in my mind when I was informed of the circumstances under which he left Norfolk [his longtime place of residence]. When Virginia voted to secede he denounced the act, and at once abandoned the State, leaving his home and property the day following, avowing openly and boldly, in the face and hearing of the Rebels by whom he was surrounded, his determination to live and die owing allegiance to no flag but that of the Union under which he had served. This firm and resolute stand caused me not only to admire the act, but led me to inquire concerning the man. I had known of him slightly during Polk's administration, and all I heard of him was well, but he was generally spoken of as were other good officers. Fox, Foote, and Dahlgren gave him a good name and D. D. Porter was emphatic in his favor, and his knowledge and estimate of men were generally pretty correct. Admiral [Joseph] Smith considered him a bold, impetuous man, of a great deal of courage, and energy, but his capabilities to command a squadron was a subject to be determined only by trial.

Had any other man than myself been Secretary of the Navy, it is not probable that either Farragut or Foote would ever have had a squadron. At the beginning of the Rebellion, neither of them stood prominent beyond others. They had not been developed; they had not possessed opportunities. . . . Neither had the showy name, the scholastic attainments, the wealth, the courtly talent, of Du Pont. But both were heroes. Du Pont is a polished naval officer, selfish, heartless, calculating, scheming, but not a hero by nature, though too proud to be a coward.

Chapter 6

Navy Department Challenges

Running the Navy Department, Welles faced a multitude of challenges that tested his administrative skills, judgment, political astuteness, and more than once, his patience. This chapter examines a diverse selection of these challenges. It concludes with diary entries recording both the criticism and the praise Welles received from various contemporaries and his own brief assessment of his performance.

Confederate Commerce Raiders

One of the most persistent problems the navy faced was the Confederacy's employment of fast commerce raiders, which played hob with American merchant ships, whalers, and ocean-going fishing boats for much of the war. Approximately a dozen raiders were active at one time or another. The two most famous – the CSS Florida *and the CSS* Alabama *– were built in English shipyards and went into service in March and July of 1862, respectively.*[1] *The* Alabama *captured or sank a total of 64 American merchant vessels and whalers and also a Union warship (the USS* Hatteras *in January 1863). The* Florida *took 37 vessels before being rammed and captured by the USS* Wachusett *in the Brazilian port of Bahia in October 1864.*

According to historian James McPherson, the most successful single raid was made by the CSS Tallahassee, *which between its departure from Wilmington, North Carolina, on August 6, 1864, and its safe return on August 25*[th], *captured 33 fishing vessels and merchantmen during a foray along the Atlantic coast as far*

---

[1] It was illegal for British shipbuilders to construct warships for a belligerent power that would use them against a friendly nation. Confederate agents and English shipbuilders managed to circumvent the law by having vessels such as the *Alabama* and *Florida* armed and otherwise outfitted as warships only after they had left British territorial waters. After mid 1863, however, a crackdown by the British government largely put a stop to this subterfuge.

SINBAD LINCOLN AND THE OLD MAN OF THE SEA

This cartoon represents Welles as a burden to Lincoln because he is too far along in years to handle the multiple demands of his job. On the left in the background is the ironclad CSS *Virginia* (originally the USS *Merrimack*) and on the right the rebel comerce raider CSS *Nashville*, both of which pose threats that Welles seems to be ignoring. Source: *Frank Leslie's Illustrated Newspaper*, May 3, 1862.

as Halifax, Nova Scotia.[2] *The following four excerpts reveal Welles's frustration at the navy's failure to snare the* Tallahassee.

August 12, 1864: Have news this evening that a new pirate craft, the Tallahassee, has appeared off New York, burning vessels.[3] Steamers ordered off in pursuit.

August 15, 1864: Depredations by the piratical Rebel Tallahassee continue. We have sixteen vessels in pursuit, and yet I feel no confidence in their capturing her. It is so easy to elude the pursuit of the most vigilant – and many in command are not vigilant – that it will not surprise me if she escapes. Should that be the case, the Navy Department will alone be held responsible. I am already censured in some of the papers for not having vessels, two or three, cruising at the time she appeared. Had that been the case we could not have communicated with them when we received intelligence, but, being in port, several were at once dispatched in pursuit. I find I have become very indifferent to the senseless complaints of the few loud grumblers.

August 18, 1864: Mr. Seward brought me this A.M. a dispatch from Consul Jackson at Halifax, saying the pirate Rebel Tallahassee had arrived at that port. I had on Sunday morning last, the 14th, sent orders to Commodore [Hiram] Paulding [commandant of the Brooklyn Navy Yard] to immediately dispatch the San Jacinto, then just arrived at New York . . . to proceed to Halifax, anticipating that the pirate craft would go thither for coal. The Commodore on the same day sent me a dispatch that orders had been given the San Jacinto to proceed to sea, and a second telegram, received that evening, said she would pass through the Sound. When, therefore, I to-day got word that the Tallahassee was in Halifax, I thought the San Jacinto should be there. I immediately inquired at what time she had sailed, that I might calculate with some certainty. This evening I have a telegram from Captain Case, Executive Officer, Brooklyn Yard, that the San Jacinto has not yet sailed but was coaled and ready and would proceed in the morning. I know not when I have been more disappointed and astonished . . . . It cannot have been otherwise than there was inattention and neglect, for there could have been no purpose or design to defeat my orders. But the sin – which is great, and almost inexcusable – of this neglect will fall on

---

[2] McPherson, *War on the Waters*, p. 201.

[3] In most cases, vessels seized by Confederate commerce raiders were burned after the crew had been removed.

me, and not on the guilty parties. They have defeated my plans and expectations, and I shall be assailed and abused by villainous partisans for it.

I trust some of the officers who have been sent in pursuit will have the perseverance and zeal to push on to Halifax, yet I have my apprehensions. They lack persistency. Not one of them is a Farragut, or Foote, or Porter, I fear. But we will see.

August 25, 1864: Most of the vessels sent out in pursuit of the Tallahassee have returned, and with scarcely an exception the commanders have proved themselves feeble and inefficient.

Welles had made a much more cheerful diary entry earlier in the summer, after news arrived of the sinking of the Alabama *by the USS* Kearsarge *off Cherbourg, France, on June 19th.*

July 9, 1864: Our Alabama news comes in opportunely to encourage and sustain the nation's heart. It does them as well as me good to dwell upon the subject and the discomfiture of the British and Rebels. The perfidy of the former is as infamous as the treason of the latter. Both were whipped by the Kearsarge, a Yankee ship.

When revising the diary, Welles reinforced the point by adding "with a Yankee commander and a Yankee crew." Presumably Welles took pride that the Kearsarge's engines had been manufactured by a Hartford firm, Woodruff and Beach.[4]

THE ISSUE OF PRIVATEERS

In early 1863, the Lincoln administration came under pressure to resort to privateers, as the United States had done during the Revolution and the War of 1812. This would have involved the president's issuance of letters of marque authorizing private citizens to arm ships and send them to sea to capture blockade-runners. If a U.S. prize court (see footnote 9, below) determined that a vessel captured by a privateer had been legitimately taken, the court would order that the ship and its cargo be sold, with most of the proceeds going to the owner(s) of the privateer, its officers, and the crew.[5] Some advocates of privateering believed that besides helping to tighten the blockade, privateers would track down and capture rebel commerce

---

[4] See William N. Peterson, "Connecticut's Naval Contributions to the Civil War," *Connecticut Explored*, Vol. 9 (Spring 2011), pp. 22-27.

[5] The term "privateer" applied to both the ship and the men involved.

raiders. Among cabinet members, Seward was especially enthusiastic about authorizing privateers, and Lincoln showed serious interest in it, while Welles was opposed, albeit with some ambivalence. Ultimately, the idea was dropped. The following excerpts illustrate Welles's role in the decision not to employ privateers – and also his deep hostility toward the British.[6]

March 31, 1863: With some effort . . . I have drawn up a communication to Mr. Seward on the subject of letters of marque [explaining why he opposed their issuance]. But at the [cabinet] council to-day he read a dispatch from Mr. [Charles Francis] Adams [the American minister in London], communicating two letters from [British Foreign Secretary] Earl [John] Russell, which are insolent, contemptuous, and they mean aggression if not war. It is evident to my mind that a devastating and villainous war is to be waged on our commerce by English capital and English men under the Rebel flag with the connivance of the English Government, which will, and is intended to, sweep our commerce from the ocean. . . . Mr. Seward is earnest to get out privateers to catch the Alabama and the blockade-runners. The President thinks they should try that policy. Chase has lately favored it. I have no faith in it as against the Rebels, who have no commerce to be injured, but if we are to have a conflict with England, letters of marque and every means in our power must be put in requisition against that faithless and wicked nation. I have, therefore, doubts about sending the letter which I have prepared.

April 2, 1863: Had a call last evening and again to-day from Senator Sumner. Our conversation was chiefly on our foreign relations, the unfortunate condition of public affairs, the inexcusable attitude of England, and the question of letters of marque. On the latter subject he is much dissatisfied with Mr. Seward. He informs me that he was opposed to the passage of the law at the late session [authorizing, but not requiring, Lincoln to issue letters of marque], and is, I am glad to see, quite sensitive on the subject. I thought the law well enough as a precautionary measure, a warning to the mischievous spirits abroad, an authorization to the President in case of necessity, and especially as a weapon to coerce England into propriety. The power granted was extraordinary and to be used with discretion, but Mr. Seward, having obtained the authority, is disposed to exercise it. The merchants having been loud and profuse in their complaints and

---

[6] In 1856, most major maritime powers and some lesser ones subscribed to the Declaration of Paris, which abolished the use of privateers. But the United States chose not to become a signatory.

promises, Mr. Seward has taken it for granted that they would at once avail themselves of the law, and make a rush in a random search for a couple of lean and hungry wolves [i.e., rebel commerce raiders] that are abroad, which it would be difficult to catch and valueless when caught. I have questioned whether he could beguile merchants into such an investment, and he begins to feel uneasy that none have come forward as he expected.

In a letter which I commenced some days since and finished Saturday night, I put upon paper some of the suggestions, views, and doubts I have from time to time expressed in our [cabinet] discussions. This letter I gave out to be copied, and it was on my table for signature when I returned yesterday from Cabinet council. The English news was such that I laid it aside unsigned, and it was lying on the table when Sumner came in. He stated . . . he had been to the State Department and that Seward had given him the substance of the last dispatches. He asked if I had seen them. I answered that I had, and was so disgusted with them that I had laid by a letter which I had prepared in opposition to the current feeling which prevailed on the subject of letters of marque. He wished to read it, and after doing so complimented the letter with emphasis, and begged I would sign and send it. . . .

The President called at my house this evening, chiefly to see the letter which I had prepared concerning letters of marque. Senator Sumner had gone directly from the Navy Department to him, and so made known his gratification at my views and the manner in which I had stated them that the curiosity of the President was excited and he desired to read the letter. I informed him that the last thing I did before leaving the Department was to sign and send it to the Secretary of State; that I perhaps should not have done it, though, as he (the President) was aware, I had differed with him and others on this subject and looked upon it as a dangerous step, but since reading the last English dispatches, I was less opposed to the measure than I had been.

The opportunity being favorable and he disposed to converse . . . I took occasion to enlarge upon the topic more fully than I had done in our Cabinet discussions. I started out with the proposition that to issue letters of marque would in all probability involve us in a war with England. That I had so viewed this question from the beginning, though he and Mr. Seward had not . . . that if we were to resort to letters of marque we should do it understandingly and with all the consequences before us. The idea that private parties would send out armed ships to capture the Alabama and other rovers of the Rebels were too absurd to be thought of for a moment. If privateers were fitted out for any purpose it would be to capture neutral vessels intended to run the blockade or supposed to be in that service – that it was not difficult for us to foresee that such a power in private hands would degenerate into an abuse for which this Government would be held responsible. The Rebels have no commerce to invite private enterprise. So far as the Rebels were concerned, therefore, I had been opposed to committing the Government to the measure. But the disclosures recently made had given a different aspect to the question. There was little doubt the British Government and British capital were encouraging the rebellion; that that Government intended to interpose no obstacle to prevent the sending out of privateers from British ports to depredate upon our commerce; that these privateers, though sailing under the Confederate flag, would be the property of British merchants; that the rich plunder would repay the lawless English adventurer, knowing he had the sanction of his Government; that this combination of British capital with Rebel malignity and desperation would despoil our commerce and drive it from the seas.[7] Our countrymen would not quietly submit to these wrongs and outrages, and allow English men to make war upon us in disguise under the Rebel flag. We ought, therefore, to have an immediate and distinct understanding with the English Government. It should be informed in terms that could not be mistaken or misunderstood that if this policy was persisted in we should in self defense be under the necessity of resorting to reprisals. In this view the law which authorized letters of marque had appeared to me proper, and might be made useful as a menace and admonition to England; and I repeated what I had said to the Secretary of State in reply to a remark of his that we must make more extensive naval operations against the Rebels by issuing letters of marque to annoy them – that letters of marque, instead of annoying them, destitute as they were of commerce, would aid them, for that step would involve war with England.

The President . . . showed much interest and accord in what I said. He assented consequently to most that I uttered and controverted nothing.

April 3, 1863: Seward tells me he already has an application from responsible parties who want a letter of marque, and assures me there will be a flood of applications, but I am still incredulous. Our merchants will not spend their money in the idle scheme of attempting to spear sharks for wool.

---

[7] Although some Confederate privateers were active against Union shipping early in the war, the practice soon gave way to blockade-running, which was much more lucrative.

April 4, 1863: Had a message from the President, who wished to see me and also Assistant Secretary Fox. Found the matter in hand to be the Prussian adventurer Sybert, who was anxious his vessel should be taken into the naval service. The President said Seward was extremely anxious this should be done and had sent Sybert to him. I inquired if he had seen Sybert. He replied that he had and that the man was now in the audience room. He learned from Seward and Sybert that he (Sybert) had a vessel of one hundred tons into which he would put a screw, if authorized, would go on blockade, and would do more than the whole squadron of naval vessels. I asked the President if he gave credit to the promises of this man, who Mr. Seward had sent to me as coming from responsible parties, though I knew none of them, had seen or heard of none but this adventurer himself – that he had first applied to me and I would not trust or be troubled with him after a slight examination, but that I sent him to Seward, who was then pushing forward his regulations for letters of marque . . . and the result was Mr. Seward wanted me to take his first case. After a little further conversation, the President, instead of sending Sybert back to Seward, said he would turn him over to the Navy Department to be disposed of. This ends Mr. Seward's first application, and probably it will be the last.

ENFORCING THE BLOCKADE

On the question of privateers, Welles was decidedly more cautious than Seward, and Lincoln sided with him, lest the issuance of letters of marque strain relations with England and perhaps lead to armed conflict. But when it came to enforcing the blockade, which was the navy's single most important task, Welles took a hard line, insisting on a maximalist interpretation of the nation's belligerent rights in combating blockade-runners.[8] In sharp contrast, when other countries – especially England – complained to the State Department that in enforcing the blockade overly zealous navy officers had infringed their rights as neutrals, Seward, although not as weak-kneed as Welles believed, tended to be conciliatory and sometimes made concessions that angered the navy secretary. More often than not, Lincoln sided with Seward, again mainly because he was determined to avoid having to fight two wars simultaneously. This is illustrated in the following diary excerpts about whether the U.S. had the legal right to open sealed mailbags found on board ships seized as suspected blockade-runners. Welles contended that there was such a right and insisted that it be upheld, since sometimes the evidence

---

[8] As noted in the Introduction, Welles had the ultimate responsibility for organizing and administering the navy's blockade of 3500 miles of Confederate coastline.

needed to convince a prize court that a ship was in fact a blockade-runner was secreted in a sealed mailbag.[9]

April 11, 1863: Seward is in great trouble about the mail of the Peterhoff, a captured blockade-runner. Wants the mail given up. Says the instructions which he prepared insured the inviolability and security of the mails. I told him he had no authority to prepare such instructions, that the law was paramount, and that anything which he proposed in opposition to and disregarding the law was not observed.

He called at my house this evening with a letter from Lord Lyons [British minister to the United States] inclosing dispatches from Archibald, English Consul at New York. [Seward] wanted me to send, and order the mail to be immediately given up and sent forward. I declined. Told him the mail was properly and legally in the custody of the [prize] court and beyond Executive control; assured him there would be no serious damage from delay if the mail was finally surrendered, but I was inclined to believe the sensitiveness of both Lord Lyons and Archibald had its origin in the fact that the mail contained matter which would condemn the vessel [i.e., convince the prize court it was a blockade-runner]. "But," said Seward, "mails are sacred; they are an institution." I replied that would do for peace but not for war; that he was clothed with no authority to concede the surrender of the mail; that by both statute and international law they must go to the court; that if his arrangement, of which I knew nothing, meant anything, the most that could be conceded or negotiated would be to mails on regular recognized neutral packets and not to blockade-runners and irregular vessels with contraband like the Peterhoff. He dwelt on an arrangement entered into between himself and the British Legation, and the difficulty which would follow a breach on our part. I inquired if he had any authority to make an arrangement that was in conflict with the express provisions of the statutes – whether it was a treaty arrangement confirmed by the Senate. Told him the law and the courts must govern in this matter. The Secretary of State and the Executive were powerless. We could not interfere.

---

[9] When a suspected blockade-runner was seized by a navy ship, it was taken to the nearest American port having a prize court. The court examined the evidence and determined whether the ship had in fact been engaged in running the blockade and thus was a "good" (i.e., legitimate) prize. If the court found that it was, the ship and its cargo were sold. Part of the proceeds went into the navy's pension fund and the rest was divided among the officers and crew of the warship that seized the vessel and the commander of the blockading squadron to which the warship belonged.

April 13, 1863: Wrote Seward a letter on the subject of captured mails, growing out of the prize Peterhoff. On the 18th of August last [1862] I prepared a set of instructions embracing the mails, on which Seward had unwittingly got committed. The President requested that this should be done in conformity with certain arrangements which Seward had made with the foreign ministers: I objected that the instructions which Mr. Seward had prepared in consultation with the foreigners were unjust to ourselves and contrary to usage and to law, but to get clear of the difficulty they were so far modified as to not directly violate the statutes. . . . The budget of concessions was, indeed, wholly against ourselves, and the covenants were made without any accurate knowledge on the part of the Secretary of State when they were given of what he was yielding. But the whole, in the shape in which the instructions were finally put, passed off very well. Ultimately, however, the circular containing among other matters these instructions . . . got into the papers, and the concessions were, even after they were cut down, so great that the Englishmen complimented the Secretary of State for his liberal views. The incense was so pleasant that Mr. Seward on the 30th of October wrote me a supercilious letter stating it was expedient [that] our naval officers should forward the mails captured on blockade-runners, etc., to their destination as speedily as possible, without their being searched or opened[10] . . . the concession [was] disreputable and unwarrantable, the surrender of our indisputable rights disgraceful, and the whole thing unstatesmanlike and illegal, unjust to the Navy and the country, and discourteous to the Secretary of the Navy and the President. . . . I said to Mr. Seward at the time, last November, that the circular of the 18th of August had gone far enough, and was yielding more than was authorized. . . . He said his object was to keep the peace, to soothe and calm the English and French for a few weeks.

Lord Lyons now writes very adroitly that the seizure of the Peterhoff mails was in violation of the order of our Government as "communicated to the Secretary of the Navy on the 31st of October." He makes no claim for surrender by right, or usage, or the law of nations, but it was by the order of our Government to the Secretary of the Navy. No such order was ever given by the Government. None could be given but by law of Congress. The Secretary of the Navy does not receive orders from the Secretary of State, and though I doubt not Mr. Seward in an excitable and

---

[10] Shortly after receiving this request, Welles wrote in his diary (November 4, 1862) that the British had "bamboozled" Seward, but there would be no "bamboozling me." He added that Seward's "course is sometimes annoying, and exhibits an ignorance which is astonishing in one of his intellectual capacity."

inflated moment promised and penned his absurd note which he called an order when conversing with them – gave it to them as such – yet I never deemed it of sufficient consequence to even answer or notice further than in a conversation to tell him it was illegal.

April 28, 1863: Sumner called this evening at the Department. Was much discomfited with an interview which he had last evening with the President. . . . A conversation then took place which greatly mortified and chagrined Sumner, who says the President is very ignorant or very deceptive. The President, he says, is horrified, or appeared to be, with the idea of a war with England. . . . He was confident we should have war if we presumed to open their mail bags, or break their seals or locks. They would not submit to it, and we were in no condition to plunge into a foreign war on a subject of so little importance in comparison with the terrible consequences which must follow our act. Of this idea of a war with England, Sumner could not dispossess him by argument, or by showing its absurdity. . . .

I have no doubts of the President's sincerity [about the risk of war]. But he has been imposed upon, humbugged, by a man in whom he confides; his confidence has been abused; he does not comprehend the principles involved nor the question itself, for Seward does not intend he shall comprehend it . . . . The Secretary of State is daily, and almost hourly, wailing in his ears the calamities of a war with England which he is striving to prevent. The President is thus led away from the real question, and will probably decide it, not on its merits, but on this false issue, raised by the man who is the author of the difficulty.

April 30, 1863: [At a meeting with Welles this afternoon] Sumner related an interesting conversation which he had last evening with Lord Lyons at Tassara's, the Spanish Minister . . . . He opened the subject [of seized mails] by regretting that in the peculiar condition of our affairs, Lord Lyons should have made a demand that could not be yielded without dishonor and said that the question was one of judicature rather than diplomacy. Lord Lyons disavowed having made a demand; said he was careful in all his transactions with Mr. Seward, that he made it a point to reduce all matters with Seward of a public nature to writing, that he had done so in regard to the mail of the Peterhoff, and studiously avoided any demand. He authorized Sumner, who is Chairman of Foreign Relations, to see all the letters in relation to the mails, etc., etc.

To-day Sumner saw the President and repeated to him this conversation, Lord Lyons having authorized him to do so. The President, he says, seemed astounded, and after some general conversation, he said in his emphatic way, "I shall have to cut this knot."

May 1, 1863: After Cabinet meeting walked over with Attorney-General Bates to his office. Had a very full and unreserved talk with him concerning the question of captured mails – the jurisdiction of the courts, the law, and usage, and rights of the Government. He is unqualifiedly with me in my views and principles – the law and our rights.

By this time the issue of the **Peterhoff's** *mailbags was moot, since the U. S. district attorney in New York, acting at Seward's direction, had already asked the prize court to turn them over, unopened, to British authorities, which the court did. Seward's action was of dubious legality, since a law enacted in August 1861 placed all federal district attorneys under the supervision of the attorney general, who presumably was the only cabinet officer authorized to give them directions.*

May 13, 1863: The last arrival from England brings Earl Russell's speech on American affairs. Its tone and views are less offensive than some things we have had, and manifest a dawning realization of what must follow if England persists in her unfriendly policy. In his speech, Earl R., in some remarks relative to the opinions of the law officers of the Crown on the subject of mails captured on blockade-runners, adroitly quotes the letter of Seward to me on the 31st of October, and announces that to be the policy of the United States Government, and the regulation which governs our naval officers. It is not the English policy, nor a regulation which they adopt or respect, but the tame, flat concession of the United States made by the Secretary of State without authority or law. The statement of Earl R. is not correct. No such orders as he represents have issued from the Navy Department. Not a naval officer or district attorney has ever been instructed to surrender the mails as stated, nor is there a court in the United States which regards it as good law. It is nothing more nor less than an attempted abandonment of our undoubted legal rights by a Secretary of State who knew not what he was about. The President may, under the influence of Mr. Seward, commit himself to this inconsiderate and illegal proceeding and direct such instructions to be issued, but if so, the act shall be his, not mine, and he will find it an unhappy error.

While Welles **may** *have been right that prize courts were legally entitled to open sealed mailbags in order to obtain evidence of blockade-running, Lincoln was too prudent to insist on a technical legal right when he feared it might lead to war with Great Britain. Two other factors may also have influenced his decision. One was Welles's inability to provide documentary proof that American prize courts* *had traditionally opened sealed mailbags when it was essential to determining whether a seized ship was a blockade-runner. The other was that back in October 1862, Lincoln had written "Approved" on Seward's note asking Welles to order naval officers to respect the sanctity of the mails, a note which Seward had shown to Lyons's attaché, who forwarded it to Lord Russell. While Lincoln may have given his approval without thinking through its implications, it would have been awkward for him now to turn around and adopt the opposite position.*

Another incident over which Welles and Seward differed involved the navy's seizure of the suspected blockade-runner Mont Blanc *about a mile off Sand Key, an uninhabited speck of land in the Bahama Archipelago. The British government protested the action on grounds that Sand Key (or Cay) was a British possession and thus the seizure of the ship was illegal because it violated an accepted principle of international law that ships were immune to capture if they were within the territorial waters of a neutral nation or one of its possessions. Such waters were usually defined as those within three miles (one marine league) of shore. Welles's unhappiness with Seward's handling of this episode is reflected in the following diary entry.*

August 24, 1863: Am annoyed and vexed by a letter from Seward in relation to the Mont Blanc. As usual, he has been meddlesome and has inconsiderately, I ought to say heedlessly and unwittingly, done a silly thing. . . .

The history of this case exemplifies the management of Mr. Seward. [Commander Napoleon] Collins in the Octorara captured the Mont Blanc on her way to Port Royal. The capture took place near Sand Key, a shoal or spit of land over which the English claim jurisdiction. I question their right to assume that these shoals, or Cays, belong to England, and that her jurisdiction extends a marine league from each, most of them being uninhabited, barren spots lying off our coast and used [by blockade-runners] to annoy and injure us. I suggested the propriety of denying, or refusing to recognize, the British claim or title to the uninhabited spots – that the opportunity should not pass unimproved to bring the subject to an issue. But Mr. Seward flinched before Lord Lyons, and alarmed the President by representing that I raised new issues, and without investigating the merits of the case of the Mont Blanc, which was in the courts, he hastened to concede to the English not only jurisdiction, but an apology and damages.

Navy Manpower Problems

During the Civil War, the number of enlisted men the navy needed was only about five percent of the number that entered the army. But many of them had to be men with nautical skills and shipboard experience, whereas there were no comparable requirements of common soldiers at the time they enlisted or were drafted. When Congress adopted the Enrollment Act in March of 1863, subjecting males between the ages of 20 and 45 to conscription into the army, it made no exception for men who were already serving in the navy or had the qualifications the navy sought in new recruits. As a result, the navy was confronted with a manpower shortage.

August 19, 1863: I called on Stanton to-day on the subject of relieving petty officers of the Navy from the draft, and permitting them to continue in the service where they are engaged, unmolested. These men are now on duty, some on blockade service, some abroad, and the law which subjects these men to draft is monstrous, and the Military Committee who, he says, drew up the law are deserving of censure for their carelessness – I do not impute to them a design in this. Stanton, who must have seen and been consulted, should have corrected the proceeding. But he seems gratified that such power should have been placed in his hands by Congress, and objects to general relief of naval men, but thinks each one, in the employ of other Departments as well as the War [Department], should make application to him for relief. The unthinking and inconsiderate legislators did not intend to compel the sailors who are performing arduous duties afloat to a draft and fine, but they are to be subjected to penalty, although engaged in battle when the draft takes place. Relief can be had if the Secretary of the Navy will make application to the Secretary of War for a discharge in each case.

December 29, 1863: There has been some vicious legislation in Congress, which I at one time supposed was inadvertent but which I begin to think was not wholly without design. The maritime towns, from which we draw most of our seamen, are allowed no credit [toward their draft quota] for men who enlist in the Navy. Of course the local authorities and public opinion in those communities are opposed to naval enlistments, which, with the high military bounties [paid to army enlistees], are telling on the naval service. We need at least five thousand of the sailors who have been enticed by high bounties and the causes alluded to into the army. They are experts, can discharge seamen's duty; landsmen cannot fill their place. Having received the bounty, they would prefer entering the Navy, but the law has given the power to allow them to do so into the hands of the Secretary of War, and he is disposed to show his authority by refusing to yield up these men to their proper trade and calling. The President can order the transfer, but he dislikes to interfere with and overrule Stanton. Congress hesitates [to revise the law]; and the result is our vessels are not manned, the service is crippled, and the country must suffer.

March 24, 1864: We are running short of sailors and I have no immediate remedy. The army officers are not disposed to lose good men, and seem indifferent to the country and general welfare if their service can get along. Commodore [Stephen C.] Rowan writes that the times of the men are running out [i.e., their period of enlistment is about to expire] and no reenlistments; the army is paying enormous bounties. Between thirty and forty vessels are waiting crews.

March 25, 1864: At Cabinet to-day, I brought up the subject of a scarcity of seamen. The President seemed concerned, and I have no doubt was. Stanton was more unconcerned than I wished, but did not object to my suggestions. I had commenced, but not completed, a letter to the President urging the importance and necessity of an immediate transfer of 12,000 men to the Navy. . . . This letter I finished and had copied after my return.

March 26, 1864: I went early this A.M. to the President on the subject of procuring a transfer of seamen from the Army to the Navy. After reading the papers he said he would take the matter in hand, and before I left the room he rang for his man Edward and told him to go for the Secretary of War, but, stopping him before he got to the door, directed him to call the Secretary of State first. In this whole matter of procuring seamen for the Navy there has been a sorry display of the prejudices of some of the military authorities. Halleck appears to dislike the Navy more than he loves his country.

March 28, 1864: The President sent for Fox and myself on Saturday evening [March 26th]. Fox, who had negotiated matters with Halleck relative to transfers, was disgusted and a little overreached and had also written as well as myself to the President. The latter desired to see us both Saturday P.M. and requested an order might be prepared which we took to him this A.M. It was less mandatory than I wished, but I know his wish not to come in conflict with the Secretary of War, certainly not in a harsh manner. The order was mild and his own, and for the Secretary of War to issue to carry it into effect. He wished me to write an order for the Secretary of War. I could see the President wished to have before him the practical working. Had an order transmitted [to] him forthwith.

THE CONSCRIPT BILL!
HOW TO AVOID IT!!
U. S. NAVY.
1,000 MEN WANTED, FOR 12 MONTHS!

Seamen's Pay, - - - - - - - **$18.00** per month.
Ordinary Seamen's Pay, ... **14.00** " "
Landsmen's Pay, ... **12.00** " "
$1.50 extra per month to all, Grog Money.

$50,000,000 PRIZES!

Already captured, a large share of which is awarded to Ships Crews. The laws for the distributing of Prize money carefully protects the rights of all the captors.

PETTY OFFICERS,—PROMOTION.—Seamen have a chance for promotion to the offices of Master at Arms, Boatswain's Mates, Quarter Gunners, Captain of Tops, Forecastle, Holds, After-Guard, &c.
Landsmen may be advanced to Armorers, Armorers' Mates, Carpenter's Mates, Sailmakers' Mates, Painters, Coopers, &c.
PAY OF PETTY OFFICERS,—From $20.00 to $45.00 per month.
CHANCES FOR WARRANTS, BOUNTIES AND MEDALS OF HONOR.—All those who distinguish themselves in battle or by extraordinary heroism, may be promoted to forward Warrant Officers or Acting Masters' Mates,—and upon their promotion receive a guaranty of $100, with a medal of honor from their country.
All who wish may leave HALF PAY with their families, to commence from date of enlistment.
Minors must have a written consent, sworn to before a Justice of the Peace.

For further information apply to U. S. NAVAL RENDEZVOUS,
E. Y. BUTLER, U. S. N. Recruiting Officer,
No. 14 FRONT STREET, SALEM, MASS.

FROM WRIGHT & POTTER'S BOSTON PRINTING ESTABLISHMENT, No. 4 SPRING LANE, CORNER OF DEVONSHIRE STREET.

U. S. Navy Recruiting Poster for a Naval Rendezvous, Salem, Mass. (probably 1864). For many men with the necessary skills, enlisting in the navy became an attractive alternative to being conscripted into the army, especially after government policy was changed in 1864 so the army could no longer draft men after they had enlisted in the navy. Source: National Archives/Naval Historical Foundation.

Coastal Defense

Residents of coastal communities often petitioned Welles to do more to defend them against what they saw as a serious danger of attacks by Confederate cruisers. He usually played down the risk, not only because he believed it was in fact small but also because he was reluctant to divert warships from blockade duty. And he was quick to point out that the army, which maintained harbor fortifications in all ports of any size, was responsible for shore defense.

September 11, 1862: Men in New York, men who are sensible in most things, are the most easily terrified and panic-stricken of any community. They are just now alarmed lest an ironclad steamer may rush in upon them some fine morning while they are asleep and destroy their city. In their imagination, under the teachings of mischievous [news]papers, they suppose every Rebel cruiser is ironclad, while the Rebels have not one ironclad afloat.

June 27, 1863: General [John] Wool, [former] Governor [Edward] Morgan, and Mayor [George] Opdyke make a combined effort to retain the Roanoke at New York, and write me most earnestly on the subject.[11] The idea that New York is in danger is an absurdity, and, with a naval force always in the harbor, and with forts and military force, is such a remote contingency that the most timid lady need not be, and is not, alarmed. Morgan and Opdyke have responsibilities and are perhaps excusable, but not General Wool, who feeds on panic and fosters excitement. It is made the duty of the military [i.e., the army] at all times to defend New York – the Navy will render incidental aid, do all that is necessary.

July 8, 1863: I yesterday informed Vice-President Hamlin and the Maine Senators we should try to keep a couple of steamers and two sailing vessels cruising off New England during the fishing season – that we could not furnish a gunboat to every place – that the shore defenses belonged properly to the War Department, etc. They on the whole seemed satisfied.

---

[11] Built as a wooden-hull steam frigate in the 1850s, in 1862-63 the *Roanoke* was converted at the Brooklyn Navy Yard into an ironclad vessel similar to the new *Passaic* class of monitors. The conversion was completed shortly before Welles wrote this diary entry. Instead of being retained in New York, the *Roanoke* was soon ordered to join the North Atlantic Blockading Squadron at Hampton Roads, Virginia, where she was stationed for the remainder of the war.

July 18, 1863: General [Gilman] Marston and others, a delegation from New Hampshire with a letter from the Governor, wanted additional defenses for Portsmouth. Letters from numerous places on the New England coast are received to the same effect. All of them want a monitor, or cruiser, or both. Few of them seem to be aware that the shore defenses belong to the military rather than the Navy Department, nor do they seem to be aware of any necessity for municipal or popular effort for their own protection.

THE POLITICIANS AND THE NAVY YARDS

Welles repeatedly came under pressure from Republican politicians who wanted hiring and firing of civilian workers at the various navy yards to be based on whether they were loyal party supporters, and also to require them to contribute a portion of their pay to party coffers. The pressure was especially intense regarding the large Brooklyn navy yard during the 1864 presidential race. The ensuing excerpts are representative of the many diary entries in which Welles discusses this issue.

June 12, 1863: The interference of Members of Congress in the petty appointments and employment of laborers in the navy yards is annoying and pernicious. The public interest is not regarded by them, but they crowd partisan favorites for mechanical positions in place of good mechanics and workmen, and when I refuse to entertain their propositions, they take offense. I can't help it if they do. I will not prostitute myself to their schemes.

December 1863 [*Welles gives no more specific date, but this presumably was written prior to December 14th, the date of his next entry*]: The interference of Members of Congress in the organization of the navy yards and the employment of workmen is annoying beyond conception. In scarcely a single instance is the public good consulted, but a demoralized, debauched system of personal and party favoritism has grown up which is pernicious.

August 8, 1864: [At a White House meeting several days before with the president and Henry J. Raymond, chairman of the National Executive Committee of the Union Party and editor of the *New York Times*] Raymond said there were complaints in relation to the Brooklyn Navy Yard – that we were having, and to have, a hard political battle the approaching fall, and that the fate of two districts depended upon the Navy Yard, and that of King's County also. It was, he said, the desire of our friends that the masters in the yard should have the exclusive selection and dismissal of hands, instead of having them subject to revision by the Commandant of the yard. The Commandant himself they wished to have removed. I told him such changes could not well be made. The present organization of the yard was in a right way, and if there were any abuses I would have them corrected. He then told me that in attempting to collect a party assessment at the yard, the Naval Constructor had objected and . . . the Commandant . . . had expressly forbidden it. This had given great dissatisfaction to our party friends, for these assessments had always been made and collected under preceding administrations. I told him I doubted if it had been done in such an offensive and public manner; that I thought it very wrong for a party committee to go into the yard on pay-day and levy a tax on each man as he received his wages for party purposes; that I was aware parties did strange things in New York, but there was no law in it, and the proceeding was indefensible; that I could make no record enforcing such assessment; that the matter could not stand investigation. He admitted that the course pursued was not a politic one, but he repeated [that] former administrations had practiced it. I questioned it still, and insisted that it was not right in itself. He said it doubtless might be done in a more quiet manner. I told him if obnoxious men, open and offensive opponents of the Administration, were there, they could be dismissed. If the Commandant interposed to sustain such men, there was an appeal to the Department. Whatever was reasonable and right I was disposed to do. We parted, and I expected to see him again, but, instead of calling himself, he has written Mr. Seward, who sent his son with . . . papers [in which] a party committee propose to take the organization of the navy yard into their keeping, to name the Commandant, to remove the Naval Constructor, to change the regulations, and make the yard a party machine and to employ men to elect candidates instead of building ships. I am amazed that Raymond could debase himself so far as to submit such a proposition, and more that he expects me to enforce it.

September 5, 1864: I am not sufficiently ductile for Mr. Raymond ...who desires to make each navy yard a party machine. The party politicians of King's County wish to make the Brooklyn Navy Yard control their county and State elections, and this not by argument, persuasion, conviction, personal effort on their part, but by the arbitrary and despotic exercise of power on the part of the Secretary of the Navy. . . . The wrong which they would perpetrate would never make a single convert, control a single vote, but it would create enmities, intensify hatred, increase opposition. They would remove any man who is not openly with us, would employ no doubtful or lukewarm men in the yard. But removing them would not get us their vote, and instead of being lukewarm or doubtful they would be active electioneers against us, exciting sympathy for themselves and hatred towards the Administration for its persecution of mechanics and laborers.

September 14, 1864: I had a formal call to-day from a committee consisting of Mr. Cook of Illinois, a member of the National Committee, Mr. Humphrey, an ex-Member of Congress from Brooklyn, and two or three other gentlemen. Mr. Cook opened the subject by presenting me a resolution, adopted unanimously by the National Committee, complaining in general terms that the employees of the Brooklyn Navy Yard were, a majority of them, opposed to the Administration. He also presented a paper which the President had given him from certain persons in Massachusetts and New Hampshire, complaining in a similar manner of the condition of affairs in the Charlestown and Kittery [officially, Portsmouth] navy yards. . . . After reading the papers, I stated that these were charges in general terms, and asked if they had any specific facts, anything tangible for us to inquire into. Was there any case within their knowledge, or the knowledge of any one to whom they could refer, of wrong, of disloyalty, of offensive political bearing? They were evidently unprepared to answer . . . . Mr. Humphrey said there were a good many disloyal men in the yard. I requested him to point them out, to give me their names, to specify one. He was not prepared, nor were either of the men with him. Mr. Humphrey said that a majority of the men in the yard were Copperheads, opposed to the Administration. I asked him how he knew that to be the case, for I could not credit it. He said he had been told so and appealed to the master joiner [the yard's supervising carpenter], who was present. . . . The master joiner thought that four sevenths were opposed to the Administration. I inquired on what data he made that statement. He said he had no data but he could tell pretty well by going round the yard and mingling with the men. I told him that his figure was mere conjecture, and asked if their ward committees in the city outside the yard did their duty – if they canvassed their wards, knew how many navy yard men were in each ward, and how they stood relatively with parties. They were aware of no such canvass, had no facts, had done nothing outside. . . .

I told [Humphrey] my impressions . . . that there was no proper party organization in Brooklyn, that they had no proper canvass, that they did not labor and exert themselves properly, but sat down leisurely and called on the President and Secretary of the Navy to do their party organization for them. That in this way they could never make themselves formidable.

They must mingle with the people, be with them and of them, convince them by intercourse that the Republicans were right. That they should invite the employees to their meetings, furnish them with arguments, get them interested, and they would, in that way, have their willing efforts and votes.

They thought, they said, they had a pretty good organization, but if allowed to go into the yard they could better organize, it would help them much. I told them I thought such a proceeding would be wrong. . . . They said if they could go near the paymaster when he was paying the men off, and get the assessment off each man, it would greatly aid them. I told them it would help them to no votes. The man who was compelled to pay a party tax could not love the party that taxed him. His contribution must, like his vote, come voluntarily, and they must persuade and convince him to make him earnest and effective.

FAVOR-SEEKERS

Welles was often importuned for special favors by politically influential figures both in and out of government, just as other cabinet members and the president himself were. In the below excerpt, Welles reacts to Vice President Hannibal Hamlin's request for a personal favor with the high-minded moralism, and also the cost-consciousness, he exhibited when dealing with favor-seekers.

July 8, 1863: The President sends me a strange letter from Hamlin, asking as a *personal* favor that prizes may be sent to Portland [Maine] for adjudication – says *he* has not had many favors, asks this on *personal* grounds. Mr. Hamlin alluded to this subject to me – said the President referred it to me, and both he and Mr. Fessenden [one of Maine's U.S. senators] made a strong local appeal in behalf of Portland. I informed them that such a matter was not to be disposed of on personal grounds or local favoritism; that Portsmouth, Providence, New Haven, and other places had equal claims . . . but that public consideration must govern, and not favoritism; that additional [prize] courts involved great additional expense; that we had no navy yard or station at Portland, to whom the captors could report, no prison to confine prisoners, no naval constructors or engineers to examine captured vessels, etc., etc. These facts, while they somewhat staggered the gentlemen, did not cause Hamlin, who is rapacious, to abate his demand for government favors. He wanted these paraphernalia, these extra persons, and extra expenditures at Portland, and solicited them of the President, as special to himself personally.

CRITICISM AND COMMENDATION

Faced with a mass of what he deemed inconsistent, contradictory, ill-informed, and often self-serving criticism by members of Congress, newspaper editors, ship owners, and others, Welles must sometimes have felt that he was damned if he did and damned if he didn't. His annoyance and frustration were evident in two diary entries he made in late 1863.

December 26, 1863: When the first turret vessel, the Monitor, was building, many naval men and men in the shipping interest sneered at her as a humbug, and at me as no sailor, until she vindicated her power and worth in that first remarkable conflict [with the *Merrimack/Virginia*]. Then I was abused by party men because I had not made preparations for and built more.

There is constant caprice in regard to the Navy. Those who know least clamor most. It is difficult to decide what course to pursue, and yet I must prescribe a policy and be held accountable for it. If I go forward and build large and expensive vessels, I shall be blamed for extravagance, particularly if peace takes place. On the other hand, if I should not build, and we have war with England or France, I shall be denounced for being unprepared. Yet it is patent that powerful, and expensive because powerful, structures are conducive to peace. A strong navy will deter commercial nations from troubling us, and if not troubled, we need no strong and expensive navy. . . .

What we needed for this war and the blockade of our extensive coast was many vessels of light draft and good speed, not large, expensive ships, for we had no navy to encounter but illicit traders to capture. I acted accordingly and I have no doubt correctly, though much abused for it. A war with one or more of the large maritime powers would require an entirely different class of vessels. . . .

I have been blamed for procuring so many small vessels from the merchant service. But those vessels were the most available and in no other way could we have established an effective blockade of our extended coast.[12] We wanted such vessels as could capture neutral unarmed

---

[12] Given the small size of the navy at the war's outbreak, the only way for the Navy Department quickly to establish a blockade of the Confederacy's 3500-mile coastline was, as Welles indicates in this passage, to buy a large number of merchant ships, arm them, and deploy them as blockaders. The biggest market for such ships was in New York City. But the naval officer assigned to make purchases there lacked the skill and experience to bargain effectively with the hardnosed ship owners and thus ended up agreeing to pay inflated prices. So Welles turned the task over to his brother-in-law George Morgan, a successful New York businessman he knew to be both honest and adept at driving hard bargains. Morgan negotiated significantly lower prices, saving the government upwards

blockade-runners. There was no [Confederate] navy, no fighting craft, to encounter. Half a dozen small vessels required no more men and were not more expensive than one first-class ship, yet either one of the six small craft of light draught was more effective than the big ship for this particular duty. It was claimed the small light vessels could not lie off the coast in winter and do blockade service. Experience has shown the contrary.

The grumblers have said our small, naval-built vessels have not great speed. Small propellers of light draught on duty for months cannot carry sufficient fuel and have great speed.

There is no little censure because fast vessels are not sent off after the Alabama, and yet it would be an act of folly to detach vessels from the blockade and send them off scouring the ocean for this roving wolf, which has no country, no home, no resting-place. When I sometimes ask the fault finders to tell me where the Alabama is or can be found, assuring them I will send a force of several vessels at once to take her on being satisfactorily informed, they are silenced. Whilst these men blame me for not sending a fleet after the marauders, they and others would blame me more were I to weaken the blockade in an uncertain pursuit. Unreasonable and captious men will blame me, take what course I may. I must, therefore, follow my own convictions.

December 30, 1863: Not long since I was blamed for not building more of the turret vessels; just now the same persons and papers abuse me for building so many . . . . I am attacked for not having more vessels before Wilmington, Mobile, and other places and thus making the blockade completely effective, and accused of neglect and indifference for not sending off twenty ships to hunt up the Alabama.

Given all of the criticism Welles confronted, it is understandable that when praise came his way, he recorded it in his diary.

December 24, 1862: [Senator James] Grimes went over the whole debate in [the Republican Senate] caucus with [Assistant Navy Secretary Fox]

---

of one million dollars on the 91 vessels he acquired. For his efforts, he earned about $70,000 in broker's fees – fees the sellers paid and were in line with what ship brokers usually received (2.5 percent of the vessel's purchase price).When Morgan concluded his work in December 1861, the navy's need for merchant ships had been largely met, and at a reasonable cost. Nevertheless, Congressional critics and many newspapers decried the arrangement as blatant nepotism and accused Welles of giving Morgan a sweetheart deal. For a time, there were even calls for Welles to be fired. West, *Welles*, pp. 121 – 123 and 138 – 142 and Niven, *Welles*, pp. 362-364

and said he believed opposition manifested itself in some degree towards every member of the Cabinet but myself. . . .[13] All who spoke were complimentary of me and the naval management, but Hale, while he uttered no complaint, was greatly annoyed with the compliments of myself.

October 10, 1863: Dining at Lord Lyons's this evening, Admiral Milne, who sat next [to] me, stated that he is the first British admiral who has visited New York since the government was established, certainly the first in forty years . . . .[14] He was exceedingly attentive and pleasant. . . . . Complimented the energy we had displayed, the forbearance exercised, the comparatively few vexatious and conflicting questions which had arisen under the extraordinary condition of affairs, the management of the extensive blockade, and the general administration of our naval matters, which he had admired . . . .

January 29, 1864: Seward says the London *Times* says the Navy Department is now the most abused of any Department, but it knows not why, for no Department could have been better managed.

February 12, 1864: [Montgomery] Blair, who, with Senator Doolittle, was at my house this evening, avers I am a fortunate man above others. He says my opponents are making me great, and that I am fortunate in the attacks and abuses that are bestowed, and repeats an aphorism of [the late] Colonel [Thomas Hart] Benton that "a man is made great by his enemies, and not by his friends." There is doubtless some truth in the remark, but not, I apprehend, as regards myself.

November 26, 1864: R. H. Gillett, formerly Solicitor of the Treasury, now a practicing lawyer, chiefly in the Supreme Court, stopped me a few mornings since to relate his last interview with Judge Taney [the chief justice of the U.S. Supreme Court, who had died the previous month]. They were discussing governmental affairs. The Chief Justice . . . said the Navy Department made less noise than some of the others, but no Department of the government was so well managed or better performed its duty.

This was, and is, high praise from a quarter that makes it appreciated. The Chief Justice could, as well as any man, form a correct opinion,

---

[13] This was the caucus of December 16th and 17th that insisted Lincoln drop Seward from his cabinet. Grimes was an influential member of the Senate Naval Affairs Committee and generally supportive of Welles's management of the Navy Department.

[14] Rear Admiral Sir Alexander Milne was commander in chief of the Royal Navy's North American and West Indies station throughout the Civil War.

and in giving it he must have been disinterested. Twenty-five and thirty years ago we were slightly acquainted, but I do not remember that I have exchanged a word with him since the days of Van Buren – perhaps I did in Polk's administration. The proceedings in the Dred Scott case alienated my feelings entirely.[15] I have never called on him, as I perhaps ought to have done, but it was not in me, for I have looked on him and his court as having contributed largely to the calamities of our afflicted country. They probably did not mean treason but thought their wisdom and official position would give national sanction to a great wrong.

Whether Judge T. retained any recollection of our former slight acquaintance, I probably shall never know, but his compliment I highly value.

December 15, 1864: In his interview with me today, it being the first time we have met since he reached Washington [for the final session of the 38th Congress], Sumner commenced by praising my [annual] report, which he complimented as a model paper – the best report he had read from a Department, etc., etc. As he is a scholar and critic, a statesman and politician capable of forming a correct opinion, has discrimination, and good judgment, I could not but feel gratified with his praise. He says he read every word of it. Very many Members [of Congress] have given me similar complimentary assurances, but no one has gratified me so much as Sumner.

Welles on Welles

While Welles often used his diary to vent his anger at his critics and to justify his actions and policies, in only one wartime entry did he offer a general assessment of his performance as navy secretary. While he expressed satisfaction with his overall record, it was perhaps characteristic of the man that he devoted most of the passage to one of the more serious blunders to occur on his watch. It involved a new type of monitor that was supposed to draw only six feet of water and thus could be used on the Mississippi River and other inland waterways. John Ericsson, the civilian inventor who initially conceived of the monitor-type warship and oversaw the construction of the USS Monitor, *sketched the basic design for these light-draft monitors. But the detailed plans and specifications were drawn up by*

---

[15] In the *Dred Scott* decision (1857), the Taney court ruled that Congress could not prohibit slavery in the territories and that African Americans, whether slave or free, were not, and could not be, United States citizens.

Chief Engineer Alban Stimers, an ambitious engineering officer who with Assistant Secretary Fox's backing was eager to demonstrate his technical expertise and thus limited to a bare minimum input from the navy's Bureau of Construction and Repair and Bureau of Steam Engineering, both of which he regarded as hostile to the monitor concept. It turned out that the Stimers design was flawed, and the problem was compounded by changes that he and others made as the vessels were under construction. Consequently, when the first of the light-draft monitors was launched in the spring of 1864, it barely stayed afloat, even though it was not yet fully loaded with coal, nor had its gun turret been installed or ammunition and other stores been put aboard. The resulting public scandal and Congressional investigation led to the removal of Stimers from the project and much criticism of Welles. Additional design changes were made to increase buoyancy, but even then the vessels were only marginally seaworthy.[16]

February 21, 1865: I have no reason to complain [about unwarranted criticism] when I look at results and the vindication of able champions. They have done me more than justice. Others could have done better, perhaps and yet, reviewing hastily the past, I see very little to regret in my administration of the Navy. In the matter of the light-draft monitors . . . I trusted too much to Fox and Stimers. In the multiplicity of my engagements, and supposing those vessels were being built on an improved model, under the approval and supervision of [John] Lenthall [head of the navy's Bureau of Construction and Repair] and the advice of John Ericsson, I was surprised to learn when they were approaching completion, that neither Lenthall nor Ericsson had participated, but that Fox and Stimers had taken the whole into their hands. Of course, I could not attempt to justify my own neglect. I had been too confiding and was compelled to pay the penalty in this searching denunciation of my whole administration. Neither of the men who brought me to this difficulty take the responsibility.

---

[16] For a detailed discussion of this episode, see Edward W. Sloan III, *Benjamin Franklin Isherwood, Naval Engineer: The Years as Engineer in Chief, 1861 – 1869* (Annapolis, Maryland: United States Naval Institute, 1965), pp. 65 – 77. Isherwood headed the Bureau of Steam Engineering at the time.

Chapter 7

HOME-STATE MATTERS

During his eight-year sojourn in Washington, Welles remained at heart a Connecticut Yankee, professing continued love for his native state and maintaining a keen interest in its people and politics. But as a member of Lincoln's cabinet, he dealt with national issues and had to adopt a national perspective. Thus he refused to give parochial Connecticut interests priority over what he regarded as the national interest, even if it meant alienating some people back home. This chapter brings together all of the home-state matters that received more than a passing reference in the diary.[1]

✳ ✳ ✳ ✳ ✳ ✳ ✳

The most troublesome Connecticut-centered issue Welles faced was whether a new navy yard for the construction, maintenance, and repair of ironclad warships should be located in New London. Given the increasingly crucial role ironclads were playing, he saw an urgent need for such a yard. But he was convinced that Philadelphia, which had offered the Navy Department League Island in the Delaware River for the facility, was definitely the preferable site. The resulting controversy dragged on until shortly before Welles left office.

December 3, 1862: Some grumbling I anticipated from New London and its vicinity for doing my duty. I last March addressed Congress through the Navy Committee on the need of a suitable navy yard and establishment for the construction of iron vessels and iron armor – and again in June. The suggestions drew from the city of Philadelphia an offer of

---

[1] Wartime Connecticut is the subject of two fine studies: John Niven, *Connecticut for the Union: The Role of the State During the Civil War* (New Haven, Conn.: Yale University Press, 1965) and Matthew Warshauer, *Connecticut in the American Civil War: Slavery, Sacrifice, and Survival* (Middletown, Conn.: Wesleyan University Press, 2011).

League Island.[2] Congress authorized me to accept it, but Senator Lafayette Foster of Connecticut procured a condition to be affixed that the Board which was to examine League Island should also examine and report on the harbor of New London, and the Rhode Island Senators had a further proviso that the waters of Narragansett Bay should be examined by the same board.

For an iron navy yard and establishment neither myself nor any one else entertained a thought of New London or Narragansett Bay, nor would either be exactly suitable for iron vessels and machinery; fresh water is essential. Neither would Congress consent, nor does the country require four navy yards east of the Hudson.[3] But the Board I appointed had some disagreement. Admiral [Silas] Stringham, Chairman of the Board, and a resident of Brooklyn, had a rival feeling as regards Philadelphia, and a partiality for New London, where he had studied in his youth. . . . The Board was divided and, forgetful of the great object in view – that of an establishment for iron vessels in fresh water – a majority reported that New London was the best place for such a navy yard. Not unlikely the fact that I am from Connecticut had its influence with some of them, though it has not with me. I am authorized by Congress to accept League Island if the Board report it suitable, but I am not authorized to accept of New London or Narragansett Bay. But I conclude to take no final step without giving Congress an opportunity to decide, though stating I propose to accept of League Island if Congress did not disapprove. I am acting for the country, not for any section and though I have a partiality for my State, and for New London, the shipping port of my father in former years, yet I should be unworthy of my place were I to permit local or selfish interests of any kind to control me against what is really best for the country. But, while convinced I am right, and deserving of approval, I shall encounter censure and abuse in quarters where I desire the good opinions of my fellow citizens.[4]

December 29, 1862: A committee has been appointed by the Legislature of Connecticut, of eight persons, to visit Washington and urge the selection of New London for a navy yard. Twelve hundred dollars are appropriated to defray their expenses. There has been no examination by the

---

[2] There was already a navy yard in Philadelphia, but it was small and located in leased facilities.

[3] The three existing yards east of the Hudson were in Brooklyn, Charlestown (Boston), and Portsmouth, New Hampshire.

[4] It was apparently around the time Welles wrote this entry that he was hanged in effigy in New London. West, *Welles*, p. 223.

Legislature of the question, or investigation of the comparative merits of this and other places, or whether an additional yard is needed, or what is required; but the idea of a government establishment for the expenditure of money controls the movement and as I am a citizen of Connecticut, there is a hope that I may be persuaded by personal considerations to debase myself – forget my duty and make this selection for that locality regardless of the true interests of the country. I propose to transfer the limited and circumscribed yard at Philadelphia to League Island, where there is an abundance of room, fresh water, and other extraordinary advantages. We do not want more yards, certainly not east of the Hudson. We do need a government establishment of a different character from any we now have, for the construction, repair, and preservation of iron vessels. League Island on the Delaware combines all these required advantages, is far in the interior, remote from assault in war, and in the vicinity of iron and coal, is away from the sea, etc., etc. New London has none of these advantages, but is located in my native State. My friends and my father's friends are there, and I am urged to forget my country and favor that place. A navy yard is for the United States, for no one State, but this the Legislature and its committee and thousands of their constituents do not take into consideration; but I must.

January 13, 1863: Was waited upon by a large committee composed mostly of old friends and associates sent here by Connecticut to procure the location of a navy yard at New London. Mr. Speaker Carter [of the state house of representatives] was chairman and chief spokesman; wanted a navy yard at New London for defensive purposes, for the benefit to be derived from a large establishment located in the State; but little had been expended in the state by the Federal Government; thought we should look out for our own State; if the Union should be broken up, it would be well to have such an establishment as I had proposed in our own limits, etc. Assured the committee if Congress decided to establish a navy yard at New London I should not oppose but would heartily cooperate to make it what was wanted and what it should be. That the small yard at Philadelphia was totally insufficient, and if, in removing it, Congress should decide to go to New London instead of remaining on the Delaware, I should submit to their decision, but I could not, in honesty, sincerity, and as an American citizen acting for all, recommend it. That I had never supposed that the true interest of the country would be promoted by such a transfer; that, much as I loved my native State, I could not forget I was acting for the whole country and for no one locality. That League Island on the Delaware had been tendered, a free gift, by the city of Philadelphia as a substitute for the present contracted wharfage in the city; that I had advised its acceptance, and that I could not do otherwise than to act in accordance with my convictions of what I deemed best for the whole country by continuing to recommend its acceptance, whatever might be determined in regard to a navy yard at New London.

December 14, 1863: The Committees of the two houses [of Congress] are announced. Hale is Chairman of the Senate Naval Committee. In the House, [Augustus] Brandegee of New London is substituted for [James] English. This exchange is not a good one, is made in bad faith, and without consulting or apprising me. Brandegee's name was not on the list which [Speaker of the House Schuyler] Colfax showed me, nor was it mentioned in either of our interviews; on the contrary we had an explicit understanding that the New England members on the committee would be retained.[5]

April 26, 1864: Sent a letter to the Naval Committee in favor of an iron navy yard, transmitting former communications. Action is required and should have been taken long since.

The sense of urgency Welles expressed in the preceding excerpt notwithstanding, the necessary Congressional approval was long deferred. Not until December 22, 1868, was he finally able to accept from the City of Philadelphia a title of deed transferring League Island to the federal government. In his diary entry for that day, Welles wrote that in favoring League Island, "I had been actuated only by a sense of duty, and yet for years I have been denounced and received the most ungenerous abuse for discharging my duty." He added that there had been "a long and angry effort on the part of a few speculators in New London to substitute that place for League Island. I was slandered and defamed because I would not give in to their schemes" and thus "the acceptance of League Island was delayed for years."

✴ ✴ ✴ ✴ ✴ ✴ ✴

---

[5] At first blush, Welles's complaint may seem odd, since Brandegee was a Republican whereas English, the man he replaced on the committee, was a Democrat (the only one in Connecticut's four-member House delegation in the 38th Congress). Presumably Welles was concerned that as a member of the Naval Affairs Committee, Brandegee would be well positioned to increase the pressure for locating a navy yard in his home city. (Interestingly, on March 1, 1865, Welles noted in his diary that in a speech in the House, Brandegee "while expressing opposition to me for not favoring New London for a navy yard, vindicated my honesty and obstinacy," which had been impugned by another Congressman.)

As a veteran politician, Welles kept an eye on his home state's annual gubernato-rial and legislative elections. His interest was all the greater because in Connect-icut the Democratic Party, many of whose leaders were vigorously anti-war, was stronger than in any other New England state except possibly New Hampshire, and a Republican loss would be interpreted as evidence the Lincoln administra-tion was losing popular support.

April 6, 1863: Great interest is felt in the result of the Connecticut elec-tion, one of the most animated and exciting elections ever known. Issues broad and distinct. Thousands will vote for [Thomas H.] Seymour under the discipline and delusion of party who have not the remotest thought of being disloyal.[6]

April 7, 1863: The result of the election in Connecticut yesterday is grati-fying. Buckingham is reelected Governor by three thousand majority.

April 5, 1864: The returns of the Connecticut election come in favorably. Buckingham is reelected by a largely increased majority, and the Union-ists have two thirds at least of the Legislature.[7] This disposes of another of the Seymours. O. S. Seymour, the defeated Democratic candidate, has respectable abilities and industry.[8] In the latter respect he is very different from T. H. Seymour, the last year's candidate. The latter was marked by indolence... from boyhood. Always lazy, proud, and opinionated, but with a fair share of talents if put to any use. He is excessively fond of adula-tion, and seeks the caresses of the young and the ignorant. Origen S. is a trimmer in politics, more pliable than Tom, though each has a trait of insincerity. [William W.] Eaton, who has been rather the leader of the anti-War faction, was a candidate for Representative [in the state legislature] in

---

[6]   Thomas H. Seymour, of Hartford, was a prominent Democrat who was elected to four consecutive terms as governor (1850- 1853) and served as American minister to Imperial Russia during the Pierce administration. He ran for governor again in 1860 but lost to the incumbent Republican, William A. Buckingham, who was soon to acquire fame as Connecticut's "War Governor." Seymour became an outspoken Copperhead Democrat who advocated a ceasefire and negotiations to restore the Union. His party nominated him to run against Buckingham again in 1863 – evidence of the Copperheads' strength in the Connecticut party – and he captured 48.3 percent of the vote, although, as Welles suggests, many of those who voted for him may have done so because they were partisan Democrats, not because they necessarily agreed with him about the war.

[7] In 1864, Republicans ran under the "Union" or "National Union" banner in hopes of attracting the votes of pro-war Democrats.

[8] Origen S. Seymour, who supported the war (though he was critical of the Lincoln administration's conduct of it), did less well than the Copperhead Thomas H. Seymour had in 1863, receiving only 45.5 percent of the vote. He ran again in 1865, and lost to Buckingham by an even larger margin.

Hartford and defeated. It is an evidence of returning sense among some of the community. Last year he was chosen by a majority of some three hundred. Now he is defeated.

✵ ✵ ✵ ✵ ✵ ✵ ✵

Conflict over the distribution of federal patronage was endemic in antebellum politics and continued to be so during the Civil War. As a member of Lincoln's cabinet, Welles sometimes was drawn into the struggles among the Connecticut Republican Party's different factions over the allocation of federal jobs in the state. He regarded two patronage cases as important enough to record in his diary. One involved the position of federal revenue collector for the Hartford district, the other the appointment of the U.S. marshal for the state. Since both of these officers would have a sizable number of subordinate patronage jobs to hand out, the two positions would be very valuable to the faction that controlled them.

August 10, 1862:[9] Governor Buckingham was here last week, and among other matters had in view the selection of Collectors and Assessors for our State. There was great competition. The State ticket [the one favored by state Republican leaders] was headed by [Mark] Howard, and the Congress ticket [the ticket favored by Connecticut's Republican members of Congress] headed by Goodman. While personally friendly to all, my convictions were for the State ticket, which was moreover much the ablest. The Secretary of the Treasury gave it the preference but made three alterations.[10]

I met Senator Dixon the next day at the Executive Mansion, he having come on to Washington with express reference to these appointments. He has written me several letters indicating much caution, but I saw at once that he was strongly committed and exceedingly disappointed. He promised to see me again, but left that P.M. to get counter support.[11]

---

[9] In his 1960 edition of the diary, Howard K. Beale reports that he did not find this entry in the manuscript diary. It is unclear whether it was added at a later time or written on August 10, 1862 but for some reason separated from the diary. The editor of the current volume thinks it is credible and sufficiently important to warrant inclusion here.

[10] These new patronage jobs resulted from tax legislation Congress enacted earlier in 1862. Mark Howard, a prominent Hartford insurance executive, had been nominated as federal revenue collector for the Hartford district. One of the founders of the Connecticut Republican Party, he had lobbied hard for Welles's inclusion in Lincoln's cabinet. During the war he was a leader of the state party's radical faction.

[11] James S. Dixon, of Hartford, was first elected to the Senate in 1856 largely by the Know-Nothing members of the state legislature; he later turned Republican. A wily politician adept at obtaining federal jobs for his henchmen, he was also one of the most conservative Republicans in the Senate and was intensely disliked by Howard and

August 15, 1862: Received yesterday a note from Chase that the President proposed to change two of the collectors under the new tax law in Connecticut. Called on the President, and stated to him I did it as a duty, that duty alone impelled me. He said he fully believed it, and was glad to do me the justice to say that in matters of appointments, patronage, I had never given him any trouble.

Having an appointment this Friday morning at 9 with the President, I met there Babcock and Platt of Connecticut.[12] They had called and stated their case, which was extremely unjust to Mr. Howard.

February 10, 1863: The nomination of Mark Howard for Collector of the Hartford District has been suspended in the Senate. Howard is a very faithful, competent, and excellent man for the office, but he and Senator Dixon, neighbors and formerly intimate friends, have latterly had some differences. Dixon takes advantage of his position as Senator to stab Howard in secret session, where H. can have no opportunity for self-defense. Senator Sumner, whom I met this evening, says Dixon came to him and asked, if a personal enemy, who abused, slandered, and defied him were before the Senate, would he vote for him. Sumner replied, No. Senator Doolittle [of Wisconsin] admits he was in like manner approached – says it was embarrassing, for there is an implied understanding – a courtesy among Senators – that they will yield to the personal appeals of a Senator in appointments to office in his own town. I asked if it was possible that the Senate prostituted itself to gratify private animosities – made itself a party to the personal quarrels of one of its members and gave him the means to wreak his vengeance on a worthy person without cause or justification. Doolittle attempted no defense; evidently did not like the attitude in which he was placed.

February 19, 1863: I wrote Senator Dixon a note, remonstrating against his misuse of power by opposing in secret session the appointment and confirmation of Howard as Collector – that it was not only wrong, officially, for he was not clothed with authority to revenge private wrongs, but it would

---

such other radicals as Calvin Day and Charles Dudley Warner, the editor of the *Hartford Evening Press*. Their animosity toward him was partly ideological, but it also reflected their resentment that he controlled so much of the federal patronage in the state. Jarlath Robert Lane, *A Political History of Connecticut During the Civil War* (Washington, D.C.: Catholic University of America Press, 1941), p. 276.

[12] James Babcock, editor of the *New Haven Palladium*, was federal revenue collector for the New Haven district. Orville H. Platt, of Meriden, was an up-and-coming young Republican who would serve in the U.S. Senate from 1879 until his death in 1905.

close the door to any reconciliation, and make lifelong enmities between those who were neighbors and should be friends – that he admitted, and every one knew, Howard was a correct officer. All was unavailing, for I hear the Senate has failed to confirm the nomination. An inexcusable and unjustifiable act on the part of the Senate, a gross wrong and outrage on an American citizen of character and worth, the peer of the Senators who are guilty of this prostitution of honor and trust. This act and this practice of the Senate are as degrading as anything in the corrupt days of Roman history, or the rotten aristocracy of modern Europe.

March 9, 1863: Had a call from Senator Dixon. Is depressed and unhappy. Regrets that he opposed the confirmation of Howard. Says if the subject was to be gone over again his course would be different. I did not attempt to soften or excuse his conduct, but told him I was sorry he did not listen to my suggestions. He proposed several names for the place. I had no other candidate than my old friend James G. Bolles, and [Dixon] fell in with it.[13]

The other patronage controversy discussed in Welles's diary arose when in late 1863 the U. S. marshal for Connecticut died and Senator Dixon quickly arranged for Lincoln to nominate one of Dixon's political operatives, Henry Hammond, for the position, a nomination the Senate promptly approved.

December 15, 1863: Senator [Lafayette] Foster called on me early this morning, concerning the appointment of Marshal in Connecticut. Said he and Mr. [Henry] Hubbard the representative of the 4th District had signed the papers for Mr. Hammond without much thought – they did not wish his appointment – considered him not a proper man for the place – had mentioned their regret to the Attorney General – would greatly prefer the appointment of Mr. Nichols, and they had referred the Attorney General to me. I suggested that he had better see the President, though it will be likely to avail little, for Dixon has interested himself in this matter to repay and attack an unscrupulous partisan and secured the influence of Seward. Foster, Hubbard, and the whole delegation have been drawn into the scheme and committed themselves against their better judgment, and now come to me to undo their own act. I shall not go for Hammond, but I can do nothing effectual in the case after their weak committals. I

---

[13] Bolles was nominated and confirmed as the collector for the Hartford district. He was friendly with the party's radical faction, and thus Dixon must have found his appointment disagreeable. But he may have decided it was in his longer-term interest to propitiate the angry Welles.

mentioned to the President that Mr. Foster had called on me and stated the circumstances. He said he had also been called upon by three gentlemen of the [Congressional] delegation who had endorsed Hammond and now wanted to take the back track. Was sorry there was disagreement – wanted the matter should rest. . . . I told him that . . . I had no partialities or favoritism in this matter – that I knew Hammond was not a proper man – but he was a sc[h]emer and intriguer for Dixon – did a great deal of nasty party work – was untruthful [and] had by falsehood deceived me once on an important matter. . . . That when men like Senator Foster, who knew Hammond as well as I did, signed the papers and then ran to me to counteract their act, it was not expedient for me to take any other part but to state to him the facts and then leave them.[14]

January 19, 1864: Friends in Connecticut are some of them acting very inconsiderately. They are outraged by the conduct of Dixon and others in procuring the nomination of Henry Hammond for marshal, a nomination eminently unfit to be made. The President was deceived into that matter by falsehood. He was told that Hammond and the clique were his true supporters and friends, and that those opposed were his enemies. This falsehood the disappointed ones seem determined to verify by making themselves opponents.[15]

✻ ✻ ✻ ✻ ✻ ✻ ✻

The following entry apparently reflected concern in Connecticut that implementation of the draft would lead to turmoil and even violence, as it had in New York City (July 13 – 16, 1863), Boston (July 14ᵗʰ), and some other localities. On July 16ᵗʰ, Calvin Day, a longtime friend and political ally of Welles's, wrote him from Hartford that "there is much excitement here and I fear we shall have resistance to the draft when the time comes to force the men into the service."[16]

July 18, 1863: Two delegations are here from Connecticut in relation to military organizations for home work [home defense?] and to preserve

---

[14] For reasons unknown this entry was omitted from the 1911 edition of the diary. It was one of a number of entries not in that edition that Professor Beale printed in his 1960 edition.

[15] Welles is alluding to the fact that some of the radicals, and especially those associated with the *Hartford Evening Press* (including Mark Howard), were so angered by Lincoln's nomination of Hammond that they began hinting they might support Chase for the presidential nomination. In strongly worded letters to several of these men, Welles put a stop to their flirtation with a Chase candidacy. Niven, *Gideon Welles*, pp. 480 – 481.

[16] Quoted in Lane, *A Political History*, p. 246, n. 30.

the peace. I went to the War Department in their behalf, and one was successful, perhaps both.[17]

✳ ✳ ✳ ✳ ✳ ✳ ✳

As in other maritime states, residents of coastal Connecticut feared that Confederate raiders would attack their communities or go after merchant ships and fishing vessels plying local waters. They looked to Welles to provide them with protection.

July 22, 1863: A delegation from Connecticut, appointed by the Legislature, called on me and consumed some time in relation to the coast defenses of the State and the waters of Long Island Sound. There is quite a panic along the whole New England coast. It is impossible to furnish all the vessels desired, and there is consequently the disagreeable result of refusal. I have very little apprehension of danger from any [Confederate] rover or predatory excursion in that quarter, yet it is possible, as it is possible some Rebel may set my house on fire. Should a rover make a dash in the [Long Island] Sound, do damage, and escape, great and heavy would be the maledictions on me after these formal applications. I am many times a day reminded and told of my responsibility.

✳ ✳ ✳ ✳ ✳ ✳ ✳

Joseph R. Hawley worked with Welles to found the Connecticut Republican Party and in 1857 took over as editor of the Hartford Evening Press, *the new party's leading editorial voice. During the war, he compiled a creditable military record, largely in engagements along the South Carolina and Florida coasts, and later in Virginia, rising to the rank of colonel. Welles was eager to see him become a brigadier general and repeatedly urged Lincoln to promote him. The promotion finally came in September 1864.[18]*

February 10, 1863: Presented Colonel Hawley's name to the President for Brigadier-General. With expressions of my regard.

---

[17] The diary contains nothing more about Welles's intervention with the War Department.

[18] Hawley was elected governor in 1866, succeeding William A. Buckingham, who did not seek reelection. Hawley later served two terms in the House of Representatives and was a U. S. Senator from 1881 to 1905. In 1867, he bought the *Hartford Courant,* into which he merged the *Evening Press.*

March 3, 1864: [At a meeting with Lincoln] I . . . brought up the subject of promoting Colonel Hawley. He said the measure was full now, but he hoped to be able to do justice to H. one of these days. I remarked that I had avoided pressing him on the subject of military appointments, but this was one for a meritorious man from my own State, that I had it much at heart, and had repeatedly brought it to his notice, etc., etc. He gave me credit for forbearance beyond others and assured me he should try not to forget this case when there was opportunity. I have no aid from the Members of Congress in this matter, and from some of them I apprehend there is opposition, or something akin to it.[19]

✳ ✳ ✳ ✳ ✳ ✳ ✳

Because of the action of the Connecticut delegation to the Union Party's convention in June 1864, Welles found himself implicated in the controversy over the convention's decision to nominate Tennessee Unionist Andrew Johnson for vice president instead of renominating the incumbent, Hannibal Hamlin.

June 8, 1864: The President was renominated to-day at Baltimore. . . . On the question of Vice-President there was greater diversity of opinion at the beginning, but ultimately and soon all united on Andrew Johnson. Personally I did not regret this result, although I took no part in its accomplishment. The delegates and people of my State generally have disapproved of Hamlin's course towards me, and I have no doubt it contributed to their [the Connecticut delegates'] casting a united vote at the start for Johnson. Hamlin and his friends will give me credit for influence which I do not possess, and for revenge or malevolence I have never felt. Without cause and because I would not extend undue favor to one of his friends by official abuse, he has treated me coldly, discourteously, and with bad temper – so much so as to attract attention and inquiry, and lead to opposition to his renomination.

June 9, 1864: There seems to be general satisfaction with the nominations made at Baltimore, and with the resolutions adopted. Except the nomination for Vice President, the whole proceedings were a matter of course. It was the wish of Seward that Hamlin should again be the Vice, and the President under Seward's lead inclined to the same policy, though

---

[19] When Lincoln said "the measure was full now," he meant that all of the brigadier general positions authorized by Congress were occupied.

personally his choice is Johnson.[20] This, I think, was the current Administration opinion, though with no particular zeal or feeling. Blair inclined to the policy of taking Hamlin, though partial to Johnson. I took no part and could not well take any. Yet to-day from several quarters it is said to me that Connecticut overthrew Hamlin, and that it was my doings which led to it. While this is not correct, I am nowise disposed to be dissatisfied with the change that has been made.

✳ ✳ ✳ ✳ ✳ ✳ ✳

The subject of the following entry, Griffin A. Stedman, was a member of a prominent Hartford family who graduated from Trinity College in 1859 and subsequently moved to Philadelphia to study law. Volunteering for army service soon after the fall of Fort Sumter, he performed ably in the war's eastern theater, rose in rank from captain to colonel, and became the commanding officer of the 11th Connecticut Volunteer Infantry Regiment. In fighting at Petersburg, Virginia, on August 5, 1864, he was mortally wounded. Liked by his men and well regarded by his superiors, he had been repeatedly recommended for promotion to brevet brigadier general.[21] He was promoted to that rank on his deathbed, and one of the forts on the Union siege lines at Petersburg was named for him. His death in combat at age 26 was widely viewed back home as exemplifying gallantry and heroism. Stedman is depicted in the monument dedicated to the "typical volunteer soldier" located in Barry Square, Hartford.

August 6, 1864: I had a telegram from Tom [Welles] this morning, stating that Colonel Stedman was mortally wounded and would probably not survive the night, that General [Edward O. C.] Ord [commanding the 18th Corps at Petersburg] desired his promotion without delay, that it might be received before his death, and wishing me to call at once on the President. I did so, who responded readily to the recommendation, and I then, at his request, saw Secretary Stanton, who met me in the right spirit.

✳ ✳ ✳ ✳ ✳ ✳ ✳

The following excerpt is included in this chapter because it deals with Isaac Toucey, who was secretary of the navy in the Buchanan administration and, more to the

---

[20] The evidence about whether Lincoln was neutral on the vice presidential nomination or exerted his influence behind the scenes to secure it for Johnson is so contradictory that the question will probably never be answered definitively.

[21] Brevet promotions were used to recognize gallant or otherwise outstanding service. Such a promotion did not increase the recipient's command authority or pay.

point, Welles's long-time adversary in the Connecticut Democratic Party. Toucey strongly sympathized with the South and led the state party's conservatives in the 1840s and '50s. Welles must have relished Stanton's account of Toucey's seemingly craven willingness to appease South Carolina secessionists during the Fort Sumter crisis, since it further confirmed his low opinion of his former party foe.

April 3, 1865: Intelligence of the evacuation of Petersburg and the capture of Richmond was received this A.M., and the city has been in an uproar through the day. . . .

Attorney-General Speed and myself met by agreement at Stanton's room last night at nine, to learn the condition of affairs with the armies.[22] We had previously been two or three times there during the day. It was about eleven before a dispatch was received and deciphered. The conversation between us three was free, and, turning on events connected with the Rebellion, our thoughts and talk naturally traveled back to the early days of the rebellion and the incipient treason in Buchanan's cabinet. Stanton [who joined Buchanan's administration as attorney general in mid December 1860, succeeding Jeremiah Black, who had been named secretary of state] became quite communicative. . . . Says Buchanan was a miserable coward, so alarmed and enfeebled by the gathering storm as to be mentally and physically prostrated, and he was apprehensive the President would not survive until the fourth of March. The discussion in regard to the course to be pursued towards [Major Robert] Anderson and the little garrison at Sumter, became excited and violent in December, 1860. [On the night of December 26, 1860, Major Anderson moved his small force from the highly vulnerable Fort Moultrie to the more defensible Fort Sumter on an island in Charleston harbor. Outraged South Carolina secessionists demanded that Buchanan order Anderson back to Moultrie.] On the 27th or 29th of that month there were three sessions of the Cabinet in council. Sitting late at night, Buchanan wrapped in an old dressing-gown or cloak, crouched in a corner near the fire, trembled like an aspen leaf. He asked what he should do. Declared that Stanton said he [Buchanan] ought to be hung and that others of the Cabinet concurred with him. This, Stanton said, grew out of his remarks that if they yielded up Sumter to the conspirators it was treason, and no more to be defended than [Benedict] Arnold's. In the

---

[22] Lincoln named James Speed, a leading Kentucky Unionist (and older brother of Lincoln's close friend Joshua Speed), attorney general in December 1864, following Edward Bates's resignation.

discussion [Joseph] Holt [a Kentuckian who was postmaster general until December 29th, when he replaced the secession-minded Virginian John Floyd as secretary of war] was very emphatic and decided in his loyalty, Toucey the most abject and mean. When called upon by the President for his opinion, Toucey said he was for ordering Anderson to return immediately to Fort Moultrie. He was asked if he was aware that Moultrie was dismantled, and replied that would make no difference, Anderson had gone to Sumter without orders, and against orders of Floyd, and he would order him back forthwith. Stanton says he inquired of Toucey if he ever expected to go back to Connecticut after taking that position, and Toucey said he did, but asked Stanton why he put the question. Stanton replied that he had inquired in good faith, that he might know the character of the people in Connecticut or Toucey's estimate of them, for were he, S., to take that position and it were known to the people of Pennsylvania, he should expect they would stone him the moment he set foot in the State, stone him through the State, and tie a stone around his neck and throw him in the river when he reached Pittsburg. Stanton gives Toucey the most despicable character in the Buchanan cabinet, not excepting Floyd or [Secretary of the Interior Jacob] Thompson [of Mississippi].[23]

---

[23] Despite strong pressure from Senator Jefferson Davis and other prominent southern political leaders whose states had not yet seceded, an angst-ridden Buchanan ultimately decided to reject South Carolina's demand that he order Anderson to return to Fort Moultrie.

Chapter 8

SIDELIGHTS AND PERSONAL NOTES

As a sober-sided Connecticut Yankee, Welles filled his diary mainly with entries about the serious business of war, government, and politics. But scattered here and there are entries of a different sort. Some of them record interesting sidelights on the wartime years, including glimpses of social life in official Washington and intriguing anecdotes. Others reveal the personal side of the man: less stern and judgmental than when acting in his official capacity, prone to sentimentality, aware of life's tragic dimension, and given to ruminations on mortality as he recorded the deaths of his youngest son and several old friends. This chapter consists of a collection of such entries presented in chronological order.

September 18, 1862: General [Joseph K. F.] Mansfield is reported slain [at Antietam]. He was from my State and almost a neighbor. He called on me last week, on his way from Norfolk to join the army above. When parting he once shook hands, there then was a farther brief conversation and he came back from the door after he left and again shook hands. "Farewell," said I, "success attend you." He remarked, with emphasis, and some feeling, "We may never meet again."

December 3, 1862: It is a month since I have opened this book and been able to make any record of current events. A pressure of public business, the preparation of my Annual Report, and domestic sorrows have consumed all my waking moments. A light, bright, cherub face, which threw its sunshine on me when this book was last opened, has disappeared forever. My dear Hubert, who was a treasure garnered in my heart, is laid beside his five brothers and sisters in Spring Grove [Cemetery in Hartford]. Well has it been for me that overwhelming public duties have borne down upon me in these sad days. Alas, frail life – amid the nation's grief I have my own.

May 19, 1863: [Former Rhode Island] Governor [William] Sprague and Miss Kate Chase [Secretary Chase's daughter] called this evening. I have been skeptical as to a match, but this means something. She is beautiful, or, more properly perhaps, interesting and impressive. He is rich and holds the position of Senator. Few young men have such advantages as he, and Miss Kate has talents and ambition sufficient for both.[1]

June 8, 1863: Spoke to the President regarding weekly performances of the Marine Band. It has been customary for them to play in the public grounds south of the Mansion once a week in summer, for many years. Last year it was intermitted, because Mrs. Lincoln objected in consequence of the death of her son [Willie, on February 20, 1862]. There was discontent, and there will be more this year if the public are denied the privilege. The public will not sympathize in sorrows which deprive them of enjoyments to which they have been accustomed, and it is a mistake to persist in it. When I introduced the subject to-day, the President said Mrs. L. would not consent, certainly not until after the 4th of July. I stated the case pretty frankly, although the subject is delicate, and suggested that the band could play in Lafayette Square. Seward and Usher, who were present, advised that course. The President told me to do what I thought best.

June 13, 1863 [a Saturday]: We had music from the Marine Band to-day in Lafayette Square. The people are greatly pleased.

June 27, 1863: A telegram last night informed me of the death of Admiral Foote. The information of the last few days made it a not unexpected event, yet there was a shock when it came. Foote and myself were schoolboys together at Cheshire Academy under good old Dr. Bronson, and, though three or four years younger than myself, we were pursuing some of the same studies, and there sprang up an attachment between us that never was broken. His profession interrupted our intimacy, but at long intervals we occasionally met, and the recollection of youthful friendship made these meetings pleasant.

When I was called to take the administration of the Navy Department, he was Executive Officer at the Brooklyn Navy Yard, and wrote me of the pleasure my appointment gave him. He soon visited Washington, when I consulted with him and procured in friendly confidence his estimate of

---

[1] By all accounts quite a beauty, Kate Chase was a charming and politically adept hostess at receptions and dinner parties given by her widowed father. After an on-again, off-again courtship, she married Senator Sprague in November 1864.

various officers. . . . In fitting out the expeditions to Fort Sumter and Fort Pickens [in March and April 1861] he displayed that energy and activity which more fully displayed itself the following autumn and winter in creating and fighting the Mississippi Flotilla.

His health and constitution were probably undermined before he took charge of the Bureau of Equipment and Recruiting [in the summer of 1862]. Our intercourse here was pleasant. His judgment good, his intentions pure, and his conduct correct, manly, and firm. Towards me he exhibited a deference that was to me, who desired a revival and continuance of the friendly and social intimacy of our earlier years, often painful. But the discipline of the sailor would not permit him to do differently, and when I once or twice spoke of it, he insisted it was proper, and said it was a sentiment which he felt even in our schoolday intercourse and friendship.

July 4, 1863: I was called up at midnight precisely by a messenger with telegram from Byington, dated at Hanover Station [Pennsylvania], stating that the most terrific battle of the War was being fought at or near Gettysburg, that he left the field at half-past 6 P.M. with tidings, and that everything looked hopeful. The President was at the War Department where this dispatch, addressed to me, was received. It was the first word of the great conflict. Nothing had come to the War Department. . . . I had remained at the War Department for news until about eleven. Some half an hour later the dispatch from Byington to me came over the wires, but nothing to Stanton or Halleck. The [telegraph] operator in the War Department gave the dispatch to the President and asked, "Who is Byington?" None in the Department knew anything of him, and the President telegraphed to Hanover Station, asking, "Who is Byington?" The operator replied, "ask the Secretary of the Navy." I informed the President that the telegram was reliable. Byington is the editor and proprietor of a weekly paper in Norwalk, Connecticut, active and stirring and is sometimes employed by the *New York Tribune*.

July 11, 1863: I directed Colonel Harris a few days since to instruct the Marine Band, when performing on public days to give us more martial and national music. This afternoon they begun [*sic*] strong. [John G.] Nicolay [the president's private secretary and a German immigrant] soon came to me aggrieved; wanted more finished music to cultivate and refine the popular taste – German and Italian airs, etc. Told him I was no proficient, but his refined music entertained the effeminate and the refined but inspired no hearty or rugged purpose. In days of peace we could lull into sentimentality, but should shake it off in these days. Martial music and not operatic airs are best adapted to all.

August 1, 1863: Went on a sail yesterday down the [Potomac] river. The day was exceedingly warm, but with a pleasant company we had an agreeable and comfortable time on the boat. The jaunt was of benefit to me. I am told by Drs. W. and H., whom I see officially almost daily, and am myself sensible of the fact, that I am too closely confined and too unremittingly employed, but I know not when or how to leave – hardly for a day. The Sabbath day is not one of rest to me.[2]

August 20, 1863: Information is received of the death of Governor [John A.] Gurley. He was a native of Manchester, Connecticut, born within a few miles of my home. He claimed to have imbibed his political principles from me and my writings; was, while in Connecticut and for some time after, an earnest reader of the *Hartford Times*. Subsequently, when new issues arose, he has often told me of the satisfaction he experienced when he found the *Times* and myself at variance, and that his convictions on the Kansas difficulties and questions in dispute in 1856 and 1860 corresponded with mine. He was here in Congress at the commencement of this administration. Mr. Lincoln thought much of him, and appointed him Governor of Arizona [Territory]. He was making his preparations to proceed and organize that Territory when death overtook him.[3]

August 29, 1863: Have reluctantly come to the conclusion to visit the navy yards. It is a matter of duty, and the physicians and friends insist it will be conducive to health and strength. If I could go quietly it would give me pleasure, but I have a positive dislike to notoriety and parade – not because I dislike well-earned applause, not because I do not need encouragement, but there is so much insincerity in their showy and ostentatious parades, where the heartless and artful are often the most prominent.

September 12, 1863: I left Washington on the 31st *ult.* on an official visit to the several navy yards. . . . Met the members of the Cabinet with the exception of Stanton at the regular meeting [today]. All appeared glad to see me – none more so than the President, who cordially and earnestly

---

[2] The physicians alluded to in this entry were William Whelan, the chief of the navy's Bureau of Medicine and Surgery, and P. J. Horwitz, the assistant chief.

[3] Originally trained as a hatter, Gurley later studied theology and was pastor of the Universalist church in Methuen, Massachusetts, from 1835 to 1838. He then moved to Cincinnati, where he continued as a Universalist pastor until 1850 and was owner and editor of a newspaper until 1854. After failing to win a Congressional race in 1856, he was elected to the 36th and 37th Congresses (March 4, 1859 to March 3, 1863). He was defeated for re-election in 1862 by Alexander Long, who became one of the most militant Copperhead Democrats in Congress and in 1864 was officially censured by the House of Representatives.

greeted me. I have been less absent than any other member and was there-fore perhaps more missed.

December 1863 [Welles gives no more-specific date]: The Russian government has thought proper to send its fleets into American waters for the winter. A number of their vessels arrived on the Atlantic seaboard some weeks since, and others in the Pacific have reached San Francisco. It is a politic movement for both Russians and Americans, and somewhat annoying to France and England.[4] I have directed our naval officers to show them all proper courtesy, and the municipal authorities in New York, Boston, and Philadelphia have exhibited the right spirit. Several of the Russian ships arrived and ascended the Potomac about the 1st instant.

On Saturday, the 5th instant, the Admiral and his staff made me an official visit, and on Monday, the 7th, the Secretary of State and myself with Mr. Usher returned the visit. Taking a steamboat at the navy yard, we proceeded down to the anchorage near Alexandria, where we were received with salutes and dined with the officers. On Monday dined with Baron Stoeckel [Russian minister to the U.S.] and the Russian officers at Seward's. Tuesday we were entertained at Stoeckel's. On Wednesday, the 9th, received and entertained fifty Russian officers, the Cabinet, foreign ministers, and the officers of our own Navy who were in Washington, and all professed to be, and I think were, gratified.

December 25, 1863: Edgar returned from college [Yale] – arrived at midnight. Greetings full, hearty, and cordial this morning. For a week preparations for the festival have been going on. Though a joyful anniversary, the day in these later years always brings sad memories. The glad faces and loving childish voices that cheered our household with "Merry Christmas" in years gone by are silent on earth forever.

January 8, 1864: At Seward's last night, who gave a party to the scientific men of the Academy now here. The Cabinet, heads of the foreign missions, the learned gentlemen and the committees on foreign relations of the two houses were present, with a goodly number of ladies. [Louis] Agassiz [Harvard], [Benjamin] Silliman [Yale], Professors Story and [Alexis] Caswell [Brown], etc., etc., were present.[5]

---

[4] During the war, U.S. relations with Imperial Russia were considerably more cordial than they were with Great Britain and France.

[5] The National Academy of Sciences was incorporated by an act of Congress adopted on March 3, 1863, and signed by Lincoln later that day. No one named "Story" (or "Storey") appears on the roster of the Academy's charter members. Perhaps Welles got the name

January 26, 1864: Stanton tells some curious matters of Jeff Davis, derived from his servant, who escaped from Richmond. The servant was a slave, born on Davis's plantation. Mrs. Davis struck him three times in the face, and took him by the hair to beat his head against the wall. At night the slave fled and after some difficulty got within our lines. He is, Stanton says, very intelligent and gives an interesting inside view of Rebel trials and suffering. It should be taken, perhaps, with some allowance.

February 5, 1864: Went last night to Blair's reception and also to a party at Riggs's, the banker. At the latter there were many semi-Secessionists whose modified views and changed opinions enable or induce them once more to mingle with the vulgar world from which they have kept secluded since these troubles commenced. The party was magnificent in its display and profusion, worthy [of] the best, and the house is baronial in its appearance. In other days the Secession aristocracy gathered there, though at Corcoran's and some others the association was more earnest and hearty. Riggs was a sympathizer, not an actor; his social affinities, rather than his political opinions, were with the Rebels.[6]

March 9, 1864: Went last evening to the Presidential reception. Quite a gathering – very many that are not usually seen at receptions were attracted thither, I presume, from the fact that General Grant was expected to be there. He came about half-past nine. I was near the centre of the reception room, when a stir and buzz attracted attention, and it was whispered that General Grant had arrived. The room was not full, the crowd having gone through to the East Room. I saw some men in uniform standing at the entrance, and one of them, a short, brown, dark-haired man, was talking with the President. There was a degree of awkwardness in the General, and embarrassment in that part of the room, and a check or suspension of the moving column. Soon word was passed around for "Mr. Seward." "General Grant is here," and Seward, who was just around me, hurried and took the General by the hand and led him to Mrs. Lincoln, near whom I was standing. The crowd gathered around the circle rapidly, and, it being intimated that it would be necessary the throng should pass on, Seward

---

wrong, or perhaps a "Story" was present but not a charter member.

[6] George Washington Riggs was a wealthy Washington banker and philanthropist. He began his career in finance as a partner of William W. Corcoran, who retired from the firm of Corcoran & Riggs in 1854 to pursue his interest in art collecting. Because of his strong southern sympathies, Corcoran chose to live out the war in Paris, returning to Washington after it ended. He is remembered today for his establishment of the Corcoran Gallery of Art.

took the General's arm and went with him to the East Room. There was clapping of hands in the next room as he passed through, and all in the East Room appeared to join in it as he entered. A cheer or two followed. All of which seemed unseemly. An hour later the General and Mr. Seward and Stanton returned. Seward beckoned me and introduced me to him as I did my two nieces.[7]

March 30, 1864: A severe storm last night and to-day. Mrs. Welles had arranged for a party this evening. The rain ceased about sundown. The evening passed off pleasantly. A large and choice company and many celebrities.

Secretary Seward fell in with Mr. [Francis] Carpenter, the artist who is getting out a large painting of the President and the Cabinet at the time of the Emancipation Proclamation. The President and Cabinet have sat several times, and the picture is well under weigh [*sic*]. Mr. C. thinks this is the great feature of the Administration, as do many others likely; but Seward said it was but an incident following and wholly subordinate to other and much greater events. When Mr. C. asked what, Seward told him to go back to the firing on Sumter, or to a much more exciting one than even that, the Sunday following the Baltimore massacre,[8] when the Cabinet assembled or gathered in the Navy Department and, with the great responsibility that was thrown upon them, met the emergency and its awful consequences, put in force the war power of the government, and issued papers and did acts that might have brought them all to the scaffold.

Few, comparatively, know or can appreciate the actual condition of things and state of feeling of the members of the administration in those days. Nearly sixty years of peace had unfitted us for any war, but the most terrible of all wars, a civil one, was upon us, and it had to be met. Congress had adjourned without making any provision for the storm, though aware it was at hand and soon to burst on the country. A new Administration, scarcely acquainted with each other, and differing essentially in the past, was compelled to act, promptly and decisively.

---

[7] At a special cabinet meeting on the 9th, Lincoln formally presented Grant with his commission as a lieutenant general, the first officer to hold that rank since George Washington. The next day Grant was appointed general in chief, succeeding Halleck.

[8] On Friday, April 19, 1861, the 6th Massachusetts Infantry, responding to Lincoln's call for troops to defend Washington, arrived in Baltimore by train. As they proceeded across the city toward the station where they could make rail connections to the capital, a boisterous pro-secession crowd jeered and threw rocks at them. Suddenly gunfire erupted, and when it ended four soldiers and an estimated nine to 12 civilians were dead.

April 29, 1864: The President to-day related to two or three of us the circumstances connected with his giving a pass to the halfsister of his wife, Mrs. White. He related the details with frankness, and without disguise. I will not go into them all, though they do him credit on a subject of scandal and abuse. The papers have assailed him for giving a pass to Mrs. White to carry merchandise. Briefly, Mrs. W. called at the White House and sent in her card to Mrs. Lincoln, her sister, who declined to receive or see her. Mrs. W. two or three times repeated these applications to Mrs. L. and the President, with the same result. The President sent her a pass, such as in some cases he has given, for her to proceed South. She sent it back with a request that she might take trunks without being examined. The President refused.[9] She then showed her pass and talked "secesh" [secession] at the hotel, and made application through Mallory first and then Brutus Clay.[10] The President refused the former and told Brutus that if Mrs. W. did not leave forthwith she might expect to find herself within twenty-four hours in the Old Capitol Prison.

May 16, 1864: I yesterday took a steamer with a small company, consisting among others of Postmaster General Blair, Senators Doolittle and Grimes, Messrs. Rice and Griswold of the [House] Naval Committee, Count Rosen of the Swedish Navy, Mr. [Charles] Hale (the newly selected Consul-General to Egypt), G. W. Blunt [publisher of nautical charts and books] and Assistant Secretary Fox, Commander Wise, Dr. Horwitz, and two or three others, and went down the Potomac to Belle Plain. The day was pleasant and the sail charming. We reached Belle Plain about two P.M. and left a little past five. Is a rough place with no dwelling – an extemporized plank-way from the shore some twenty or thirty rods in the rear. Some forty or fifty steamers and barges, most of them crowded with persons, were there. Recruits going forward to reinforce Grant's army, or the wounded and maimed returning from battle.[11] Rows of stretchers, on each of which was a maimed or wounded Union soldier, were wending towards the steamers which were to bear them to Washington, while from the newly arrived

---

[9] Lincoln undoubtedly knew that Confederate sympathizers granted permission to pass through Union lines often tried to smuggle medicines or other contraband into the Confederacy by concealing it in their baggage. Hence his refusal to give Mrs. White a pass exempting her from having her trunks inspected.

[10] Brutus Clay, a Kentuckian, was a Unionist member of the House of Representatives in the 38th Congress. The Mallory to whom Welles refers was the Confederate secretary of the navy, Stephen R. Mallory.

[11] Grant's Overland Campaign to crush Lee's army and take Richmond was now into its second week and casualties were mounting rapidly, necessitating the dispatch of large numbers of replacement troops.

boats were emerging the fresh soldiers going forward to the field. Working our way along the new and rough-made road, through teams of mules and horses, we arrived at the base of a hill some two or three hundred feet in height, and went up a narrow broken footpath to the summit, on which were the headquarters of General [John J.] Abercrombie and staff. The ascent was steep and laborious. We had expected to find the prisoners here, but were told they were beyond, about one and a half miles. The majority were disposed to proceed thither, and, though tired and reluctant, I acquiesced. The prisoners, said to be about 7000 in number, were encamped in a valley surrounded by steep hills, the circumference of the basin being some two or three miles. . . . The prisoners were rough, sturdy looking men, good and effective soldiers, I should judge. Most of them were quiet and well-behaved, but some few of them were boisterous and inclined to be insolent.

One of the prisoners, a young man of some twenty-five, joined me and inquired if I resided in the neighborhood. I told him at a little distance. He wished to exchange some money, Rebel for greenbacks. When I told him that his was worthless, he claimed it was better than greenbacks though not current here. I asked him if they had not enough of fighting, opposing the Union and lawful authority. He said no, there was much more fighting yet to be done. Claimed that Lee would be in Fredericksburg before the Union army could get to Richmond. Would not believe that [the Confederate cavalry commander] J. E. B. Stuart was killed, news of which I received just as I came on board the boat this morning.[12] He was earnest, though uninformed, and said he was from western North Carolina. Returning, we reached Washington at 9 P.M.

July 1, 1864: This day is the anniversary of my birth. I am sixty-two years of age. Life is brief. Should I survive another year, I shall then have attained my grand climacteric.[13] Yet it is but the journey of a day, and of those who set out with me in the morning of life how few remain! Each year thins out the ranks of those who went with me to the old district school in my childhood.

July 20, 1864: My son, Thomas G. Welles, left to-day for the Army of the Potomac, having received orders from the War Department to report to

---

[12] The news Welles had received about Stuart's death was accurate; he had been mortally wounded at the Battle of Yellow Tavern on May 11th.

[13] Although "grand climacteric" has several meanings, Welles probably was referring to the belief that a person's sixty-third year brings important changes in health, fortune, and other life circumstances.

General Grant. To part with him has been painful to me beyond what I can describe. Were he older and with more settled principles and habits, some of the anxieties which oppress me would be relieved. But he is yet a mere youth and has gone to the camp with boyish pride and enthusiasm, and will be in danger of being misled when beyond a parent's control. He is just eighteen and goes alone on his mission. I have tried to dissuade him so far as I could with propriety, but there was a point beyond which I could not well go. In the condition of the country and when others were periling their lives and the lives of their children, how could I refrain, and resist the earnest appeals of my son, whose heart was set upon going? To have positively prohibited him would have led to bad results, and perhaps not have accomplished the end desired. Yet it has been hard to part with him, and as he left me, I felt that it was uncertain whether we should ever meet again, and if we do he may be mutilated, and a ruined man. I have attended closely to my duties, but am sad, and unfit for any labor.

February 10, 1865: On Wednesday evening Mrs. W. held a levee, which always disarranges. The season has thus far been one of gaiety. Parties have been numerous. Late hours I do not like, but I have a greater dislike to late dinners. The dinner parties of Washington are to be deprecated always by those who regard health.

March 13, 1865: Rear Admiral Porter spent the evening at my house. Among other things he detailed what he saw and knew of Jeff Davis and others in the early days of the Rebellion. He was on intimate terms with Davis and Mrs. Davis, and had been for some years. On the evening after reception of the news that South Carolina passed the secession ordinance he called at Davis's house.[14] A number of Secession leaders were there. It was a rainy, disagreeable evening, but Mrs. Davis came down stairs bonneted and prepared to go out. She caught him and congratulated him on the glorious news. South Carolina had declared herself out of the Union, which was to be broken up. She was going to see the President, Buchanan, and congratulate him. Wanted to be the first to communicate the intelligence to him. Porter told her the weather and roads were such she could not walk, and, one of the Members of Congress having come in a hack, he, Porter, took it and accompanied her. On the way he inquired why she should feel so much elated. She said she wanted to get rid of the old government; that they would have a monarchy South, and gentlemen

---

[14] South Carolina adopted its secession ordinance on December 20, 1860.

to fill official positions. This, he found, was the most earnest sentiment, not only of herself but others. Returning in the carriage to Davis's house, he found that the crowd of gentlemen was just preparing to follow Mrs. D. to call on the President and interchange congratulations. They all spoke of Buchanan, he says, as being with them in sentiment, and Porter believes him to have been one of the most guilty in that nefarious business; that he encouraged the active conspirators in his intercourse with them, if he did not openly approve them before the world.

April 3, 1865: Intelligence of the evacuation of Petersburg and the capture of Richmond was received this A.M., and the city has been in an uproar through the day. Most of the clerks and others left the Departments, and there were immense gatherings in the streets. Joy and gladness lightened every countenance. Secessionists and their sympathizers must have retired, and yet it seemed as if the entire population, the male portion of it, was abroad in the streets. Flags were flying from every house and store that had them. Many of the stores were closed, and Washington appeared patriotic beyond anything ever before witnessed.

Chapter 9

REFLECTIONS ON THE WAR

The material in this chapter derives from those occasions when Welles stepped back from the daily rush of events and viewed the war in broader perspective. Section I consists of his reflections on the progress of the war effort (or the lack thereof) and such related questions as how to restore national unity once the war was won and how the defeated leaders of the rebellion should be dealt with (a topic on which his views fluctuated widely). In Section II, he discusses the pro-Confederate attitude of the British aristocracy and of Emperor Louis Napoleon of France and how it could lead to catastrophic consequences for the international order and the ruling elites in Great Britain and on the Continent. Section III contains a single long entry in which Welles criticizes Confederate President Jefferson Davis and the quality of southern political leadership both before and during the war. The chapter concludes with Welles's reflections on the role of South Carolina's planter oligarchy in fostering sectional hatred and bringing on the war.

Viewed in the light of modern historical scholarship, some of Welles's reflections are at best dubious (for instance, his claim that Jefferson Davis was a "despot"); and he certainly was not free of bias, most notably regarding England. Yet many of these reflections still resonate 150 years later, despite having been written in the highly emotional atmosphere of a protracted civil war and without the benefit of historical perspective.

I

December 31, 1862: The year closes less favorably than I had hoped and expected, yet some progress has been made. It is not to be denied, however, that the national ailment seems more chronic. The disease is deep-seated.

Energetic measures are necessary, and I hope we may have them. None of us appear to do enough, and yet I am surprised that we have done so much. We have had some misfortunes, and a lurking malevolence exists towards us among nations, that could not have been anticipated. Worse than this, the envenomed, remorseless and unpatriotic spirit of party demoralizes and weakens the strength of the Government and country.

January 10, 1863: In the insurgent States patriotism seems extinguished, the flag and country are hated. There is great suffering on the part of the [southern] people from all the direful calamities which war can bring, yet there is no evidence of returning sense or affection for that union which conferred upon them happiness and prosperity. Greater calamities, greater sufferings must be endured.

Some things have taken place which will undoubtedly for a time exasperate the Southern mind, for they will affect Southern society, habits, labor, and pursuits. For a period emancipation will aggravate existing differences, and a full generation will be necessary to effect and complete the change which has been commenced.

July 18, 1863: There is some talk, and with a few, a conviction, that we are to have a speedy termination of the war. Blair is confident the Rebellion is about closed. I am not so sanguine. As long as there is ability to resist, we may expect it from Davis and the more desperate leaders, and when they quit, as they will if not captured, the seeds of discontent and controversy which they have sown will remain, and the social and political system of the insurrectionary States is so deranged that small bodies may be expected to carry on for a time, perhaps for years, a bushwhacking warfare. It will likely be a long period before peace and contentment will be fully restored.[1]

August 22, 1863: The reestablishment of the Union and harmony will be a slow process, requiring forbearance and nursing rather than force and

---

[1] Welles's concern that after the Confederacy surrendered bitter-enders would continue the struggle by means of guerrilla warfare was shared by Lincoln and some other Union leaders. And Jefferson Davis did advocate such resistance after Richmond fell. For an analysis of why no widespread guerrilla resistance emerged, see George M. Fredrickson, "Why the Confederacy Did Not Fight a Guerrilla War After the Fall of the Confederacy: A Comparative View" (35th Annual Fortenbaugh Memorial Lecture, Gettysburg College, 1996). During Reconstruction, however, the struggle to restore "home rule" and white supremacy often involved the use of violence and intimidation and thus did somewhat resemble a guerrilla insurgency, as Mark Grimsley suggests in "Wars for the American South: The First and Second Reconstructions Considered as Insurgencies," *Civil War History*, V. 58 (March 2012), pp. 6 – 36.

coercion. The bitter enmities which have been sown, the hate which has been generated, the blood which has been spilled, the treasure, public and private, which has been wasted, and the lives which have been sacrificed, cannot be forgotten and smoothed over in a day – we can hardly expect it in a generation. By wise and judicious management, the States may be restored to their place and the people to their duty, but let us not begin by harsh assumptions, for even with gentle treatment the work of reconciliation and fraternity will be slow.

December 31, 1863: The year closes more satisfactorily than it commenced. The wretched faction in the Free States which makes country secondary to party had then an apparent ascendency. They were dissatisfied with the way in which the War was conducted – with what they called the imbecility of the Administration – and uniting with another faction which is opposed to the War, they swept the States. The country understands them better than it did.[2] The War has been waged with success, although there have been errors and misfortunes. But the heart of the nation is sounder and its hopes brighter. The national faith was always strong, and grows firmer. The Rebels show discontent, distrust, and feebleness. They evidently begin to despair, and the loud declarations that they do not and will not yield confirm it.

June 1, 1864: This war is extraordinary in all its aspects and phases, and no man was prepared to meet them. It is much easier for the censorious and factious to complain than to do right. I have often thought that greater severity might well be exercised, and yet it would tend to barbarism.

No traitor has been hung. I doubt if there will be, but an example should be made of some of the leaders, for present and for future good. They may, if taken, be imprisoned or driven into exile, but neither would be lasting. Parties would form for their relief, and ultimately succeed in restoring the worst of them to their homes and the privileges they originally enjoyed. Death is the proper atonement, and will be enduringly beneficent in its influence.

There was, moreover, an aristocratic purpose in this Rebellion. An

---

[2] Welles is alluding to the setbacks the Republicans suffered in many state and congressional elections in the fall of 1862 and early 1863, including a net loss of 28 seats in the House of Representatives. The two party factions to which he refers were the regular Democrats, who supported the war with varying degrees of enthusiasm but opposed most Lincoln administration policies, and the anti-war Copperhead Democrats. Thanks mainly to the Union victories at Gettysburg and Vicksburg, the Republicans rebounded in the fall of 1863, winning, for example, key gubernatorial elections in Ohio and Pennsylvania against Copperhead candidates.

aristocracy of blood and wealth was to have been established. Consequently a contrary effect would work a benignant influence. Were the leaders to be stripped of their possessions, and their property confiscated, their families impoverished, the result would be salutary in the future. But I apprehend there will be very gentle measures in closing up the Rebellion. The authors of the enormous evils that have been inflicted will go unpunished, or will be but slightly punished.[3]

In late June and early July 1864, Confederate troops under General Jubal Early conducted a raid northward through the Shenandoah Valley toward Washington. Its purpose was to clear the Valley of Union forces and to relieve pressure on Lee's army by forcing Grant to transfer troops from the Petersburg front to defend the capital. Early reached Washington's outskirts on July 11th, but finding that Grant had reinforced the city's defenses, he ordered a retreat to Virginia the next day. On the 11th, rebel soldiers burned Montgomery Blair's home in suburban Silver Spring, Maryland. That prompted Welles to record two reflections about whether it was legitimate, as a matter of policy, for armies purposely to destroy private property belonging to enemy civilians.

July 13, 1864: The Rebels, before leaving, burnt the house of Judge Blair, Postmaster-General. This they claimed to have done in retaliation for the destruction of the house of [former Virginia] Governor [John] Letcher – a disgraceful act and a disgraceful precedent. I have no idea that General [David] Hunter or any officer authorized the burning of Letcher's house. It was doubtless done by some miscreants, hangers-on, stragglers, who ought to be punished. But men in authority appear to have had direction in burning Blair's house.[4]

July 26, 1864: The papers contain a letter from Governor Letcher stating that General Hunter gave the order for burning his (L.'s) house. I shall wish to hear from H. before believing that he could give such an order, and yet I confess I am not without apprehensions, for Hunter is not possessed of so much wisdom as one should possess who holds so responsible a position.

---

[3] This harsh prescription for how to deal with leaders of the rebellion notwithstanding, Welles would end up supporting President Johnson's lenient treatment of them.

[4] Welles was wrong about the burning of former Governor Letcher's home not being authorized (as he had come to suspect when he wrote the July 26th entry). On June 11th, Hunter's small Army of West Virginia entered Lexington, Virginia, and torched a number of houses, including Letcher's, and also most of the buildings on the Virginia Military Institute campus. Hunter ordered these actions, apparently in retaliation for the hit-and-run attacks local guerrillas had made on his forces.

The burning of the [Virginia Military] Institute at the same place and time was disgraceful to the army, and if there is any justification or ameliorating circumstances, they should be made to appear. The crude and indefensible notions of some of our people, however, are not general.

Indiscriminate warfare on all in the insurrectionary region is not general, and few would destroy private property wantonly.

With regard to the last two sentences in the preceding entry, it should be noted that during the war's early phases, Union army policy was to avoid the intentional destruction of private dwellings, farm buildings, stores, and other structures that, unlike railroads and manufacturing facilities, were not regarded as integral to the enemy's war effort.[5] Over time, however, and particularly during the final year or so of the war, there was a significant increase in the severity with which invading Union armies treated the property of southern civilians who supported the rebellion, and especially those who were financially well off or politically prominent. When such generals as Sherman, during his extended raid through Georgia and the Carolinas in late 1864 and early 1865, and Philip Sheridan, during his campaign in the Shenandoah Valley in the fall of 1864, subjected the Confederate home front to what historian Mark Grimsley calls "the hard hand of war," their main objective was to hasten Union victory by depriving the rebel armies of essential supplies and demoralizing Confederate civilians and soldiers. Grimsley emphasizes, however, that "hard war" differed from the so-called total wars of the 20th Century, since the severity was largely "directed" instead of indiscriminate, relatively little private property was wantonly destroyed, and few civilians were killed intentionally or as victims of what is now termed "collateral damage."[6] So Welles was essentially correct that "indiscriminate warfare" and wanton destruction were not general.[7]

---

[5] From early in the war onward, however, private dwellings were sometimes destroyed, either accidentally by errant artillery fire or intentionally because they harbored enemy sharpshooters or in order to provide troops with a clear field of fire at enemy positions.

[6] Grimsley, *The Hard Hand of War: Union Military Policy Toward Southern Civilians* (New York: Cambridge University Press, 1995), *passim*. Also see Mark S. Neely, Jr., *The Civil War and the Limits of Destruction* (Cambridge, Mass.: Harvard University Press, 2007) and Megan Kate Nelson, *Ruin Nation: Destruction and the American Civil War* (Athens: University of Georgia Press, 2012), especially Chapters 1 and 2. Nelson sees hard war beginning much earlier in the conflict than Grimsley does and places more emphasis on pilfering and vandalism by Union soldiers.

[7] In areas where Union troops had to cope with bushwhacking and other forms of irregular warfare, destruction of homes, barns, other farm buildings, and the like was authorized earlier than it was elsewhere, largely in retaliation against members of the local civilian population who were believed to be aiding the irregulars. For the most part, the Union army began the practice of "hard war" in the western theater of operations earlier than it did in the eastern.

October 15, 1864: The speeches of Jeff Davis betoken the close of the War. The rebellion is becoming exhausted, and I hope ere many months will be entirely suppressed. Not that there may not be lingering banditti to rob and murder for a while longer, the offspring of a demoralized state of society, but the organized rebellion cannot long endure.

January 1, 1865: The date admonishes me of passing time and accumulating years. Our country is still in the great struggle for national unity and national life; but progress has been made during the year that has just terminated, and it seems to me the Rebellion is not far from its close. The years that I have been here have been oppressive, wearisome, and exhaustive, but I have labored willingly, if sometimes sadly, in the cause of my country and of mankind.

What mischief has the press performed and is still doing in the Rebel States by stimulating the people to crime by appeals to their manhood, to their courage, to all that they hold dear, to prosecute the war against the most benignant government that a people ever had! Violent misrepresentation and abuse, such as first led them to rebel, are still continued. The suppression for a period of the Rebel press in Richmond, Charleston, and one or two other points would do more than armies in putting an end to this unnatural war.

January 21, 1865: At the Cabinet meeting yesterday Stanton gave an interesting detail of his trip to Savannah and the condition of things in that city . . . . There is, he says, little or no loyalty in Savannah and the women are frenzied, senseless partisans. . . .

I am apprehensive, from the statement of Stanton, and of others also, that the Rebels are not yet prepared to return to duty and become good citizens. They have not, it would seem, been humbled enough, but must be reduced to further submission. Their pride and arrogance must be brought down. They have assumed superiority, and boasted and blustered, until the wretched boasters had brought themselves to believe they really were better than the rest of their countrymen, or the world. Generally these vain fellows were destitute of any honest and fair claim to higher lineage or family, but are adventurers, or the sons of adventurers, who went South as mechanics or slave-overseers. The old stock have been gentlemanly aristocrats, to some extent, but lack that common-sense energy which derives its strength from toil. The Yankee and Irish upstarts or their immediate descendants have been more violent and extreme than the real Southerners, but working together they have wrought their own destruction. How soon they will possess the sense and judgment to seek and have peace is a problem. Perhaps there must be a more thorough breakdown of the whole framework of society, a greater degradation, and a more effectual wiping out of family and sectional pride in order to eradicate the aristocratic folly which has brought the present calamities upon themselves and the country. If the fall of Savannah and Wilmington will not bring them to conciliatory measures and friendly relations, the capture of Richmond and Charleston will not effect it. They may submit to what they cannot help, but their enmity will remain.

February 21, 1865: We have made great progress in the Rebel War within a brief period. Charleston and Columbia have come into our possession without any hard fighting.[8] The brag and bluster, the threats and defiance which have been for thirty years the mental aliment of South Carolina are most impotent and ridiculous. They have displayed a talking courage, a manufactured bravery, but no more, and I think not so much inherent heroism as others. Their fulminations that their cities would be Saragossas were mere gasconade.[9]

April 7, 1865 [*This was two days before Lee's surrender at Appomattox*]: It is desirable that Lee should be captured. He, more than any one else, has the confidence of the Rebels, and can, if he escapes, and is weak enough to try and continue hostilities, rally for a time a brigand force in the interior. I can hardly suppose he would do this, but he has shown weakness, and his infidelity to the country which educated, and employed, and paid him shows gross ingratitude. His true course would be to desert the country he has betrayed, and never return.

II

March 31, 1863 [*Welles wrote this entry during the controversy over whether to authorize privateers – see Chapter 6.*]: Earl Russell [the British foreign secretary] gives us to understand the English Government do not intend to interpose to prevent the Rebels from building, buying, and sending out

---

[8] Sherman took Columbia on February 17th. As noted in Chapter 5, Charleston, which Sherman chose to bypass, was evacuated by its Confederate defenders on the same day and occupied by federal troops on the 18th. The contempt for South Carolinians Welles expresses in this excerpt prefigures his extended criticism of them in the passage that concludes this chapter.

[9] In the 12th-Century French poem *The Song of Roland*, Saragossa was the last Saracen (i.e., Muslim) city in Spain to hold out against Charlemagne's invading army in 788.

from England cruisers, semi-pirates, to prey upon our commerce. In plain language, English capital is to be employed in destroying our shipping interests. If we are silent and submissive, they will succeed, and we shall waken to our condition when our vessels and merchant seamen are gone.

The condition of affairs opens a vast field before us. Should a commercial war commence, it will affect the whole world. The police of the seas will be broken up and the peaceful intercourse of nations destroyed. Those governments and people that have encouraged and are fostering our dissensions will themselves reap the bitter fruits of their malicious intrigues. In this great conflict, thus wickedly begun, there will be likely to ensue an uprising of nations that will shatter existing governments and overthrow the aristocracies and dynasties not only of England but of Europe.

I close my book this month of March with painful forebodings. The conduct and attitude of Great Britain, if persisted in, foreshadow years of desolation, of dissolution, of suffering and blood.

Should April open, as we hope, with success at Charleston and Vicksburg, there will be a change in the deportment and conduct of England. Her arrogance and subtle aggression will be checked and suppressed by our successes, and by that alone. She has no magnanimity, no sense of honor or of right. She is cowardly, treacherous, and mean, and hates and fears our strength. In that alone is our security.

July 27, 1863: The last arrivals [of news from Europe] bring us some inklings of the reception of the news that has begun to get across the Atlantic of our military operations. John Bull is unwilling to relinquish the hope of our national dismemberment. There is, on the part of the aristocracy of Great Britain, malignant and disgraceful hatred of our government and people. In every way that they could, and dare, they have sneakingly aided the Rebels. The tone of their journals shows a reluctance to believe that we have overcome the Rebels, or that we are secure in preserving the Union. The Battle of Gettysburg they will not admit to have been disastrous to Lee, and they represent it as of little importance compared with Vicksburg and Port Hudson, which they do not believe can be taken. Palmerston [the British prime minister] and [French Emperor] Louis Napoleon are as much our enemies as Jeff Davis.[10]

---

[10] A month before Welles wrote this passage, French troops, which Louis Napoleon had dispatched to Mexico late in 1861, finally occupied Mexico City, setting the stage for Napoleon to achieve his goal of reestablishing a monarchy in Mexico.

III

July 18, 1863: [Jefferson] Davis, who strove to be, and is, the successor of Calhoun, is ambitious and has deliberately plunged into this war as the leader, and, to win power and fame, has jeopardized all else.[11] The noisy, gasconading politicians of the South who figured in Congress for years and had influence have, in their new Confederacy, sunk into insignificance. The Senators and Representatives who formerly loomed up in Congressional debate in Washington, and saw their harangues spread before the country by a thousand presses, have all been dwarfed, wilted, and shriveled. The Confederate Government, having the element of despotism, compels its Congress to sit with closed doors. Davis is the great "I am." . . .

Strange that such a man as Davis, though possessing some talent, should mislead and delude millions, some of whom have far greater intellectual capacity than himself. They were, however, and had been, in a course of sectional and pernicious training under Calhoun and his associates, who for thirty years devoted their time and talents to the inculcation of hate and division, or a reconstruction of the federal government on a different basis. When Calhoun closed his earthly career several men of far less ability sought to wear his mantle. I have always entertained doubts whether Calhoun intended a dismemberment of the Union. He intended special privileges for the South – something that should secure perpetuity to the social and industrial system of that section, which he believed, not without reason, was endangered by the advancing spirit of the age. Many of the lesser lights – shallow political writers and small speech-makers – talked flippantly of disunion, which they supposed would enrich the South and impoverish the North. "Cotton is king," they said and believed, and with it they would dictate terms not only to the country but the world. The arrogance begotten of this folly led to the great Rebellion.

Davis is really a despot and the people of the South are abject subjects, demoralized, subdued, but frenzied and enraged, without individual independence – an impoverished community, hurrying to swift destruction. "King Cotton" furnishes them no relief. Men are not permitted in that region of chivalry to express their views if they tend to

---

[11] John C. Calhoun (1782-1850) was from the mid 1820s to the time of his death the South's most intellectually gifted and articulate exponent of states' rights and state sovereignty. He also defended slavery as a "positive good" rather than as a "necessary evil."

national unity. Hatred of the Union, of the government, and of the country is the basis of the Confederate despotism. Hate, sectional hate, is really the fundamental teaching of Calhoun and his disciples. How is it to be overcome and eradicated? Can it be extinguished in a day? I fear not. It will require time.

It is sad and humiliating to see men of talents, capacity and of reputed energy and independence, cower and shrink and humble themselves before the imperious master who dominates over the Confederacy. Association and the tyranny of opinion and of party first led them astray, and despotism holds them in the wrong as with a vise. The whole political, social, and industrial fabric of the South is crumbling to ruin. They see and feel the evil, but dare not attempt to resist it. There is little love or respect for Davis among such intelligent Southern men as I have seen.

IV

Although lacking the nuance and complexity of modern historical treatments of the subject, the following depiction of how elite South Carolinians viewed themselves and their Yankee adversaries has, in broad outline, considerable validity (and also applicability to many members of the "master class" in other southern states).[12]

April 7, 1865: *Memo.* This Rebellion which has convulsed the nation for four years, threatened the Union, and caused such sacrifice of blood and treasure may be traced in a great degree to the diseased imagination of certain South Carolina gentlemen, who some thirty and forty years since studied [Sir Walter] Scott's novels, and fancied themselves cavaliers, imbued with chivalry, a superior class, not born to labor but to command, brave beyond mankind generally, more intellectual, more generous, more hospitable, more liberal than others. Such of their countrymen as did not own slaves, and who labored with their own hands, who depended on their own exertions for a livelihood, who were mechanics, traders, and tillers of the soil, were, in their estimate, inferiors who would not fight, were religious and would not gamble, moral and would not countenance duelling, were serious and minded their own business, economical and

---

[12] For an account of southerners' perceptions of the people of the free states and the belief of many members of the southern elite that they belonged to a "race" different from – and superior to – that of northerners, see Ritchie Devon Watson, Jr., *Normans and Saxons: Southern Race Mythology in the Intellectual History of the American Civil War* (Baton Rouge: Louisiana State University Press, 2008).

thrifty, which was denounced as mean and miserly. Hence the chivalrous Carolinian affected to, and actually did finally, hold the Yankee in contempt. The women caught the infection. They were to be patriotic, Revolutionary matrons and maidens. They admired the bold, dashing, swaggering, licentious, boasting, chivalrous slave-master who told them he wanted to fight the Yankee but could not kick and insult him into a quarrel. And they disdained and despised the pious, peddling, plodding, persevering Yankee who would not drink, and swear, and fight duels.

The speeches and letters of James Hamilton [13] and his associates from 1825 forward will be found impregnated with the romance and poetry of Scott, and they came ultimately to believe themselves a superior and better race, knights of blood and spirit.

Only a war could wipe out this arrogance and folly, which had by party and sectional instrumentalities been disseminated through a large portion of the South. Face to face in battle and in field with these slandered Yankees, they learned their own weakness and misconception of the Yankee character. Without self-assumption of superiority, the Yankee was proved to be as brave, as generous, as humane, as chivalric as the vaunting and superficial Carolinian to say the least. Their ideal, however, in Scott's pages of "Marmion," "Ivanhoe," etc., no more belonged to the Sunny South than to other sections less arrogant and presuming but more industrious and frugal. [14]

---

[13] Hamilton was an ardent champion of nullification. In 1832, as governor of South Carolina he initiated the process that led to the calling of a special convention that nullified the tariffs of 1828 and 1832 and precipitated a crisis that might have ultimately led to the state's secession.

[14] When later revising the diary, Welles added the following paragraph: "On the other hand, the Yankees, and the North generally, underestimated the energy and enduring qualities of the Southern people who were slave-owners. It was believed they were effeminate idlers, living on the toil and labor of others, who themselves could endure no hardship such as is indispensable to soldiers in the field. It was also believed that a civil war would, inevitably, lead to servile insurrection, and that the slave-owners would have their hands full to keep the slaves in subjection after hostilities commenced. Experience has corrected these misconceptions in each section." In this passage, Welles overlooks the fact that although there was no servile insurrection, the slaves did do much to undermine the Confederate war effort by escaping to Union lines, where many of the adult males joined the army; or, if they remained behind, by engaging in work slow-downs and other forms of largely non-violent resistance. Moreover, the *fear* that the slaves would revolt necessitated precautionary measures that diverted resources from the military struggle. See, for example, Stephanie McCurry, *Confederate Reckoning: Power and Politics in the Civil War South* (Cambridge, Mass.: Harvard University Press, 2010), especially Chapters 6 – 8, and Ira Berlin, *et al., Slaves No More: Three Essays on Emancipation and the Civil War* (Cambridge, UK: Cambridge University Press, 1992). A stimulating recent study of the reasons the Confederacy failed to win its independence, including the role slavery and the slaves played in its demise, is Bruce Levine, *The Fall of the House of Dixie: The Civil War and the Social Revolution That Transformed the South* (New York: Random House, 2013).

Chapter 10

LINCOLN'S ASSASSINATION

Welles's extended diary entry is the only account of Lincoln's assassination written by a member of the cabinet at the time of the event. (The two other cabinet members who kept diaries – Bates and Chase – had left the administration in 1864.) It is notable for its narrative drama, its attention to small but revealing details, such as the black mourning ribbons displayed on the dwellings of many poor white and black Washingtonians, and, above all, its poignancy.[1]

April 14, 1865: Last night there was a general illumination in Washington, fireworks, etc. To-day is the anniversary of the surrender of Sumter, and the flag is to be raised by General [Robert] Anderson [commander at Fort Sumter when it was forced to surrender on April 13, 1861][2] . . . .

Inquiry had been made as to army news on the first meeting of the Cabinet, and especially if any information had been received from Sherman.[3] None of the members had heard anything, and Stanton, who makes it a point to be late, and who has the telegraph in his Department, had not arrived. General Grant, who was present, said he was hourly expecting word. The President remarked it would, he had no doubt, come soon, and come favorable for he had last night the usual dream which he had preceding nearly every great and important event of the War. Generally

---

[1] Although Welles's entry on the assassination is dated April 14th, it refers to events occurring as late as April 21st. Howard K. Beale, editor of the 1960 edition of the diary, concluded that none of the entry was written later than April 25th and that except for several paragraphs written on the 16th, the portion covering the period from the assassination itself through April 18th was written on the 18th.

[2] The formal surrender proceedings took place a day later; thus the anniversary ceremony to which Welles refers was held on April 14th.

[3] By this time, Sherman and his army were in the vicinity of Goldsboro, North Carolina. It was expected that General Joseph Johnston, commander of the last major Confederate army in the field, would soon surrender to Sherman, which he did on the 18th.

the news had been favorable which succeeded this dream, and the dream itself was always the same. I inquired what this remarkable dream could be. He said it related to the water – that he seemed to be in some singular, indescribable vessel and that he was moving with great rapidity[4] – that he had this dream preceding Sumter, Bull Run, Antietam, Gettysburg, Stone['s] River, Vicksburg, Wilmington, etc. General Grant said Stone['s] River was certainly no victory, and he knew of no great results which followed from it. The President said however that might be, his dream preceded that fight.

"I had," the President remarked, "this strange dream again last night, and we shall, judging from the past, have great news very soon. I think it must be from Sherman. My thoughts are in that direction, as are most of yours." I write this conversation two days after it occurred, in consequence of what took place Friday night, but for which the mention of this dream would probably have never been noted. Great events did, indeed, follow, for within a few hours the good and gentle, as well as truly great, man who narrated his dream closed forever his earthly career.

I had retired to bed about half past-ten on the evening of the 14th of April, and was just getting asleep when my wife said some one was at our door. Sitting up in bed, I heard some one twice call to John, my son, whose sleeping-room was on the second floor directly over the front entrance. I arose at once and raised a window, when my messenger, James Smith, called to me that Mr. Lincoln, the President, had been shot, and Secretary Seward and his son, Assistant Secretary Frederick Seward, were assassinated. James was much alarmed and excited. I told him his story was very incoherent and improbable, that he was associating men who were not together and liable to attack at the same time. "Where," I inquired, "was the President when shot?" James said he was at Ford's Theatre on 10th Street. "Well," said I, "Secretary Seward is an invalid in bed in his house on 15th Street."[5] James said he had been there, stopped in at the house to make inquiry before alarming me.

I immediately dressed myself, and, against the earnest remonstrance and appeals of my wife, went directly to Mr. Seward's, whose residence was on the east side of the square, mine being on the north. James accompanied me. As we were crossing 15th Street, I saw four or five men in earnest consultation, standing under the lamp on the corner by St. John's

---

[4] Later, Welles added at this point the words "toward an indefinite shore." Many writers include this phrase when discussing Lincoln's dream.

[5] Seward had been seriously injured in a carriage accident on April 5th and was still bedridden when the attempt was made on his life.

Church. Before I had got half across the street, the lamp was suddenly extinguished and the knot of persons rapidly dispersed. For a moment and but a moment I was disconcerted to find myself in darkness, but, recollecting that it was late and about time for the moon to rise, I proceeded on, not having lost five steps, merely making a pause without stopping. Hurrying forward into 15th Street, I found it pretty full of people, especially so near the residence of Secretary Seward, where there were many soldiers as well as citizens already gathered.

Entering the house, I found the lower hall and office full of persons, and among them most of the foreign legations, all anxiously inquiring what truth there was in the rumors afloat. I replied that my object was to ascertain the facts. Proceeding through the hall to the stairs, I found one, and I think two, of the servants there holding the crowd in check. The servants were frightened and appeared relieved to see me. I hastily asked what truth there was in the story that an assassin or assassins had entered the house and assaulted the Secretary. I was assured that it was true, and that Mr. Frederick was also badly injured. They wished me to go up, but no others. At the head of the first stairs I met the elder Mrs. Seward, who desired me to proceed up to Mr. Seward's room. I met Mrs. Frederick Seward on the third story, who, although evidently distressed, was, under the circumstances, exceedingly composed. I inquired for the Secretary's room, which she pointed out – the southwest room. As I entered, I met Miss Fanny Seward [Seward's daughter], with whom I exchanged a single word, and proceeded to the foot of the bed. Dr. [Tullio]Verdi and, I think, two others were there. The bed was saturated with blood. The Secretary was lying on his back, the upper part of his head covered by a cloth, which extended down over his eyes. His mouth was open, the lower jaw dropping down. I exchanged a few whispered words with Dr. V. Secretary Stanton, who came almost simultaneously with me, spoke in a louder tone till admonished by a word from one of the physicians. We almost immediately withdrew and went into the adjoining front room, where lay Frederick Seward on his right side. His eyes were open but he did not move them, nor a limb, nor did he speak. Doctor White told me he was unconscious and more dangerously injured than his father.

As we descended the stairs, I asked Stanton what he had heard in regard to the President that was reliable. He said the President was shot at Ford's Theatre, that he had seen a man who was present and witnessed the occurrence. I remarked that I would go immediately to the White House. Stanton told me the President was not there but was down at the theatre. "Then," said I, "let us go immediately there." He said that was his intention, and asked me, if I had not a carriage, to go with him. In the lower hall we met General Meigs, whom he requested to take charge of the house, and to clear out all who did not belong there. General Meigs requested Stanton not to go down to 10th Street; others also remonstrated against his going. Stanton, I thought, hesitated. I remarked that I should go immediately, and I thought it his duty also. He said he should certainly go, but the remonstrants increased and gathered round him. I remarked that we were wasting time, and, pressing through the crowd, entered the carriage and urged Stanton, who was detained after he had placed his foot on the step. I was impatient. Stanton, as soon as he had seated himself, said the carriage was not his. I said that was no objection. He invited Meigs to go with us, and Judge Cartter of the Supreme Court [of the District of Columbia] mounted with the driver. At this moment Major Eckert [assistant superintendent of the military telegraph] rode up on horseback beside the carriage and protested vehemently against Stanton's going to 10th Street; said he had just come from there, that there were thousands of people of all sorts there, and he considered it very unsafe for the Secretary of War to expose himself. I replied that I knew not where he would be safe, and the duty of both of us was to attend the President immediately. Stanton concurred. Meigs called to some soldiers to go with us, and there was one on each side of the carriage. The streets were full of people. Not only the sidewalk but the carriage-way was to some extent occupied, all or nearly all hurrying towards 10th Street. When we entered that street we found it pretty closely packed.

The President had been carried across the street from the theatre, to the house of a Mr. Peterson [correct spelling: Petersen]. We entered by ascending a flight of steps above the basement and passing through a long hall to the rear, where the President lay extended on a bed, breathing heavily. Several surgeons were present, at least six, I should think more. Among them I was glad to observe Dr. Hall, who, however, soon left. I inquired of Dr. H., as I entered, the true condition of the President. He replied the President was dead to all intents, although he might live three hours or perhaps longer.

The giant sufferer lay extended diagonally across the bed, which was not long enough for him. He had been stripped of his clothes. His large arms, which were occasionally exposed, were of a size which one would scarce have expected from his spare appearance. His slow, full respiration lifted the [bed]clothes with each breath that he took. His features were calm and striking. I had never seen them appear to better advantage than for the first hour, perhaps, that I was there. After that, his right eye began to swell and that part of his face became discolored.

Senator Sumner was there, I think, when I entered. If not he came in soon after, as did Speaker Colfax, Mr. Secretary [of the Treasury] McCulloch, and the other members of the Cabinet, with the exception of Mr. Seward.[6] A double guard was stationed at the door and on the sidewalk, to repress the crowd, which was of course highly excited and anxious.

The room was small and overcrowded. The surgeons and members of the Cabinet were as many as should have been in the room, but there were many more, and the hall and other rooms in the front or main house were full. One of these rooms was occupied by Mrs. Lincoln and her attendants. Mrs. Dixon and Mrs. Kinney came to her about twelve o'clock.[7] About once an hour Mrs. Lincoln would repair to the bedside of her dying husband and remain until overcome by emotion.

A door which opened upon a porch or gallery, and the windows, were kept open for fresh air. The night was dark, cloudy, and damp, and about six it began to rain. I remained until then without sitting or leaving it, when, there being a vacant chair at the foot of the bed, I occupied it for nearly two hours, listening to the heavy groans, and witnessing the wasting life of the good and great man who was expiring before me.

About 6 A.M. a fainting sickness came over me and for the first time since entering the room, a little past eleven, I left it and the house, and took a short walk in the open air. It was a dark and gloomy morning, and rain set in before I returned to the house, some fifteen minutes later. Large groups of people were gathered every few rods, all anxious and solicitous. Some one stepped forward as I passed, to inquire into the condition of the President, and to ask if there was no hope. Intense grief exhibited itself on every countenance when I replied that the President could survive but a short time. The colored people especially – and there were at this time more of them, perhaps, than of whites – were painfully affected.

Returning to the house, I seated myself in the back parlor, where the Attorney-General and others had been engaged in taking evidence concerning the assassination. Stanton, and Speed, and Usher were there, the latter asleep on the bed. There were three or four others also in the room. While I did not feel inclined to sleep, as many did, I was somewhat indisposed. I had been for several days. The excitement and bad atmosphere from the crowded rooms oppressed me physically.

A little before seven, I went into the room where the dying President was rapidly drawing near the closing moments. His wife soon after

---

[6] Hugh McCulloch became secretary of the treasury on March 9, 1865, shortly after Secretary Fessenden resigned the post upon being elected to the Senate.

[7] Elizabeth L. C. Dixon, the wife of Senator James Dixon of Connecticut, and Mary C. Kinney, her sister, were both part of Mrs. Lincoln's small circle of female friends in Washington, as was Welles's wife, Mary.

made her last visit to him. The death-struggle had begun. Robert, his son, stood at the head of the bed. He bore himself well, but on two occasions gave way to overpowering grief and sobbed aloud, turning his head and leaning on the shoulder of Senator Sumner. The respiration of the President became suspended at intervals, and at last entirely ceased at twenty-two minutes past seven.

A prayer followed from Dr. Gurley;[8] and the Cabinet with the exception of Mr. Seward and Mr. McCulloch, immediately thereafter assembled in the back parlor, from which all other persons were excluded, and there signed a letter which had been prepared by Attorney-General Speed to the Vice-President, informing him of the event, and that the government devolved upon him.

Mr. Stanton proposed that Mr. Speed, as the law officer, should communicate the letter to Mr. Johnson with some other member of the Cabinet. Mr. Dennison named me.[9] I saw that it disconcerted Stanton, who had expected and intended to be the man and to have Speed associated with him. As I was disinclined to any effort for myself personally I named Mr. McCulloch as the first in order after the Secretary of State.

I arranged with Speed, with whom I rode home, for a Cabinet meeting at twelve meridian at the room of the Secretary of the Treasury, in order that the government should experience no detriment, and that prompt and necessary action might be taken to assist the new Chief Magistrate in preserving and promoting the public tranquility. We accordingly met at noon. Mr. Speed reported that the President had taken the oath, which was administered by the Chief Justice, and had expressed a desire that the affairs of the government should proceed without interruption. Some discussion took place as to the propriety of an inaugural address, but the general impression was that it would be inexpedient. I was most decidedly of that opinion.

President Johnson, who was invited to be present, deported himself with gentlemanly and dignified courtesy, and on the subject of an inaugural was of the opinion that his acts would best disclose his policy. In all essentials it would, he said, be the same as that of the late President. He desired the members of the Cabinet to go forward with their duties without any interruption. Mr. [William] Hunter, Chief Clerk of the State Department, was designated to act *ad interim* as Secretary of State. I suggested Mr.

---

[8] The Reverend Phineas Gurley was pastor of the New York Avenue Presbyterian Church, which the Lincolns sometimes attended.

[9] William Dennison, a former governor of Ohio, succeeded Montgomery Blair as postmaster general on September 24, 1864.

Speed, but I saw it was not acceptable in certain quarters. Stanton especially expressed a hope that Hunter should be assigned.

A room for the President as an office was proposed, and Mr. McCulloch offered the adjoining room. I named the State Department as appropriate and proper until there was a Secretary of State, or so long as the President wished, but objections arose at once. The papers of Mr. Seward would be disturbed; it would be better here, etc., etc. Stanton, I saw, had a purpose.[10]

On returning to my house this morning, Saturday [the 15th], found Mrs. Welles, who had been confined to the house from indisposition for a week, had been twice sent for by Mrs. Lincoln and had yielded, and imprudently gone, although the weather was inclement. She remained at the Executive Mansion through the day. For myself, wearied, shocked, exhausted, but not inclined to sleep, the day passed strangely.

Welles subsequently inserted at this point the following two paragraphs. The editor believes they deserve to be put in the body of the text instead of being relegated to a footnote, the fact they were a later addition notwithstanding.

I went after breakfast to the Executive Mansion. There was a cheerless cold rain and everything seemed gloom. On the Avenue in front of the White House were several hundred colored people, mostly women and children weeping and wailing their loss. This crowd did not appear to diminish through the whole of that cold, wet day; they seemed not to know what was to be their fate since their great benefactor was dead, and their hopeless grief affected me more than almost anything else, though strong and brave men wept when I met them.

At the White House all was silent and sad. Mrs. W. was with Mrs. L. and came to meet me in the library. Speed came in, and we soon left together. As we were descending the stairs, "Tad," who was looking from the window at the foot, turned and, seeing us, cried aloud in his tears, "Oh, Mr. Welles, who killed my father?" Neither Speed nor myself could restrain our tears, nor give the poor boy any satisfactory answer.

---

[10] Welles later inserted here a claim that Stanton feared President Johnson would see papers Stanton did not want him to see if he was temporarily housed at the State Department.

Sunday, the 16th, the President and Cabinet met by agreement at 10 A.M. at the Treasury. The President was half an hour behind time. Stanton was more than an hour late. He brought with him papers, and had many suggestions relative to the measure [regarding the reconstruction of North Carolina and Virginia] before the Cabinet at our last meeting with President Lincoln. The general policy of treating the Rebels and the Rebel States was fully discussed. President Johnson is not disposed to treat treason lightly, and the chief Rebels he would punish with exemplary severity.[11] . . .

On Monday, the 17th, I was actively engaged in bringing forward business, issuing orders, and arranging for the funeral solemnities of President Lincoln. Secretary Seward and his son continue in a low condition, and Mr. Fred Seward's life is precarious.

Tuesday 18th. Details in regard to the funeral, which takes place on the 19th, occupied general attention and little else than preliminary arrangements and conversation was done at the Cabinet meeting. From every part of the country comes lamentation. Every house, almost, has some drapery, especially the homes of the poor. Profuse exhibition is displayed on the public buildings and the houses of the wealthy, but the little black ribbon or strip of black cloth from the hovel of the poor negro or the impoverished white is more touching.

I have tried to write something consecutively since the horrid transactions of Friday night, but I have no heart for it, and the jottings down are mere mementos of a period, which I will try to fill up when more composed and I have some leisure or time for the task.

Sad and painful, wearied and irksome, the few preceding incoherent pages have been written for future use, for the incidents are fresh in my mind and may pass away with me but cannot ever be forgotten by me.

The funeral on Wednesday, the 19th, was imposing and sorrowful beyond conception by the whole people. The lamentation was sincere. All felt the solemnity, and sorrowed as if they had lost one of their own household. By voluntary action business was everywhere suspended and the people crowded the streets.

The Cabinet met by arrangement in the room occupied by the President at the Treasury. We left a few minutes before meridian so as to be in the East Room at precisely twelve o'clock, being the last to enter. Others will give the details.

---

[11] Johnson later softened his stance and issued pardons to numerous leading Confederates who had been expressly excluded from the proclamation granting amnesty to the mass of former rebels that he issued on May 29th.

I rode with Stanton in the procession to the Capitol. The front of the procession reached the Capitol, it was said, before we started, and there were as many, or more, who followed us. A brief prayer was made by Mr. Gurley in the rotunda, where we left the remains of the good and great man we loved so well. Returning, I left Stanton, who was nervous and full of orders as usual, and took in my carriage President Johnson and Preston King, their carriage having been crowded out of place. Coming down Pennsylvania Avenue after this long detention, we met the marching procession in broad platoons all the way to the Kirkwood House on Twelfth Street.

There were no truer mourners, when all were sad, than the poor colored people who crowded the streets, joined the procession, and exhibited their feelings and anxiety for the man whom they regarded as a benefactor and father. Women as well as men, with their little children, thronged the streets, trouble and distress depicted on their countenances and in their bearing. The vacant holiday expression had given way to real grief. Seward, I am told, sat up in bed and viewed the procession and hearse of the President, and I know his emotion. Stanton, who rode with me, was uneasy.

On the morning of Friday, the 21st, I went by appointment or agreement to the Capitol at 6 A.M. Stanton had agreed to call for me before six and take me in his carriage, the object being to have but few present when the remains were taken from the rotunda, where they had lain in state through Thursday, and were visited and seen by many thousands. As I knew Stanton to be uncertain and in some respects unreliable, I ordered my own carriage to be ready, and I wished also to take my sons with me to the last opportunity they or I would have to manifest our respect and love for the man who had been the steady and abiding friend of their father. Stanton, as I expected, was late, and then informed me he had not, as he agreed, informed Governor Dennison of our purpose. He said he had to go for another friend, and wished me to take up Governor D. Not until I had got to Dennison's house was I aware of Stanton's neglect. It was then about six. Governor D. sent me word he would be ready in three minutes. I think he was not five. Stanton, I perceived, did not tell me the truth about another visitor. He [Stanton] moved in great state, being escorted by the cavalry corps which had usually attended the President.

We reached the Capitol, and entered the rotunda just as Mr. Gurley was commencing an earnest impressive prayer. When it was concluded, the remains were removed and taken to the depot, where a car and train were prepared for the commencement of the long and circuitous journey to his last earthly resting place in Springfield, in the great prairies of the West. We were, as we had intended, an hour in advance of the time, and thus avoided the crowd, which before the train departed thronged the road and depot.

❋ ❋ ❋ ❋ ❋ ❋ ❋

The following entry, which Welles did not date but he apparently wrote on May 23rd or soon thereafter, provides a fitting conclusion to his account of Lincoln's assassination.

On the 22d and 23d [of May], the great review of the returning armies of the Potomac, the Tennessee, and Georgia took place in Washington. I delayed my proposed Southern trip in order to witness this magnificent spectacle. I shall not attempt at this time and here to speak of these gallant men and their distinguished leaders. It was computed that about 150,000 passed in review, and it seemed as if there were as many spectators. For several days the railroads and all communications were overcrowded with the incoming people who wished to see and welcome the victorious soldiers of the Union. The public offices were closed these two days. On the spacious stand in front of the Executive Mansion the President, Cabinet, generals, and high naval officers, with hundreds of our first citizens and statesmen, and ladies, were assembled. But Abraham Lincoln was not there. All felt this.

Afterword

Late in the afternoon of March 3, 1869 – the day before Ulysses S. Grant's inauguration as president – Gideon Welles left his office at the Navy Department for the final time. He and Seward were the only cabinet officers to have served from the start of Lincoln's administration through the end of Andrew Johnson's. He apparently departed with few regrets. In his April 17th diary entry he admitted missing "the daily routine which has become habitual," but he declared that the "relief from many perplexities more than counterbalances it." He then proceeded to sum up his years as secretary of the navy in a passage combining pride in his achievements with a characteristic bit of Wellesian pessimism (or "realism," as he probably would have preferred to call it):

> My duties were faithfully discharged and they have passed into history. I look back upon the eight years of my Washington official life with satisfaction and with a feeling that I have served my country well. My ambition has been gratified, and with it a consciousness that the labors I have performed, the anxieties I have experienced, the achievements I have been instrumental in originating and bringing to glorious results, and the great events connected with them will soon pass in a degree from remembrance or be only slightly recollected. Transient are the deeds of men, and often sadly perverted and misunderstood.

Whatever satisfaction Welles felt, he had more cause for it during his first four years in office than during the second four. After the Confederacy's surrender, his main task was to convert the large wartime naval force he had worked so hard to create into a much smaller peacetime force. This meant cutting the number of ships from well over 600 to about 100, sharply reducing the number of active-duty officers and men, shrinking the civilian work force at the navy yards, and reorganizing and consolidating the various squadrons.[1] While Welles carried out this task with his usual dispatch, successful demobilization could not have been half as gratifying as meeting the challenges of mobilization when the nation's very existence was at stake.

During the Johnson years, Welles was deeply troubled by the triumph of what he viewed as *Radical* Reconstruction, but that many modern-day historians believe is more accurately termed *Congressional* Reconstruction.[2] He opposed every Reconstruction measure the Republican majority in Congress adopted during Johnson's term of office, including the Freedmen's Bureau Act, the Civil Rights Act, and the proposed 14th Amendment to the Constitution in 1866 and a series of Military Reconstruction Acts in 1867 and 1868. All of these were enacted over presidential vetoes, except for the 14th Amendment, which did not require Johnson's signature before being sent to the states for ratification, but which he urged the states to reject.

Although he confided doubts about Johnson's political judgment to his diary, no member of the cabinet was stauncher than Welles in supporting the president's vetoes and his opposition to the 14th Amendment. True to his bedrock belief in states' rights and his fear of centralized government power, Welles regarded all of the Reconstruction laws as unconstitutional federal intrusions into matters falling exclusively within the states' jurisdiction.[3] And he opposed the 14th Amendment because he thought it would upset the balance between state and federal authority, skewing it toward the latter, and also because he regarded it as wrong for Congress to propose altering the Constitution when the former rebel states remained unrepresented in both the Senate and the House.[4]

---

[1] Welles discussed these changes in his annual report of December 1865.

[2] Since the late 1950s, a wealth of historical scholarship has fundamentally revised the extremely negative traditional view of Reconstruction, demonstrating, among numerous other important findings, that its radicalism had been exaggerated by earlier writers and that Republican *moderates* played a key role in shaping Reconstruction measures. Classic examples of such scholarship are Eric McKitrick, *Andrew Johnson and Reconstruction* (Chicago: University of Chicago Press, 1960), John Hope Franklin, *Reconstruction After the Civil War* (Chicago: University of Chicago Press, 1961), Kenneth Stampp, *The Era of Reconstruction* (New York: Alfred A. Knopf, 1965) and Eric Foner, *Reconstruction: America's Unfinished Revolution, 1863-1877* (New York: Harper & Row, 1988).

[3] According to Welles's March 22, 1866, diary entry, for example, he had urged the president to veto the Civil Rights bill because it "breaks down all barriers to protect the rights of the States, concentrates power in the General Government, which assumes to itself the enactment of municipal regulations between the States and citizens, and between citizens of the same State. No bill of so contradictory and consolidating a character has ever been enacted." For good measure, he added that "the Alien and Sedition Laws were not so objectionable."

[4] Under Johnson's restoration plan, the former Confederate states had elected senators and representatives during the summer and fall of 1865, but Congress refused to seat them when it met in December.

Welles saw the Republicans' entire Reconstruction program as the product of rank partisanship, unbridled extremism, and fanatical hatred of the South. A clumsily phrased diary passage of March 1, 1867, typifies his racially inflected (mis)reading of what motivated Congressional Republicans: "Hate of the Rebels, and of all whites in the Rebel States, and with intense love for the negro for whom the rights and feelings of white men are freely sacrificed, characterizes Congress."

What Welles failed to grasp was that the strongest driving force behind the various Reconstruction measures was the fear of the great majority of Congressional Republicans, moderates as well as radicals, that the North, having won the war, risked losing the peace. In order to secure the victory, they believed effective measures must be adopted to prevent white southerners from reducing the freed people to quasi-slavery, as many of them seemed bent on doing, and also to shore up the minority of white southerners who had remained loyal and now faced sometimes deadly animosity from the defeated rebels.[5]

Black suffrage was the most controversial of all the contentious issues raised during Reconstruction. Welles was generally opposed to it, at least until African Americans had become educated. Yet when in October 1865, Connecticut voters defeated a proposed amendment to the state constitution that would have eliminated a provision that only white men could qualify for the franchise, he noted in his diary that he might have voted for the measure had he been at home for the balloting, though he added that its defeat had not caused him any great distress.[6]

The far more important question for Welles was whether the federal government had the authority to enfranchise the former slaves. His answer was an emphatic "no," for a basic tenet of his states' rights and strict-constructionist ideology was that decisions about something as fundamental as the suffrage must be left entirely to the individual states. Thus, when the Military Reconstruction Act of March 1867 granted the vote to black men in 10 of the 11 former Confederate states,[7] Welles reacted with indignation. He attributed the measure to the radicals' determination "to

---

[5] Welles recognized that both the freed people and southern Unionists were often subjected to threats, coercion, and violence at the hands of former rebels. But he believed federal intervention to protect them, which would have necessitated the creation of a national police power operative in the former Confederate states, would be unconstitutional and also serve to exacerbate the situation.

[6] Connecticut had a literacy qualification for voting that would have disqualified many blacks even if the constitutional amendment had passed. This may explain why Welles could imagine himself voting for it.

[7] Tennessee was exempted from the act since it had ratified the 14th Amendment, whereas the ten other former Confederate states had rejected it.

pull down the pillars of the Republic," and he thought it was hypocritical for Congressional Republicans to impose black suffrage on the southern states when most of them represented northern states that denied African Americans the ballot.[8] Subsequently, Welles also condemned the 15th Amendment, which barred all the states, northern as well as southern, from denying the vote to adult male citizens on the basis of race, color, or previous condition of servitude. Shortly before Congress approved the amendment in late February 1869 (his last full month in office) and sent it on to the states for ratification, he characterized it in his diary as "giving the suffrage to negroes and fools . . . in total disregard of the rights of the States, and of the fundamental principles of our system."

Welles was appalled when in early 1868 the House voted to impeach President Johnson. He testified at Johnson's Senate trial, and the president's counsel used information in the diary to document part of Johnson's defense. After the Senate acquitted the president (by a one-vote margin) on May 26th, Welles wrote that the senators who voted to convict were "partisan knaves or blockheads."

In 1868, Welles was so alienated from the Republican mainstream and so contemptuous of Grant, the party's presidential nominee, that he thought a victory by the Democratic candidate, Horatio Seymour, would be the lesser evil. But in multiple diary entries he criticized the Democrats for choosing a candidate whose support for the war had been less than wholehearted. If the party had instead nominated a prominent War Democrat such as General Winfield S. Hancock, Welles was sure it would have gained the votes of enough of his fellow conservative "Union men" to win the election.

Grant's conduct during President Johnson's struggle to remove Stanton from the cabinet, which was a major reason for his impeachment, convinced Welles that the general was an unprincipled and duplicitous self-seeker who had willfully betrayed the president. Furthermore, he believed, as he put it in his February 10, 1869, diary entry, that Grant had been "elected by illegal votes and unconstitutional practices." So great was his animosity toward the president-elect that when Johnson asked the cabinet's advice about whether he and they should attend Grant's inauguration, as was customary when the presidency changed hands, Welles argued passionately against it. Several of his colleagues disagreed, but in the end neither Johnson nor anyone from the cabinet went.

---

[8] Welles was also outraged that the act subjected the ten states to a period of military rule (albeit a relatively brief one in most of those states).

* * * * * * *

During his waning days in office, Welles considered remaining in Washington. Friends there encouraged him to stay. He found the capital's climate – especially in the spring and fall – preferable to Connecticut's and its social life more agreeable. He also knew that during his eight-year absence Hartford had changed and many of his old friends had moved away or died. But as his wife, Mary, and his three surviving sons had urged, he ultimately decided to return home and, as he put it in his May 2, 1869 diary entry, "pass my few remaining days in the land of my ancestors. Here I shall in all probability," he continued, "close my earthly pilgrimage, here close the record of my life, and here lie down beside my children who have gone before me."

The morning of April 27th, Welles and Mary boarded a train to New York, where they spent the night and part of the next day. (During the stopover, Welles visited the ailing Admiral Farragut at his home in the city.) They then caught the 3:00 o'clock train to Hartford, arriving there in early evening. They lodged at the Allyn House hotel while he and their sons searched for a suitable dwelling.

Although dismayed by the high cost of real estate, Welles finally decided to buy a 12-room house on Charter Oak Place. He paid the seller, J. Woodbridge White, $29,200 for it, plus several thousand dollars more for two vacant lots, one adjoining the house lot and the other across the street from it.[9] By the end of May, Mary and he had moved in.

Welles had continued keeping his diary since returning to Hartford. But on June 6th he recorded the final entry in it, grousing about the high cost and poor quality of domestic servants and commenting on the continuing controversy over whether Great Britain should pay compensation for the destruction that English-built Confederate raiders had visited on American commercial vessels (the so-called *Alabama* claims). By drawing to a close the diary he had faithfully kept since late summer 1862, he symbolically marked the end of the Washington phase of his life.

Despite Welles's gloomy comment about spending his "few remaining days" in Connecticut, he lived another nine years. They were years filled with achievement, owing to his still-prolific pen. Almost immediately, he began placing articles in the Democratic *Hartford Times* (where he often skewered Grant and his administration) and sometimes in the Republican *Hartford Courant* as well. Soon he was also contributing editorials to the

---

[9] The house was razed in the 1950s.

New York Times. And from time to time he presumably worked on revising the diary.

Welles's writing life took an important turn in the summer of 1870. The June issue of *The Galaxy* magazine carried an article about the dramatic events of March and April 1861 by Thurlow Weed, the longtime New York political boss and Seward's political alter ego. Welles was distressed by the article's factual errors and Weed's exaggeration of the influence he had exerted on the Lincoln administration during the tense weeks surrounding the firing on Fort Sumter. Even worse, Weed faulted Welles for not preventing the rebels' seizure of the Gosport navy yard shortly after Virginia seceded.

Drawing on his memory and some of the trove of letters and docments he had brought with him from Washington, Welles quickly composed an 11-page response that appeared in the July number of *The Galaxy*. He corrected Weed's errors of fact, provided a detailed account of the loss of the Gosport yard, and in the process cleared himself of culpability.

In responding to Weed, Welles had discovered a congenial form of expression: the relatively short historical essay combining narrative with a participant's sharply etched judgments of men and events. Over the next seven years, he would write 20 more such essays, ranging in length from nine to 25 pages. They all appeared in *The Galaxy*, except the final two, which *The Atlantic Monthly* published posthumously after absorbing *The Galaxy* early in 1878. All of them dealt with the Civil War period, and a majority of them centered on Lincoln, whose leadership Welles repeatedly described in very positive terms.

In 1874, Welles published a short book entitled *Lincoln and Seward*. It was based on three articles he had been provoked into writing the previous year by Charles Francis Adams's glowing eulogy of Seward, who had died in 1872.[10] In the articles, and in more detail in the book, Welles took issue with Adams's depiction of Seward as Lincoln's intellectual superior and the administration's dominant figure. While acknowledging that the secretary of state was a talented and influential, if not especially principled, member of the cabinet, Welles argued that Lincoln, with his exceptionally astute and penetrating intellect and remarkable political skills, firmly controlled the administration. Even on key foreign policy issues, he emphasized, it was Lincoln, not Seward, who made the decisions.

---

[10] Adams prepared the eulogy at the request of the New York state legislature and delivered it before that body.

Despite serious illnesses in 1874 and 1875, advancing age failed to reduce Welles's output. In fact, during the three-year period 1875 – 1877 he wrote nine of his 21 historical essays, including a five-part series published in 1877 under the umbrella title "Administration of Abraham Lincoln."

✻ ✻ ✻ ✻ ✻ ✻ ✻

As the year 1878 opened, Welles seemed to be in reasonably good health. But then a painful carbuncle developed on his neck. Unlike several previous carbuncles, it did not respond to treatment, and the infection spread to his throat. By the evening of February 9th, he could no longer swallow, and breathing had become difficult. The next day, he was unable to speak, and it was clear death was imminent. Although he seemed a little better the morning of the 11th, that evening he succumbed. He had outlived Seward, Stanton, Chase, Sumner, Farragut, and many of his other wartime associates. And as a result of his diary, he had achieved a measure of immortality.

Appendix
The Members of Lincoln's Cabinet

Note: Those who served beyond April 14, 1865, were members of Andrew Johnson's cabinet as well as Lincoln's.

Edward Bates,
    Attorney General

March 5, 1861 – November 24, 1864

Montgomery Blair,
    Postmaster General

March 5, 1861 – September 24, 1864

Simon Cameron,
    Secretary of War

March 5, 1861 – January 14, 1862

Salmon P. Chase,
    Secretary of the Treasury

March 7, 1861 – June 30, 1864

William Dennison, Jr.,
    Postmaster General

September 24, 1864 – July 25, 1866

William P. Fessenden,
    Secretary of the Treasury

July 5, 1864 – March 3, 1865

Hugh McCulloch,
    Secretary of the Treasury

March 9, 1865 – March 3, 1869

William H. Seward,
    Secretary of State

March 5, 1861 – March 4, 1869

Caleb B. Smith,
    Secretary of the Interior

March 5, 1861 – December 31, 1862

James Speed,
    Attorney General

December 2, 1864 – July 22, 1866

Edwin M. Stanton,
    Secretary of War

January 20, 1862 – May 28, 1868

John P. Usher,
    Secretary of the Interior

January 1, 1863 – May 15, 1865

Gideon Welles,
    Secretary of the Navy

March 7, 1861 – March 4, 1869

Current Members of the Acorn Club
As of January 1, 2014

Richard J. Buel, Jr., Essex – 1993*

David W. Dangremond, Old Lyme – 2009

James F. English, Jr., Noank – 1981

Jay Gitlin, North Branford – 2011

Briann Greenfield, New Britain – 2010

Helen Higgins, Guilford – 2000

Karen Ordahl Kupperman, Mansfield Center – 2012

Richard C. Malley, Simsbury – 2002

J. Bard McNulty, Glastonbury – 1980

Brenda Miller, Simsbury – 2011

Curtis Patton, New Haven – 2008

William N. Peterson, North Stonington – 2010

Patrick L. Pinnell, Higganum – 2012

Judith Ann Schiff, New Haven – 1995

John W. Shannahan, Suffield – 1998

Ann Smith, Roxbury – 2007

Robert H. Smith, Jr., Hartford – 2007

Clayton B. Spencer, Litchfield – 2011

J. Ronald Spencer, West Hartford – 2007

Thomas Truxes, Westbrook – 2009

Carolyn Wakeman, Old Lyme – 2013

Kendall Wiggin, Windsor Locks – 2011

George J. Willauer, Lyme – 1998

Walter W. Woodward, Manchester – 2006

Honorary Members
Christopher Collier, Orange – 1986

Howard Lamar, North Haven – 1998

---

* Indicates the year the member joined the Club.

CPSIA information can be obtained at www.ICGtesting.com
Printed in the USA
BVOW07s1850120614

356017BV00002B/5/P